FEAR AGENT™

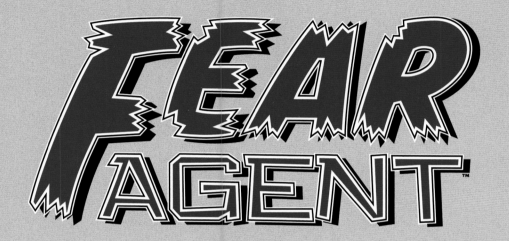

SENSES-SHATTERING!

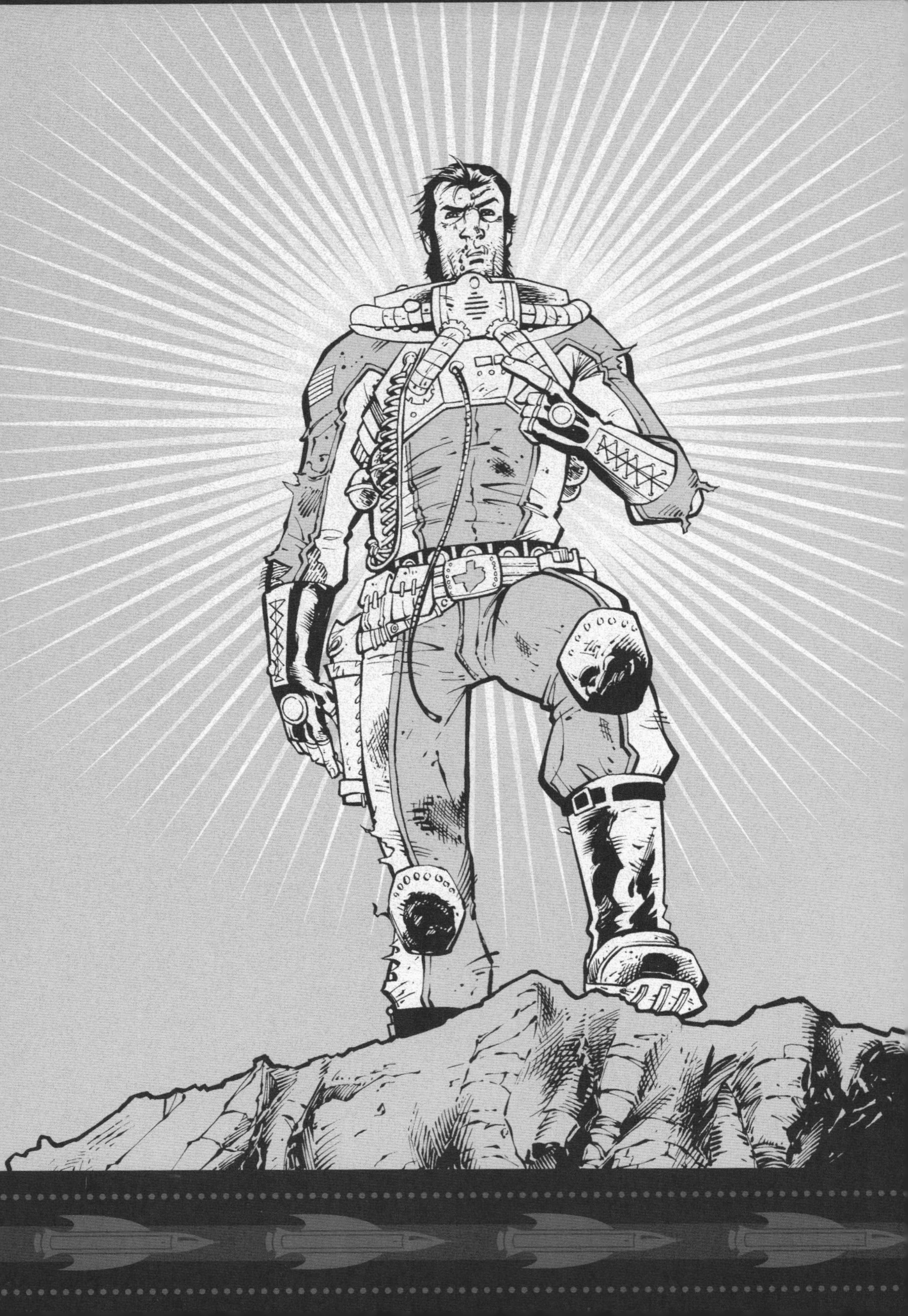

Space thrills and chills

FEAR AGENT

Volume Three
THE LAST GOODBYE

story **RICK REMENDER**

pencils **TONY MOORE**

inks Ande Parks & Rick Remender

colors Lee Loughridge

letters Rus Wooton

covers Tony Moore

DARK HORSE BOOKS

Publisher ⚡ Mike Richardson
Art Director ⚡ Lia Ribacchi
Designer ⚡ M. Joshua Elliott
Assistant Editor ⚡ Katie Moody
Editor ⚡ Dave Land

Dark Horse Comics, Inc.
10956 SE Main Street
Milwaukie, OR 97222

DarkHorse.com

To find a comic shop in your area, call the Comic Shop
Locator Service toll-free at (888) 266-4226
International Licensing: (503) 905-2377

Second edition: June 2014
ISBN 978-1-61655-452-1

1 3 5 7 9 10 8 6 4 2
Printed in China

FEAR AGENT VOLUME 3: THE LAST GOODBYE

This book collects issues twelve through fifteen of the
Dark Horse comic-book series *Fear Agent*.

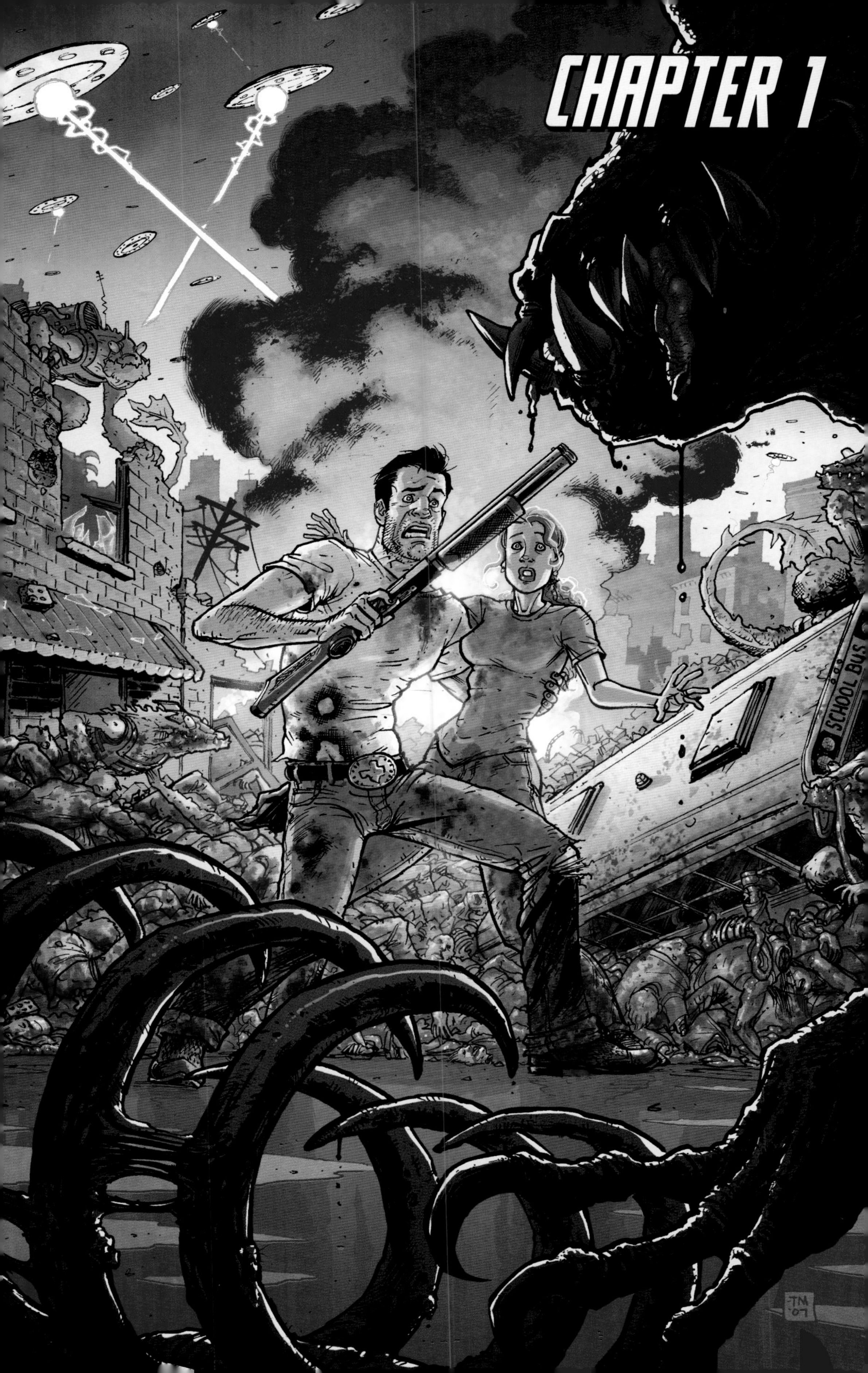
CHAPTER 1
SCHOOL BUS
TM '07

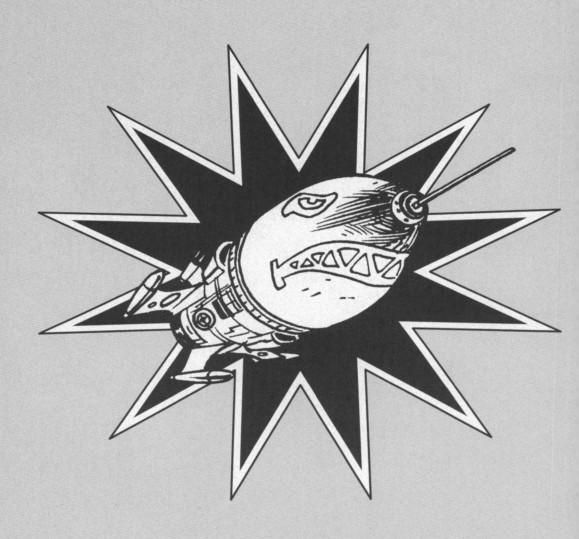

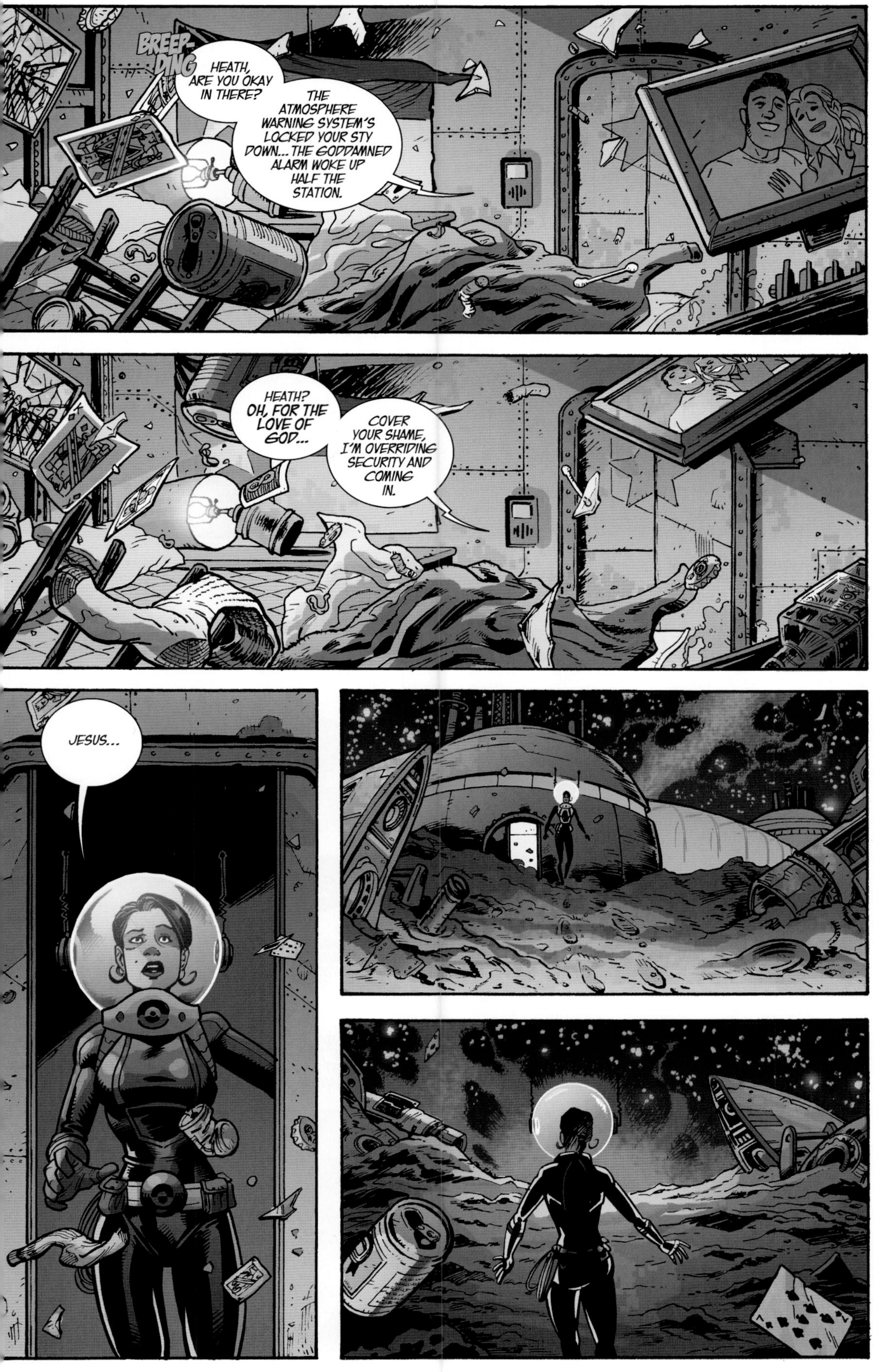
BREEP-DING
HEATH, ARE YOU OKAY IN THERE?
THE ATMOSPHERE WARNING SYSTEM'S LOCKED YOUR STY DOWN... THE GODDAMNED ALARM WOKE UP HALF THE STATION.
HEATH? OH, FOR THE LOVE OF GOD...
COVER YOUR SHAME, I'M OVERRIDING SECURITY AND COMING IN.
JESUS...

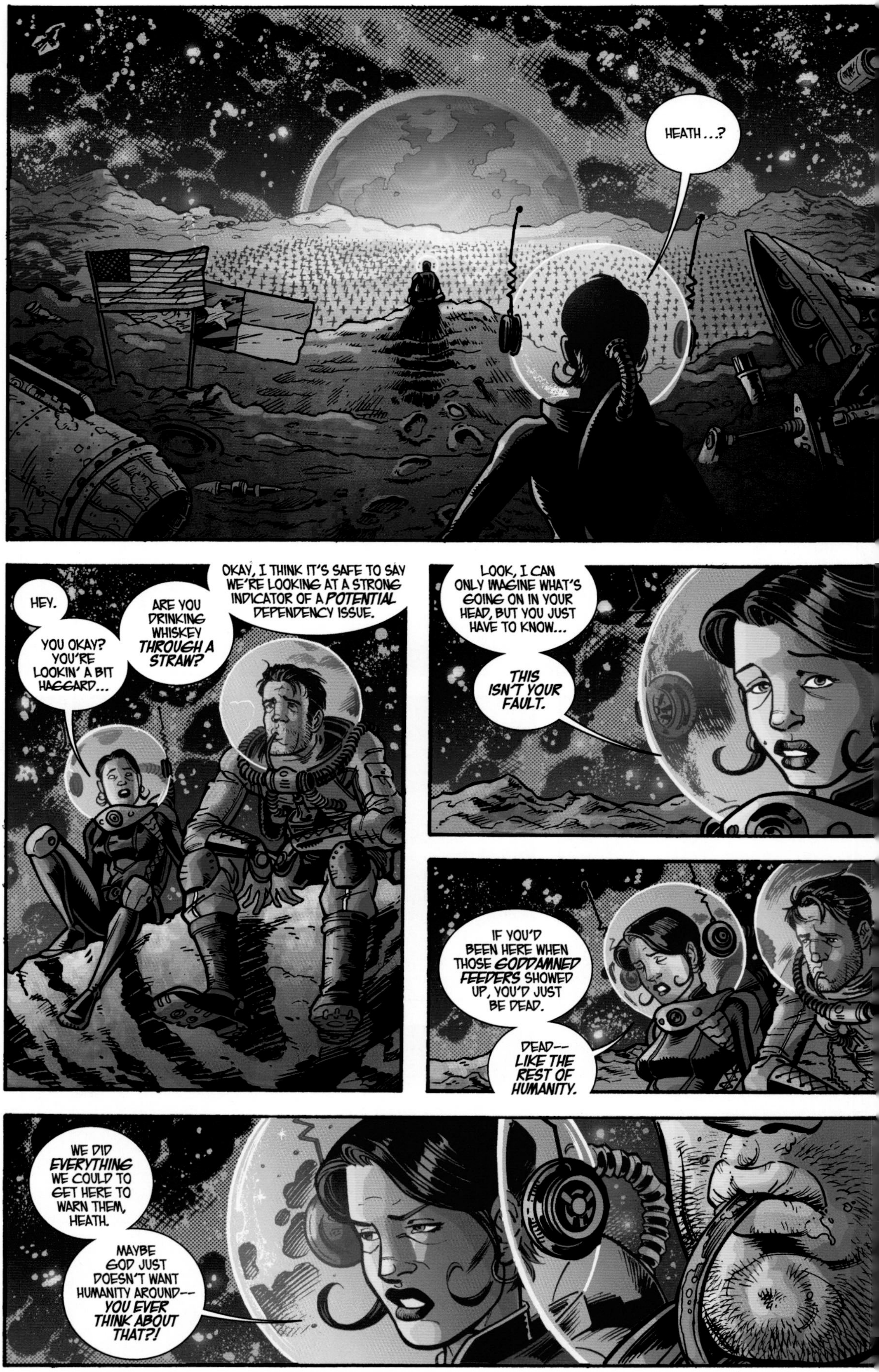
HEATH...?
HEY.
YOU OKAY? YOU'RE LOOKIN' A BIT HAGGARD...
ARE YOU DRINKING WHISKEY *THROUGH A STRAW?*
OKAY, I THINK IT'S SAFE TO SAY WE'RE LOOKING AT A STRONG INDICATOR OF A *POTENTIAL* DEPENDENCY ISSUE.
LOOK, I CAN ONLY IMAGINE WHAT'S GOING ON IN YOUR HEAD, BUT YOU JUST HAVE TO KNOW...
THIS ISN'T YOUR FAULT.
IF YOU'D BEEN HERE WHEN THOSE *GODDAMNED FEEDERS* SHOWED UP, YOU'D JUST BE DEAD.
DEAD-- *LIKE THE REST OF HUMANITY.*
WE DID *EVERYTHING* WE COULD TO GET HERE TO WARN THEM, HEATH.
MAYBE GOD JUST DOESN'T WANT HUMANITY AROUND-- *YOU EVER THINK ABOUT THAT?!*

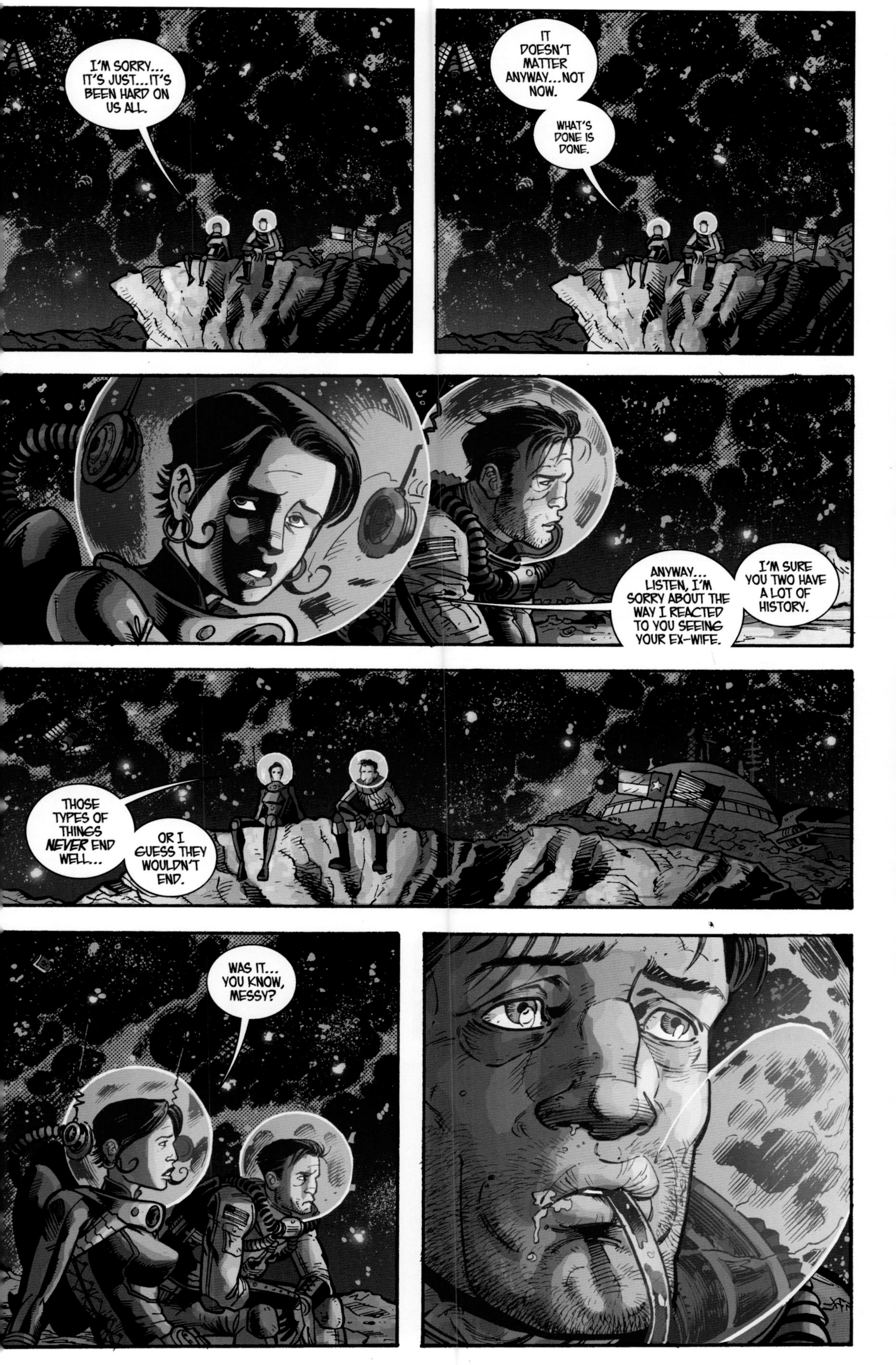
I'M SORRY... IT'S JUST...IT'S BEEN HARD ON US ALL.
IT DOESN'T MATTER ANYWAY...NOT NOW.
WHAT'S DONE IS DONE.
ANYWAY... LISTEN, I'M SORRY ABOUT THE WAY I REACTED TO YOU SEEING YOUR EX-WIFE.
I'M SURE YOU TWO HAVE A LOT OF HISTORY.
THOSE TYPES OF THINGS NEVER END WELL...
OR I GUESS THEY WOULDN'T END.
WAS IT... YOU KNOW, MESSY?

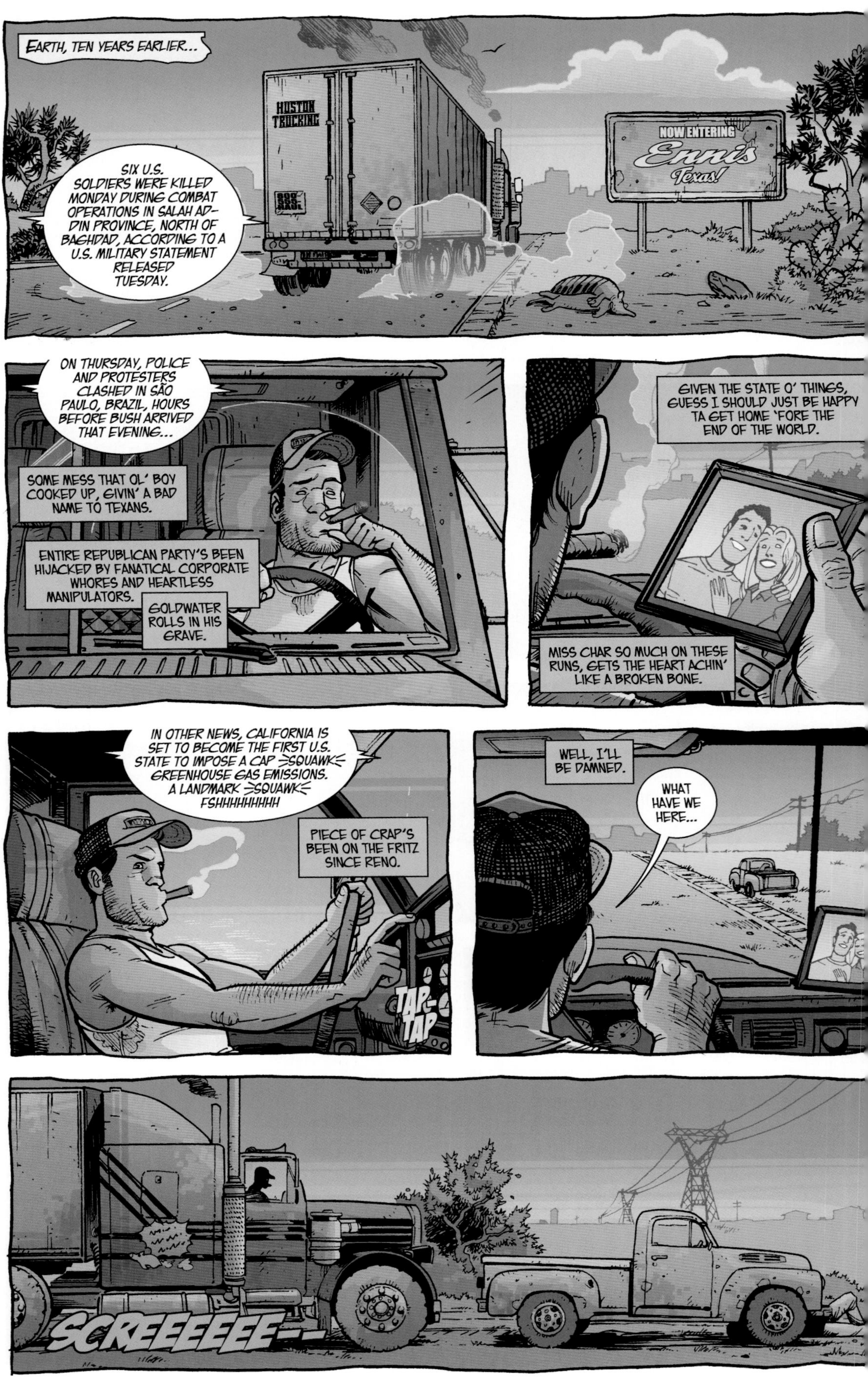
EARTH, TEN YEARS EARLIER...
HUSTON TRUCKING
NOW ENTERING Ennis Texas!
SIX U.S. SOLDIERS WERE KILLED MONDAY DURING COMBAT OPERATIONS IN SALAH AD-DIN PROVINCE, NORTH OF BAGHDAD, ACCORDING TO A U.S. MILITARY STATEMENT RELEASED TUESDAY.
ON THURSDAY, POLICE AND PROTESTERS CLASHED IN SÃO PAULO, BRAZIL, HOURS BEFORE BUSH ARRIVED THAT EVENING...
SOME MESS THAT OL' BOY COOKED UP, GIVIN' A BAD NAME TO TEXANS.
ENTIRE REPUBLICAN PARTY'S BEEN HIJACKED BY FANATICAL CORPORATE WHORES AND HEARTLESS MANIPULATORS.
GOLDWATER ROLLS IN HIS GRAVE.
GIVEN THE STATE O' THINGS, GUESS I SHOULD JUST BE HAPPY TA GET HOME 'FORE THE END OF THE WORLD.
MISS CHAR SO MUCH ON THESE RUNS, GETS THE HEART ACHIN' LIKE A BROKEN BONE.
IN OTHER NEWS, CALIFORNIA IS SET TO BECOME THE FIRST U.S. STATE TO IMPOSE A CAP =SQUAWK= GREENHOUSE GAS EMISSIONS. A LANDMARK =SQUAWK= FSHHHHHHHHH
PIECE OF CRAP'S BEEN ON THE FRITZ SINCE RENO.
TAP-TAP
WELL, I'LL BE DAMNED.
WHAT HAVE WE HERE...
SCREEEEEEE--

JUNKYARD'S ABOUT THREE MILES SOUTH O' TOWN, OLD-TIMER.

YOU WANT I KIN HELP YOU CART THIS BUCKET DOWN OVER.

DAMN, YOU MUST BE WAY DOWN ON YER LUCK...

...THAT IS ONE *SORRY* OL' PAIR A BOOTS.

BOUGHT THESE NINETEEN-SEVENTY-THREE SO I HAD A CLEAN NEW PAIR TA STICK UP THE ASS OF THE AWFUL CUR MY WIFE'D JUST GIVEN BIRTH TA.

SOUNDS LIKE THAT KID WAS ONE TOUGH SON OF A BITCH. I RECKON THE ONLY TIME YOU HAD THE UPPER HAND ON THAT BOY WAS INFANCY?

ACTUALLY, I WAS JUST ON MY WAY TA POLISH THESE OL' BEAUTS UP SIDE THE PUNK'S POSTERIOR.

IT'S GOOD TA SEE YA, POPS.

I'LL HELP YER ENFEEBLED OL' HIDE FIX THIS JALOPY BUT YER BUYING FIRST ROUND AT JUDD'S.

I SEEN YER HANDY WORK... DON'T SEEM I'M ON THE WINNIN' END OF THIS DEAL.

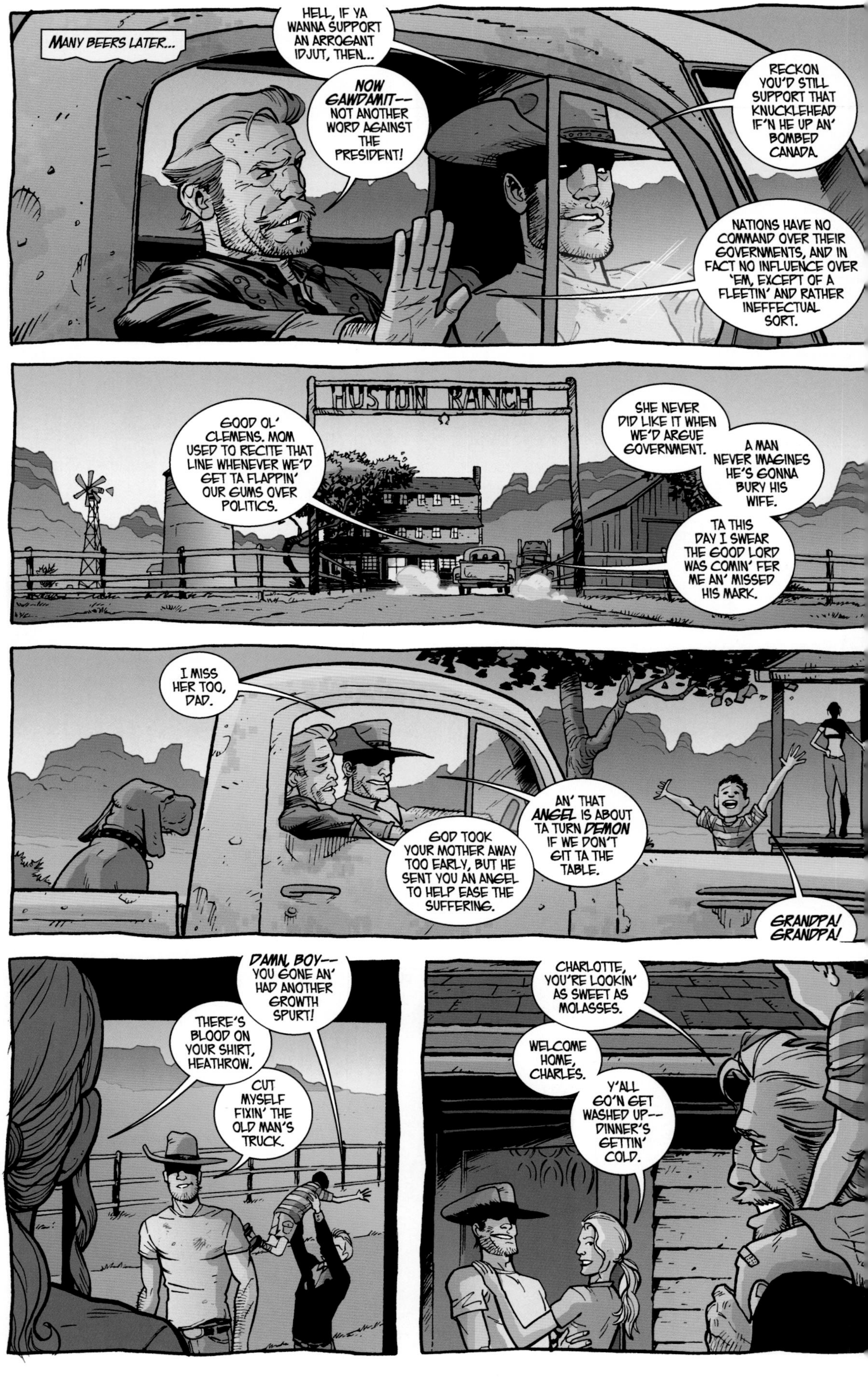
MANY BEERS LATER...
HELL, IF YA WANNA SUPPORT AN ARROGANT IDJUT, THEN...
NOW GAWDAMIT-- NOT ANOTHER WORD AGAINST THE PRESIDENT!
RECKON YOU'D STILL SUPPORT THAT KNUCKLEHEAD IF'N HE UP AN' BOMBED CANADA.
NATIONS HAVE NO COMMAND OVER THEIR GOVERNMENTS, AND IN FACT NO INFLUENCE OVER 'EM, EXCEPT OF A FLEETIN' AND RATHER INEFFECTUAL SORT.
HUSTON RANCH
GOOD OL' CLEMENS. MOM USED TO RECITE THAT LINE WHENEVER WE'D GET TA FLAPPIN' OUR GUMS OVER POLITICS.
SHE NEVER DID LIKE IT WHEN WE'D ARGUE GOVERNMENT.
A MAN NEVER IMAGINES HE'S GONNA BURY HIS WIFE.
TA THIS DAY I SWEAR THE GOOD LORD WAS COMIN' FER ME AN' MISSED HIS MARK.
I MISS HER TOO, DAD.
GOD TOOK YOUR MOTHER AWAY TOO EARLY, BUT HE SENT YOU AN ANGEL TO HELP EASE THE SUFFERING.
AN' THAT ANGEL IS ABOUT TA TURN DEMON IF WE DON'T GIT TA THE TABLE.
GRANDPA! GRANDPA!
DAMN, BOY-- YOU GONE AN' HAD ANOTHER GROWTH SPURT!
THERE'S BLOOD ON YOUR SHIRT, HEATHROW.
CUT MYSELF FIXIN' THE OLD MAN'S TRUCK.
CHARLOTTE, YOU'RE LOOKIN' AS SWEET AS MOLASSES.
WELCOME HOME, CHARLES.
Y'ALL GO'N GET WASHED UP-- DINNER'S GETTIN' COLD.

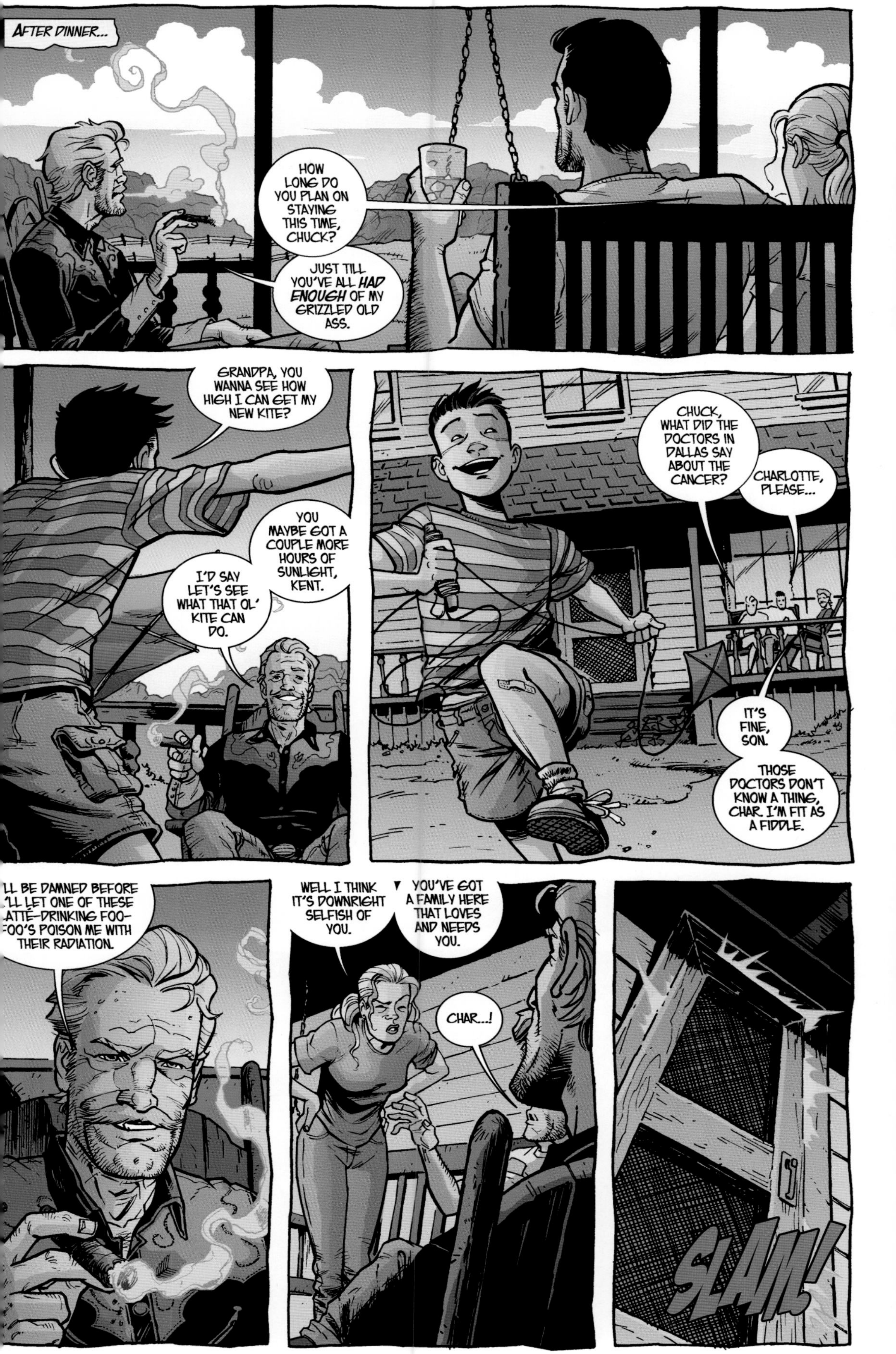
AFTER DINNER...
HOW LONG DO YOU PLAN ON STAYING THIS TIME, CHUCK?
JUST TILL YOU'VE ALL ***HAD ENOUGH*** OF MY GRIZZLED OLD ASS.
GRANDPA, YOU WANNA SEE HOW HIGH I CAN GET MY NEW KITE?
YOU MAYBE GOT A COUPLE MORE HOURS OF SUNLIGHT, KENT.
I'D SAY LET'S SEE WHAT THAT OL' KITE CAN DO.
CHUCK, WHAT DID THE DOCTORS IN DALLAS SAY ABOUT THE CANCER?
CHARLOTTE, PLEASE...
IT'S FINE, SON.
THOSE DOCTORS DON'T KNOW A THING, CHAR. I'M FIT AS A FIDDLE.
LL BE DAMNED BEFORE
'LL LET ONE OF THESE
ATTÉ-DRINKING FOO-
FOO'S POISON ME WITH
THEIR RADIATION.
WELL I THINK IT'S DOWNRIGHT SELFISH OF YOU.
YOU'VE GOT A FAMILY HERE THAT LOVES AND NEEDS YOU.
CHAR...!
SLAM!

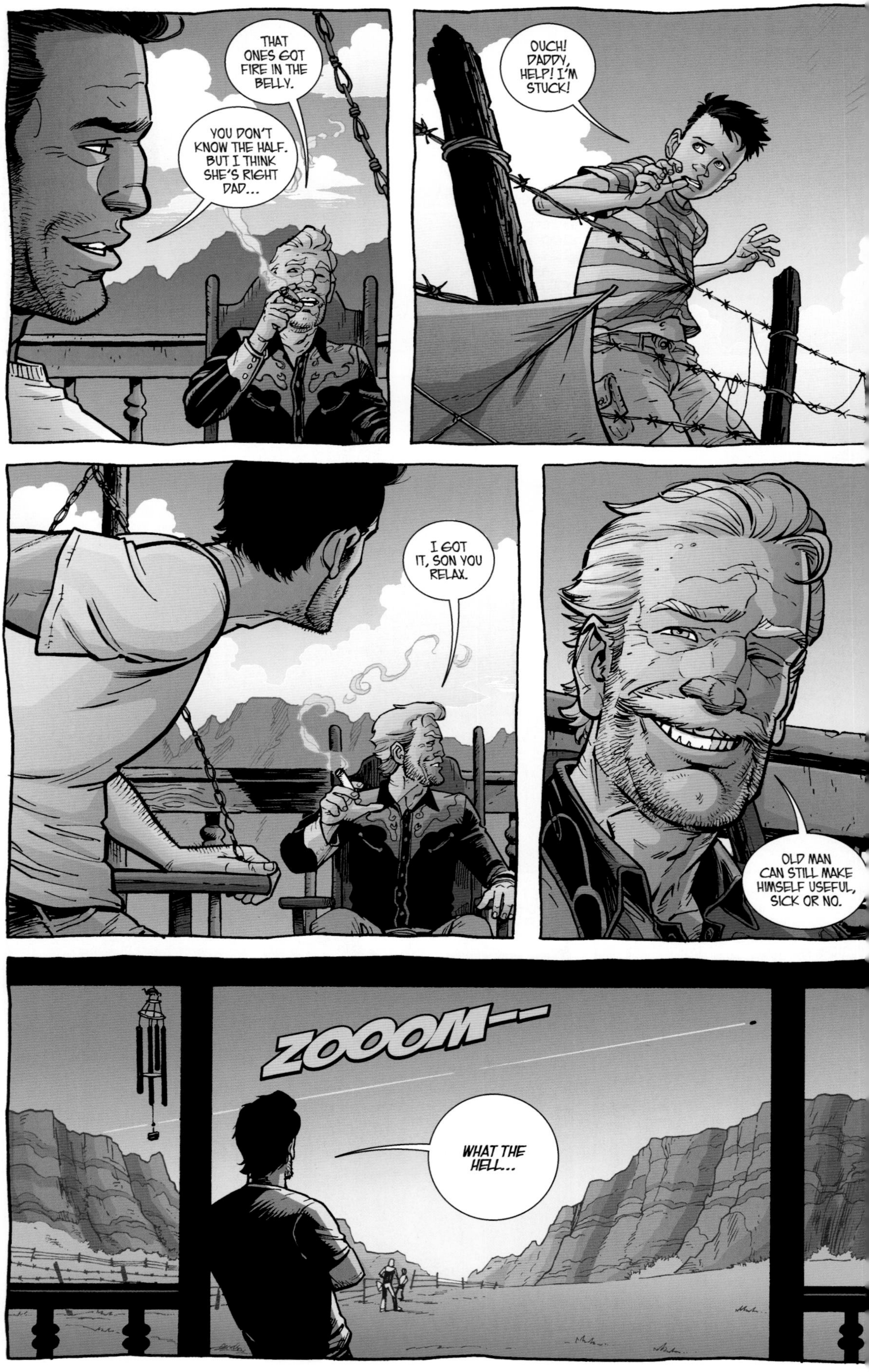
THAT ONES GOT FIRE IN THE BELLY.
YOU DON'T KNOW THE HALF. BUT I THINK SHE'S RIGHT DAD...
OUCH! DADDY, HELP! I'M STUCK!
I GOT IT, SON YOU RELAX.
OLD MAN CAN STILL MAKE HIMSELF USEFUL, SICK OR NO.
ZOOOM--
WHAT THE HELL...

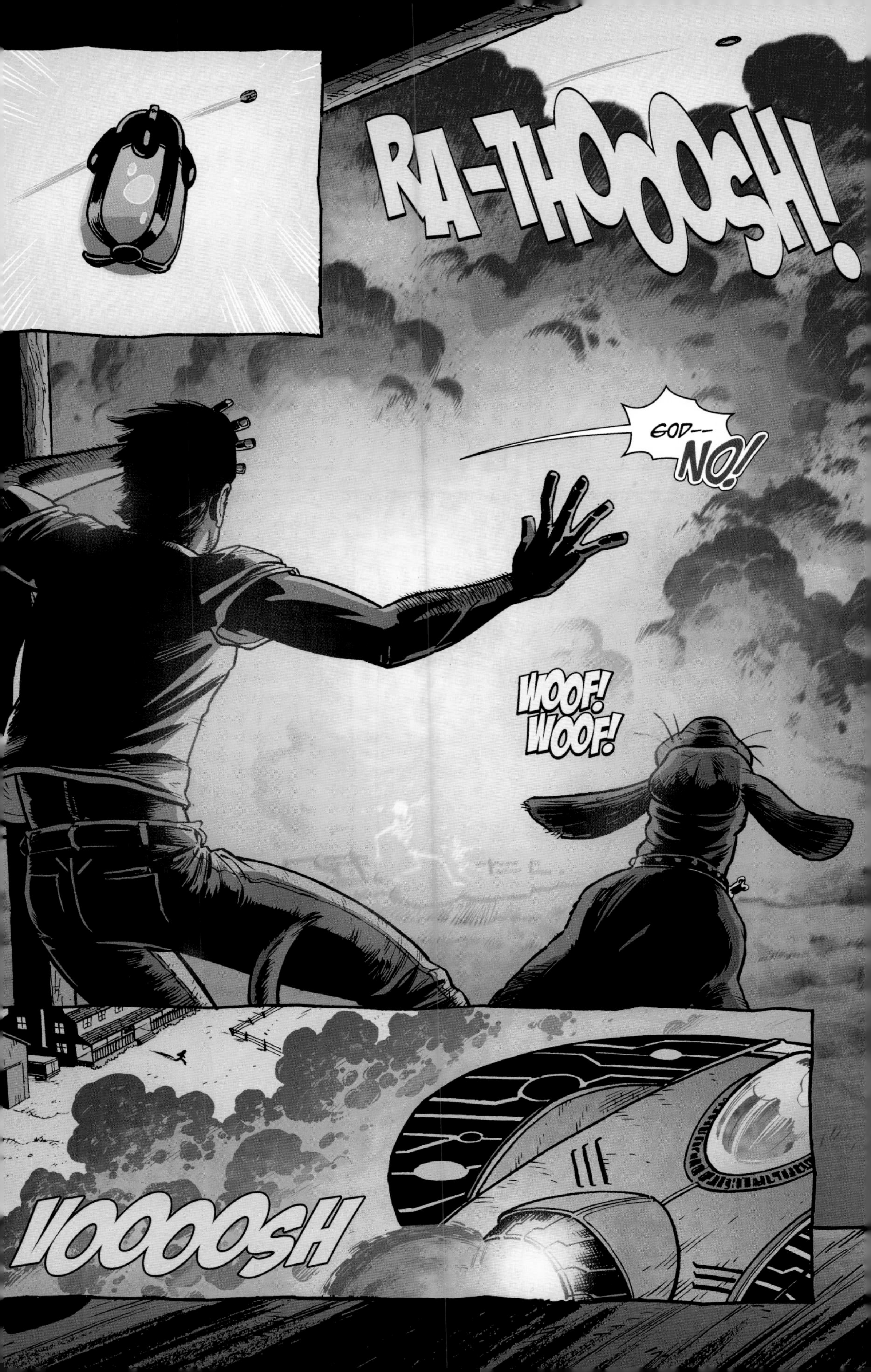
RA-THOOOOSH!
GOD--
NO!
WOOF! WOOF!
VOOOOSH

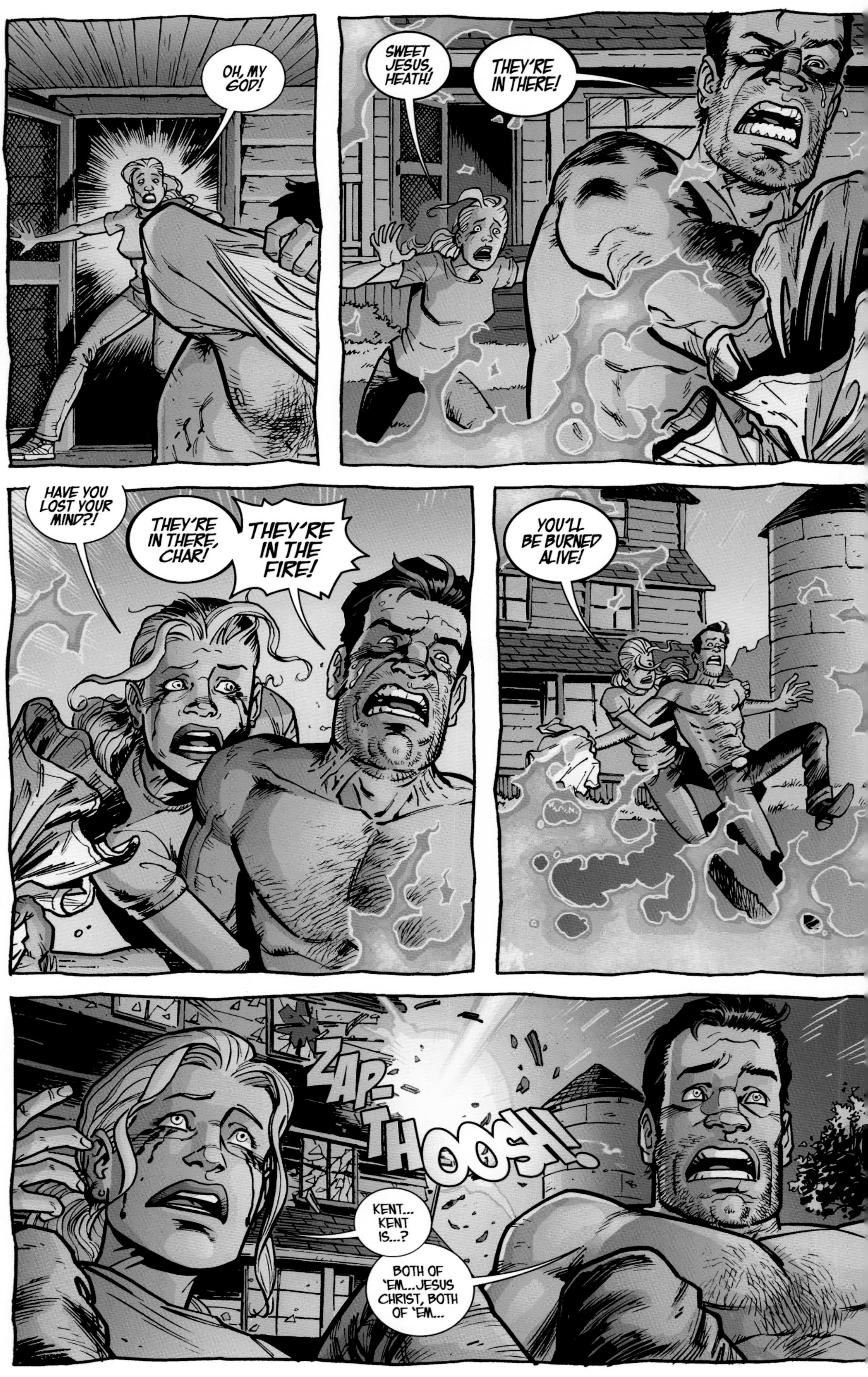
OH, MY GOD!
SWEET JESUS, HEATH!
THEY'RE IN THERE!
HAVE YOU LOST YOUR MIND?!
THEY'RE IN THERE, CHAR!
THEY'RE IN THE FIRE!
YOU'LL BE BURNED ALIVE!
ZAP-THOOSH!
KENT... KENT IS...?
BOTH OF 'EM...JESUS CHRIST, BOTH OF 'EM...

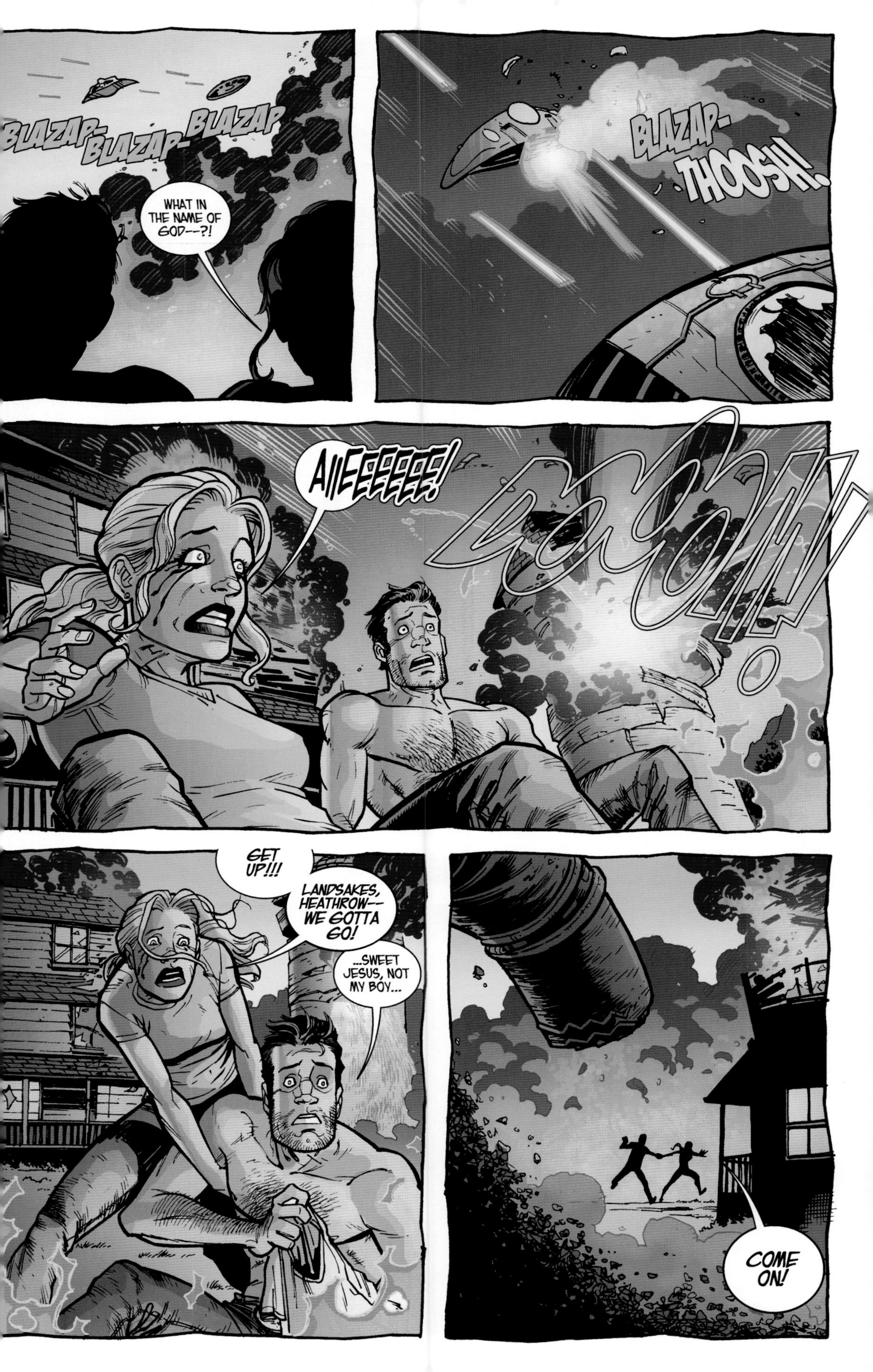
BLAZAP-BLAZAP-BLAZAP
WHAT IN THE NAME OF GOD--?!
BLAZAP-THOOSH!
AIIEEEEEE!
GET UP!!!
LANDSAKES, HEATHROW-- WE GOTTA GO!
...SWEET JESUS, NOT MY BOY...
COME ON!

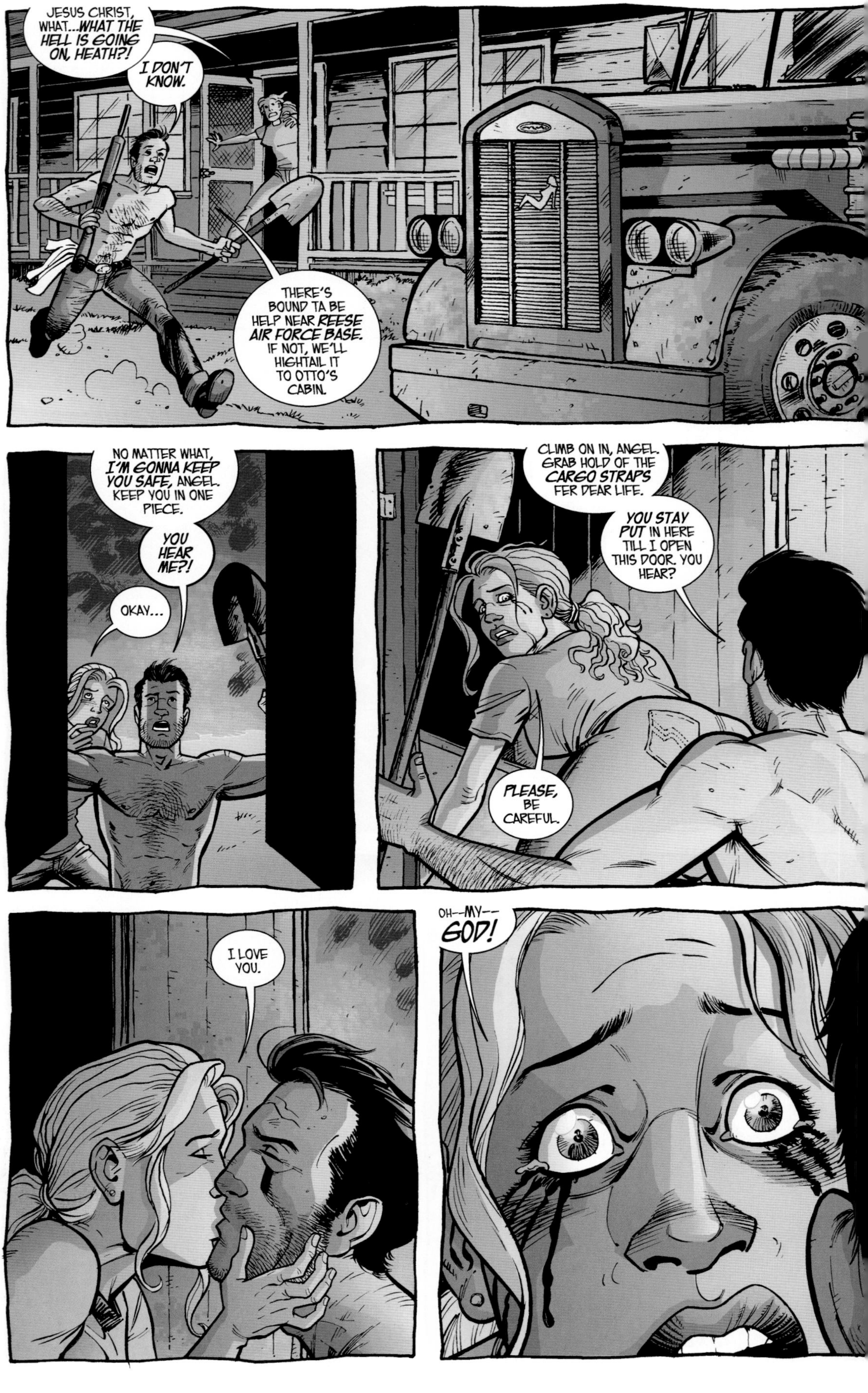
JESUS CHRIST, WHAT...WHAT THE HELL IS GOING ON, HEATH?!
I DON'T KNOW.
THERE'S BOUND TA BE HELP NEAR REESE AIR FORCE BASE. IF NOT, WE'LL HIGHTAIL IT TO OTTO'S CABIN.
NO MATTER WHAT, I'M GONNA KEEP YOU SAFE, ANGEL. KEEP YOU IN ONE PIECE.
YOU HEAR ME?!
OKAY...
CLIMB ON IN, ANGEL. GRAB HOLD OF THE CARGO STRAPS FER DEAR LIFE.
YOU STAY PUT IN HERE TILL I OPEN THIS DOOR. YOU HEAR?
PLEASE, BE CAREFUL.
I LOVE YOU.
OH--MY--
GOD!

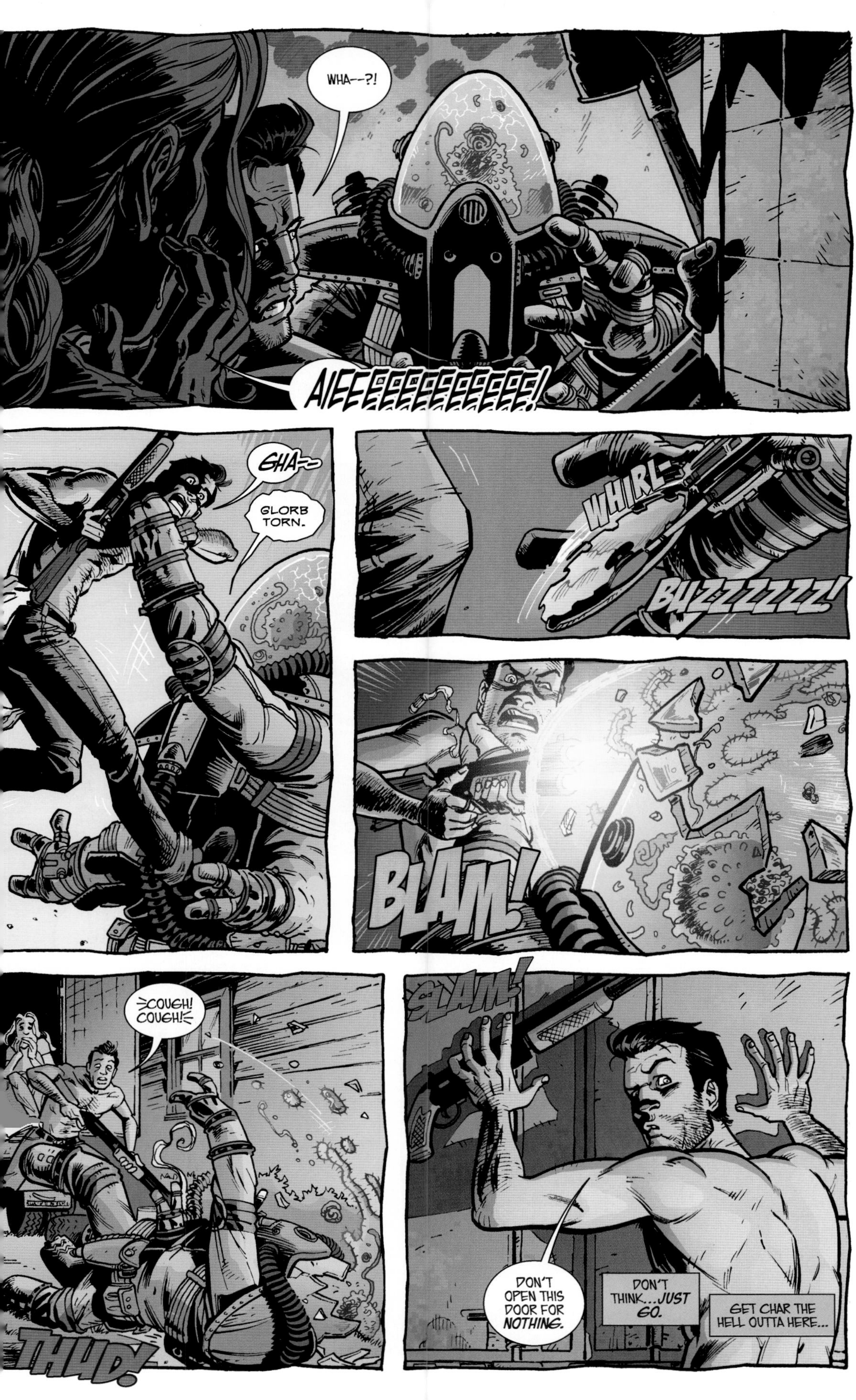
WHA--?!
AIEEEEEEEEEEEEE!
GHA--
GLORB TORN.
WHIRL
BUZZZZZZ!
BLAM!
COUGH! COUGH!
THUD!
SLAM!
DON'T OPEN THIS DOOR FOR NOTHING.
DON'T THINK... JUST GO.
GET CHAR THE HELL OUTTA HERE...

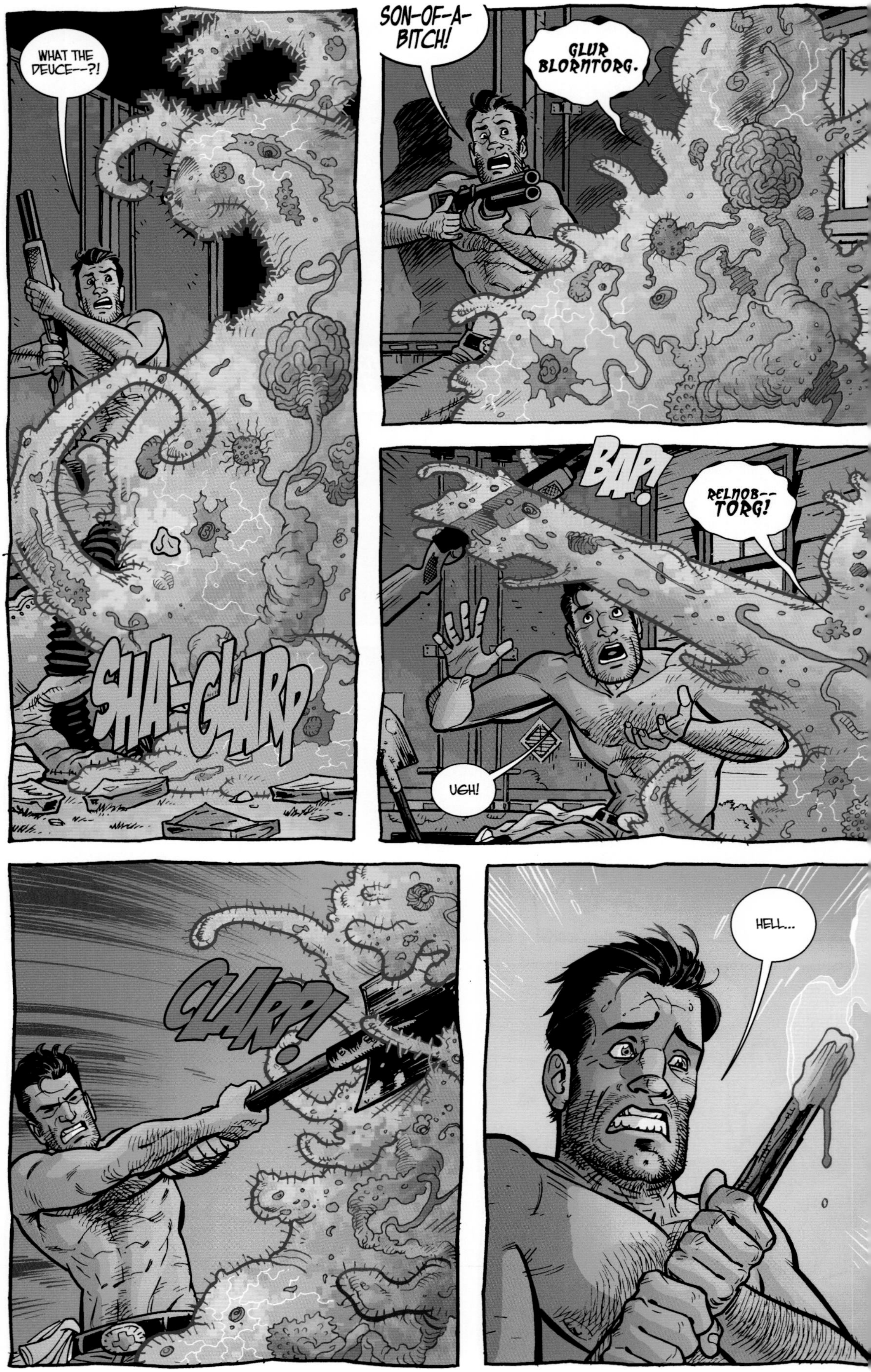
WHAT THE DEUCE--?!
SHA-GLARP
SON-OF-A-BITCH!
GLUR BLORNTORG.
BAP!
RELNOB--TORG!
UGH!
CLARP!
HELL...

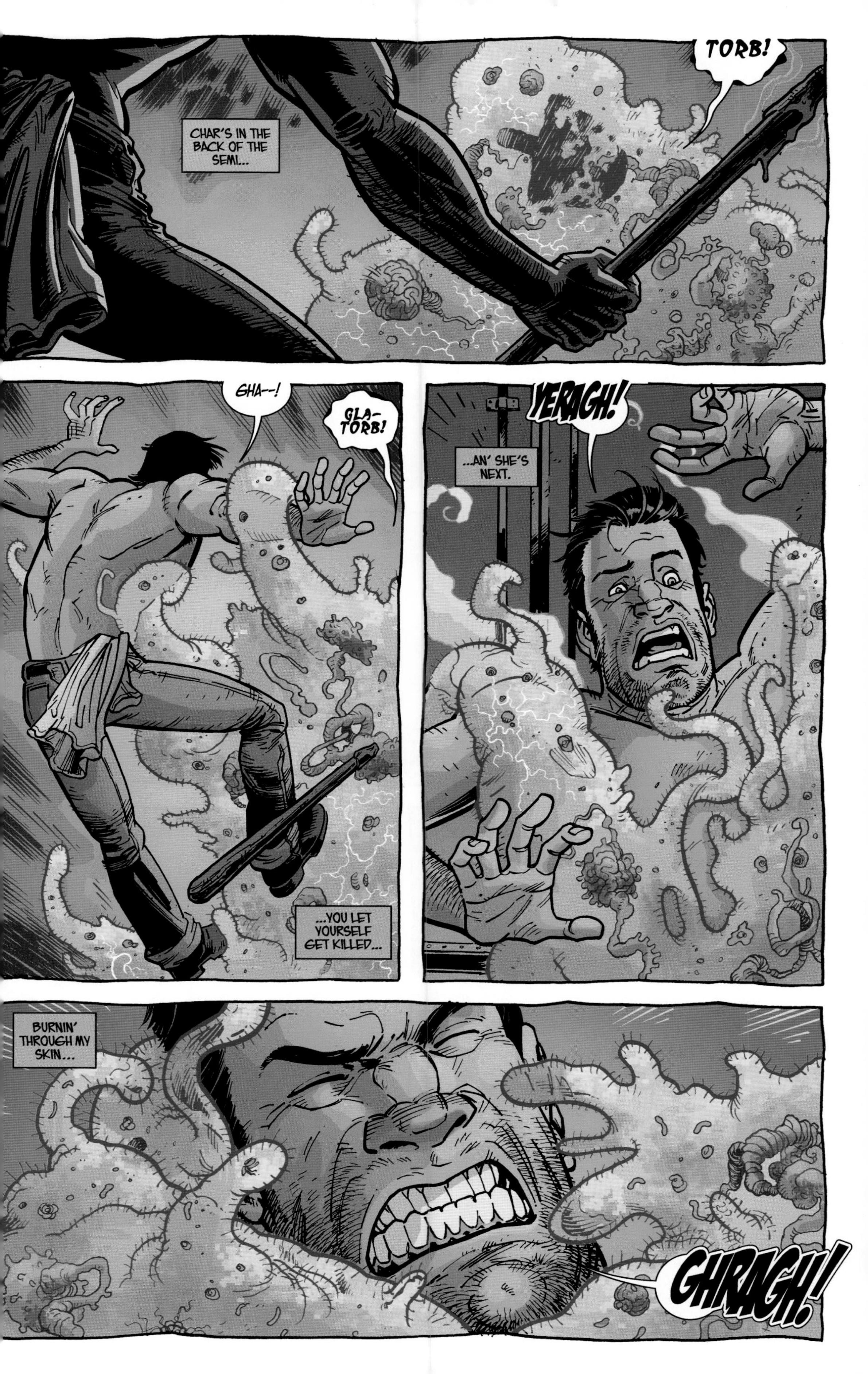

CHAR'S IN THE BACK OF THE SEMI...
TORB!
GHA--!
GLA-TORB!
...YOU LET YOURSELF GET KILLED...
YERAGH!
...AN' SHE'S NEXT.
BURNIN' THROUGH MY SKIN...
GHRAGH!

YERASH!

...I'M SORRY, ANGEL...

BLOGOOSH!

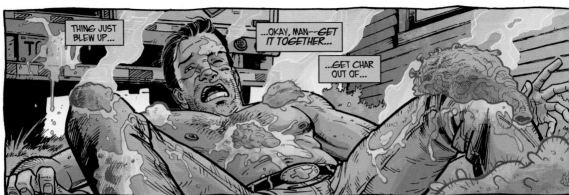

THING JUST BLEW UP...

...OKAY, MAN--GET IT TOGETHER...

...GET CHAR OUT OF...

...DEAR MOTHER OF GOD.

ZERTEEB-THUM.

RUN...

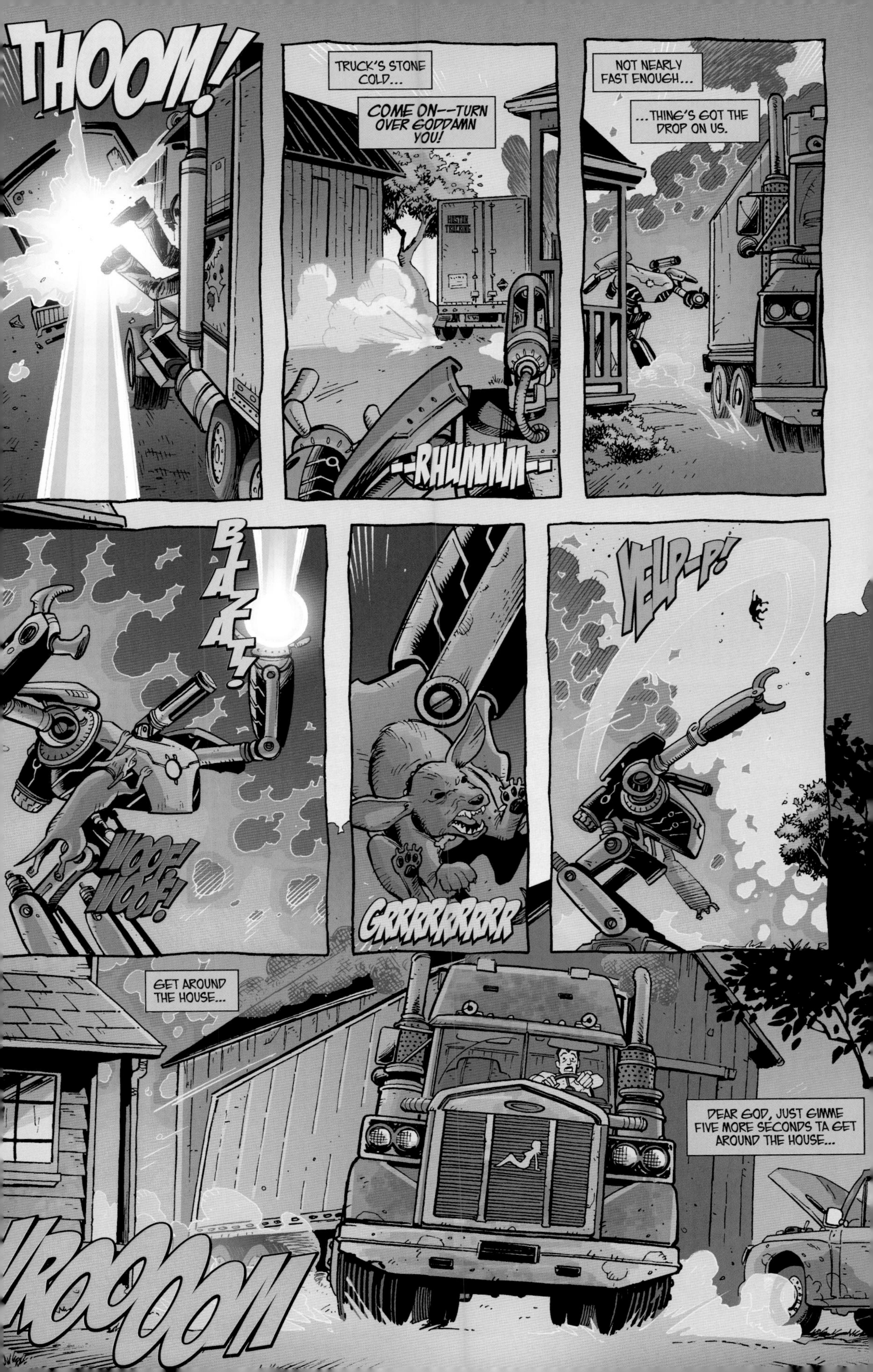

THOOM!
TRUCK'S STONE COLD...
COME ON--TURN OVER GODDAMN YOU!
--RHUMMM--
NOT NEARLY FAST ENOUGH...
...THING'S GOT THE DROP ON US.
BZZAT!
WOOF! WOOF!
GRRRRRRRRR
YELP-P!
GET AROUND THE HOUSE...
DEAR GOD, JUST GIMME FIVE MORE SECONDS TA GET AROUND THE HOUSE...
VROOOOOM

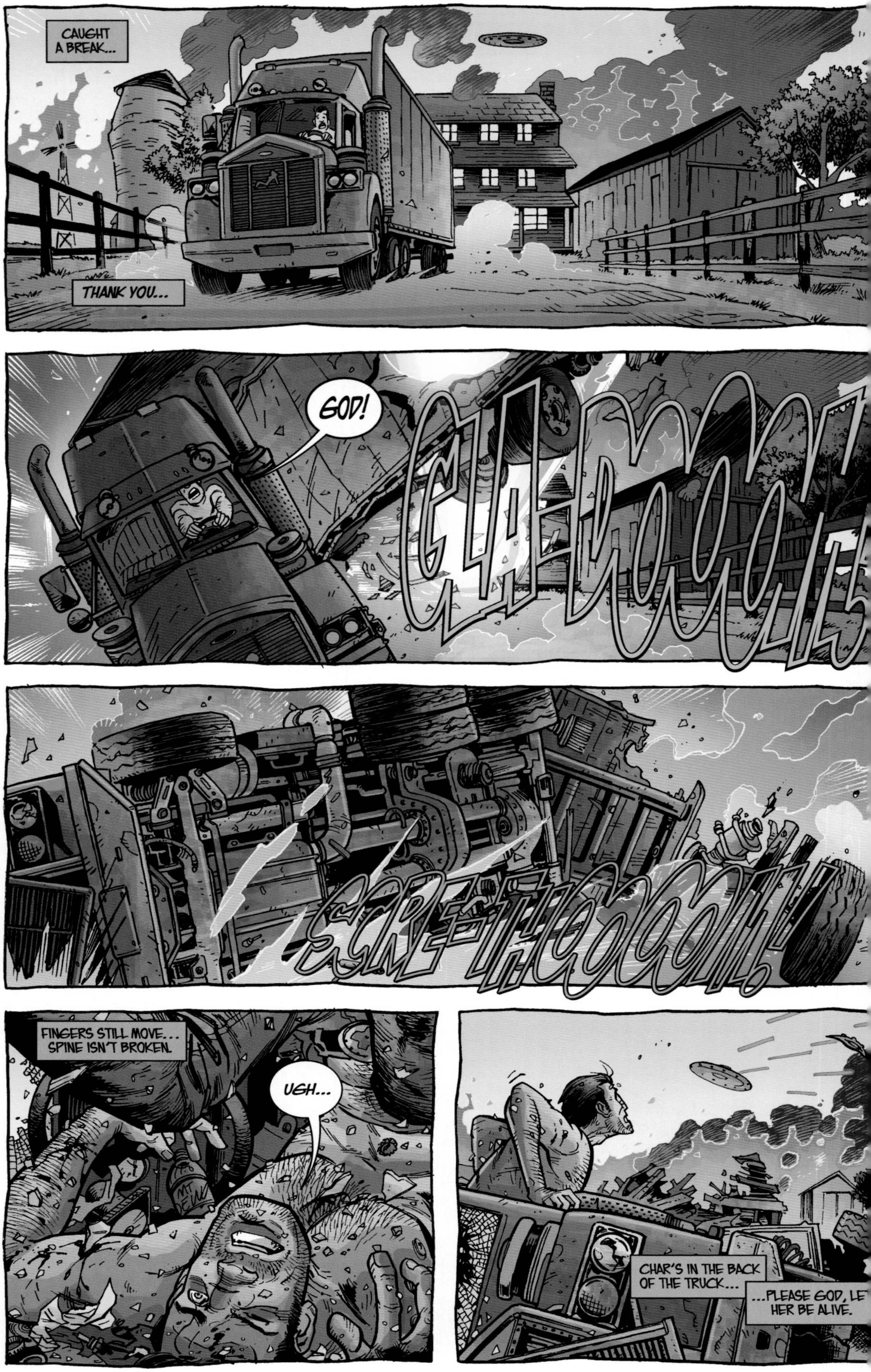
CAUGHT A BREAK...
THANK YOU...
GOD!
FINGERS STILL MOVE... SPINE ISN'T BROKEN.
UGH...
CHAR'S IN THE BACK OF THE TRUCK...
...PLEASE GOD, LET HER BE ALIVE.

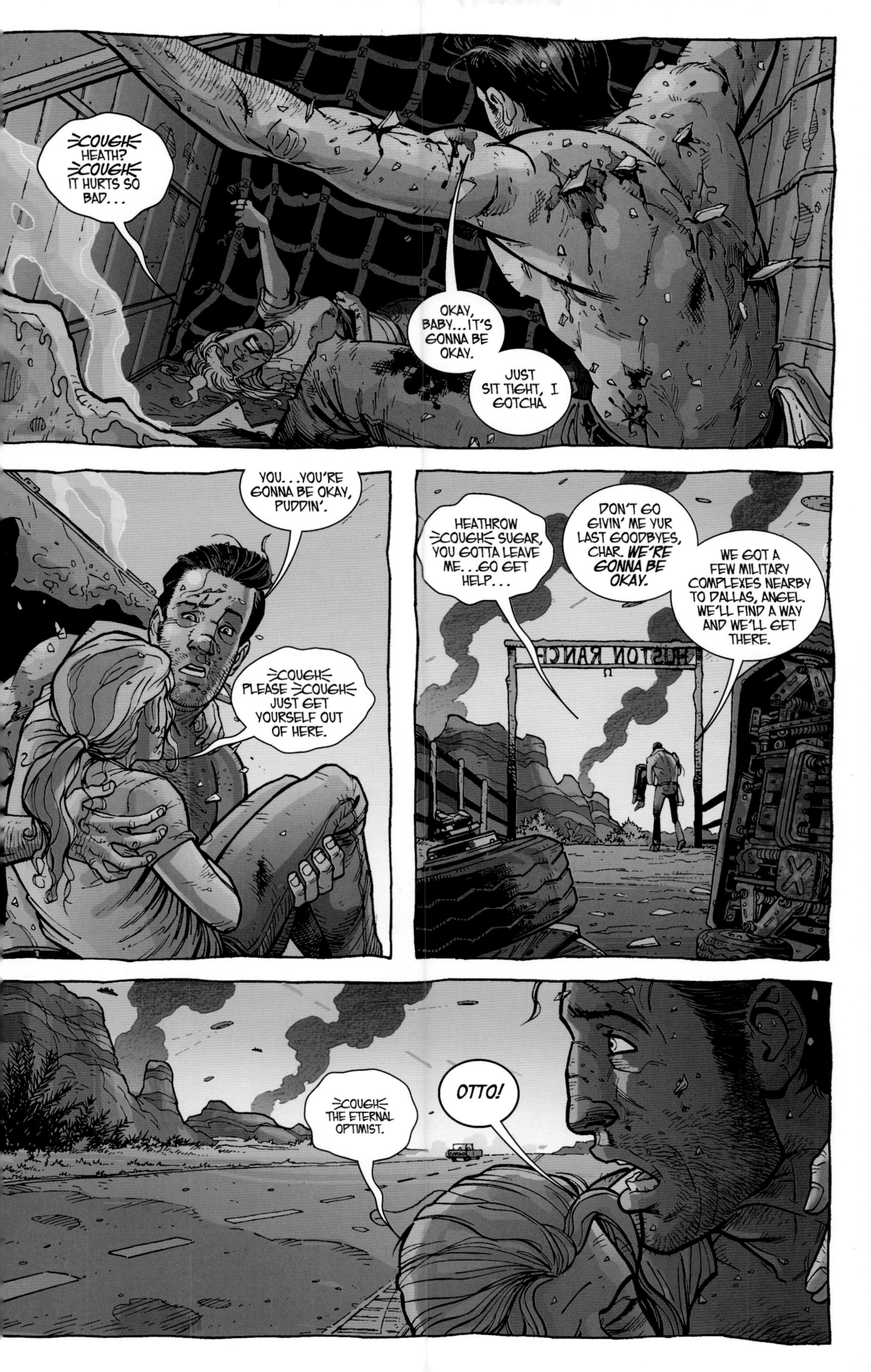

≥COUGH≤ HEATH? ≥COUGH≤ IT HURTS SO BAD...
OKAY, BABY...IT'S GONNA BE OKAY.
JUST SIT TIGHT, I GOTCHA.
YOU...YOU'RE GONNA BE OKAY, PUDDIN'.
≥COUGH≤ PLEASE ≥COUGH≤ JUST GET YOURSELF OUT OF HERE.
HEATHROW ≥COUGH≤ SUGAR, YOU GOTTA LEAVE ME...GO GET HELP...
DON'T GO GIVIN' ME YUR LAST GOODBYES, CHAR. *WE'RE GONNA BE OKAY.*
WE GOT A FEW MILITARY COMPLEXES NEARBY TO DALLAS, ANGEL. WE'LL FIND A WAY AND WE'LL GET THERE.
HUSTON RANCH
≥COUGH≤ THE ETERNAL OPTIMIST.
OTTO!

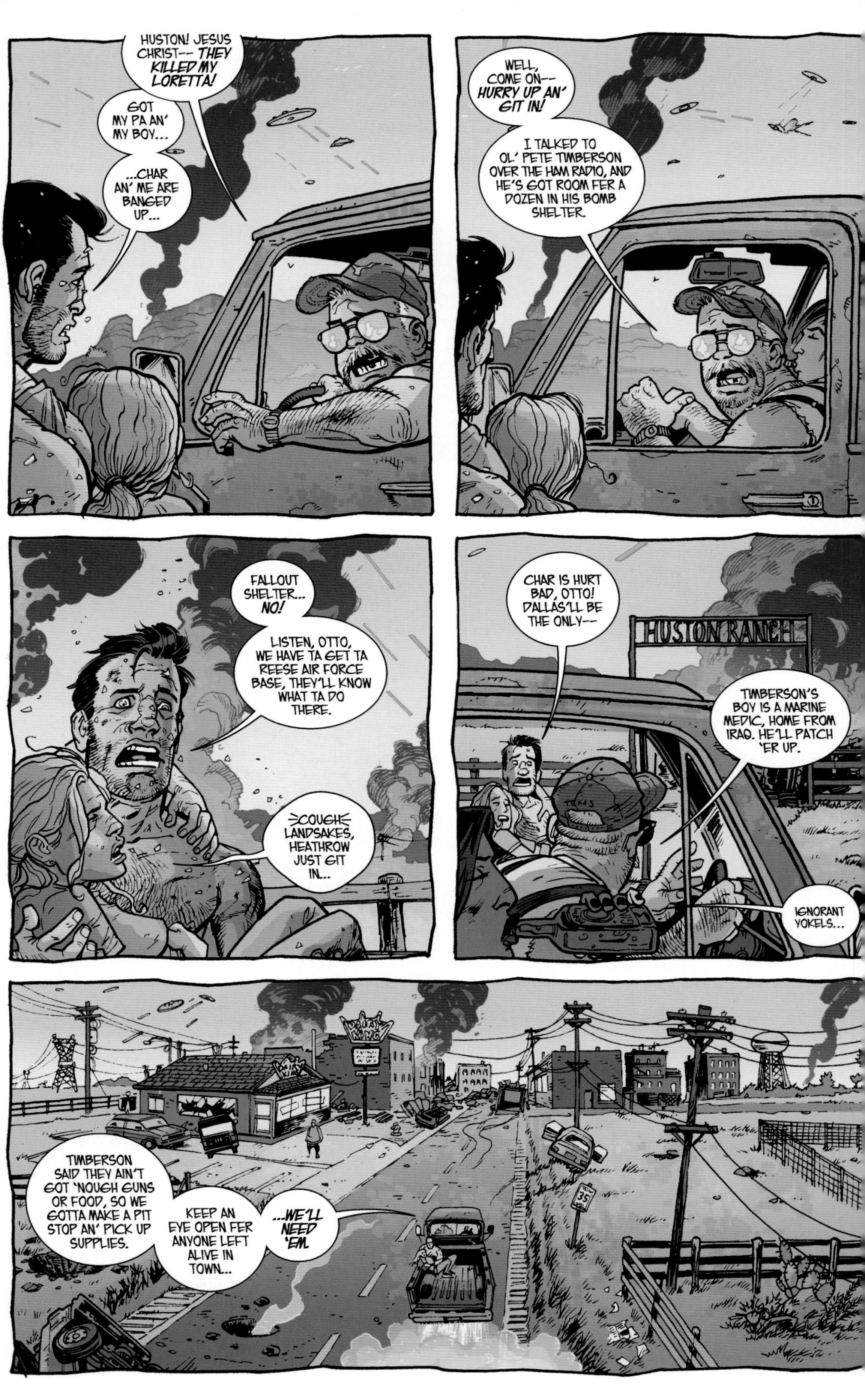
HUSTON! JESUS CHRIST-- THEY KILLED MY LORETTA!
GOT MY PA AN' MY BOY...
...CHAR AN' ME ARE BANGED UP...
WELL, COME ON-- HURRY UP AN' GIT IN!
I TALKED TO OL' PETE TIMBERSON OVER THE HAM RADIO, AND HE'S GOT ROOM FER A DOZEN IN HIS BOMB SHELTER.
FALLOUT SHELTER... NO!
LISTEN, OTTO, WE HAVE TA GET TA REESE AIR FORCE BASE, THEY'LL KNOW WHAT TA DO THERE.
=COUGH= LANDSAKES, HEATHROW JUST GIT IN...
CHAR IS HURT BAD, OTTO! DALLAS'LL BE THE ONLY--
HUSTON RANCH
TIMBERSON'S BOY IS A MARINE MEDIC, HOME FROM IRAQ. HE'LL PATCH 'ER UP.
IGNORANT YOKELS...
TIMBERSON SAID THEY AIN'T GOT 'NOUGH GUNS OR FOOD, SO WE GOTTA MAKE A PIT STOP AN' PICK UP SUPPLIES.
KEEP AN EYE OPEN FER ANYONE LEFT ALIVE IN TOWN...
...WE'LL NEED 'EM.
35

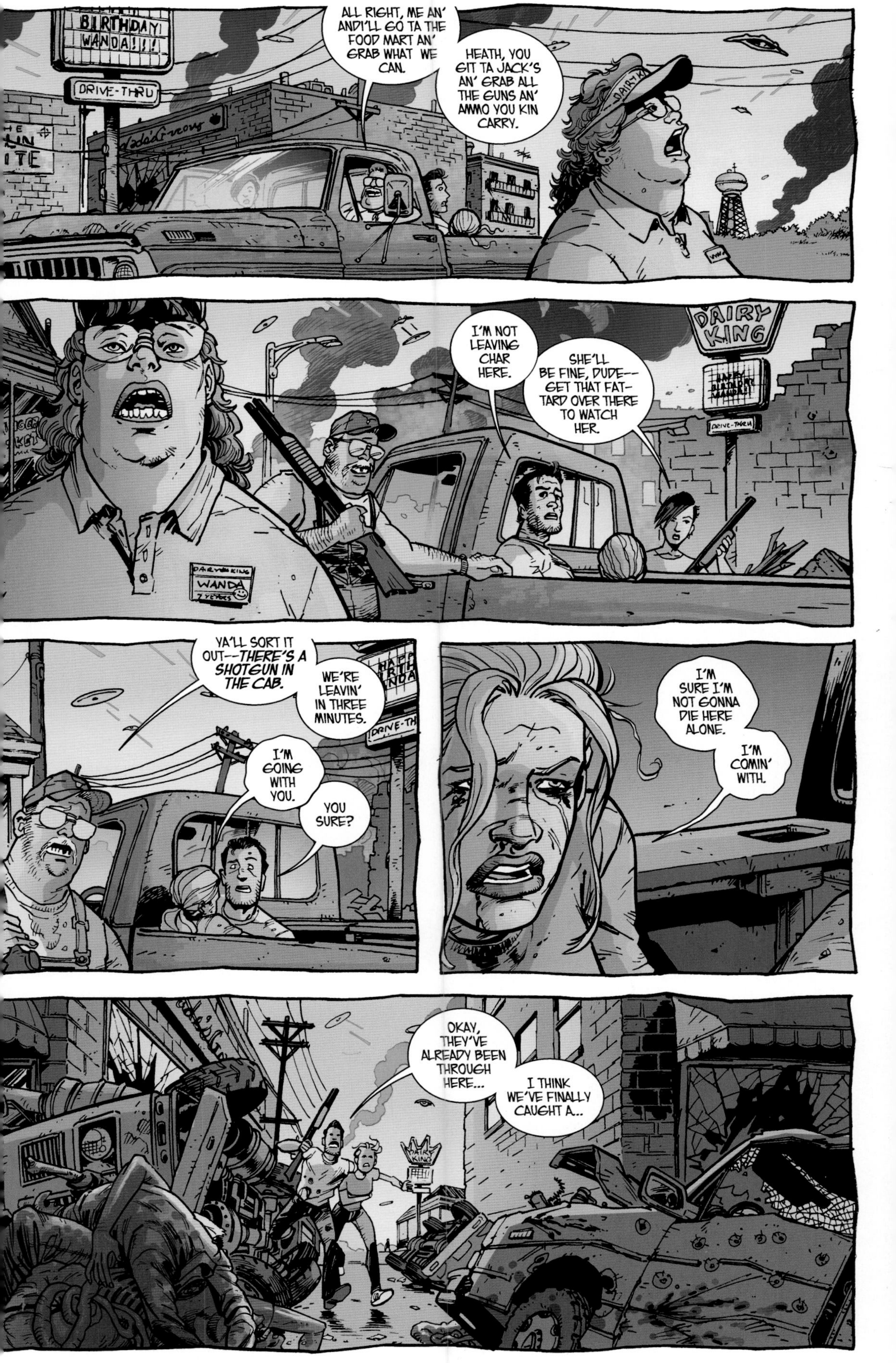
BIRTHDAY WANDA!!!
DRIVE-THRU
ALL RIGHT, ME AN' ANDI'LL GO TA THE FOOD MART AN' GRAB WHAT WE CAN.
HEATH, YOU GIT TA JACK'S AN' GRAB ALL THE GUNS AN' AMMO YOU KIN CARRY.
DAIRY KING
I'M NOT LEAVING CHAR HERE.
SHE'LL BE FINE, DUDE-- GET THAT FAT-TARD OVER THERE TO WATCH HER.
DAIRY KING WANDA 7 YEARS
YA'LL SORT IT OUT--*THERE'S A SHOTGUN IN THE CAB.*
WE'RE LEAVIN' IN THREE MINUTES.
I'M GOING WITH YOU.
YOU SURE?
I'M SURE I'M NOT GONNA DIE HERE ALONE.
I'M COMIN' WITH.
OKAY, THEY'VE ALREADY BEEN THROUGH HERE...
I THINK WE'VE FINALLY CAUGHT A...

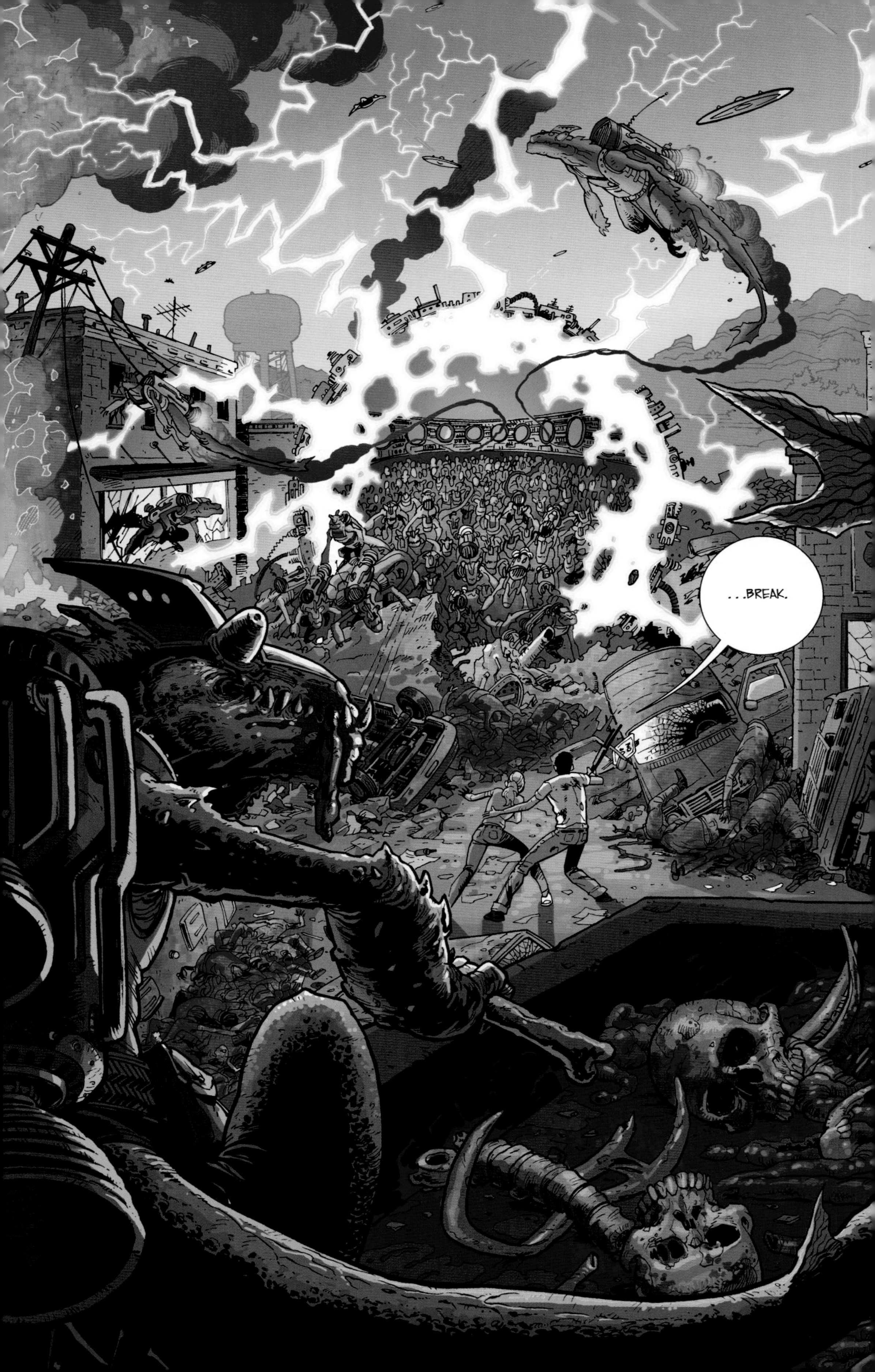
. . .BREAK.

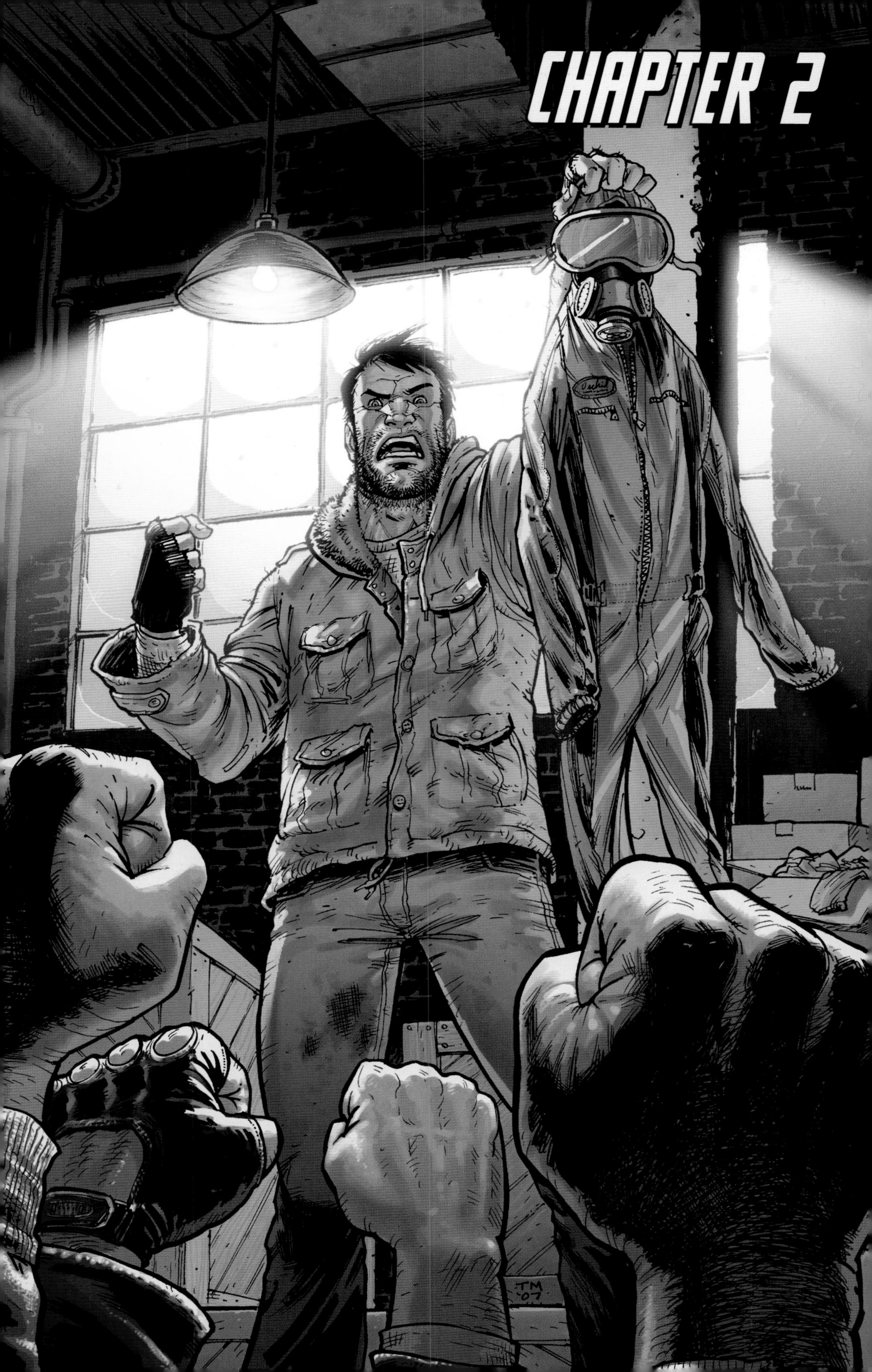
CHAPTER 2
TM
'07

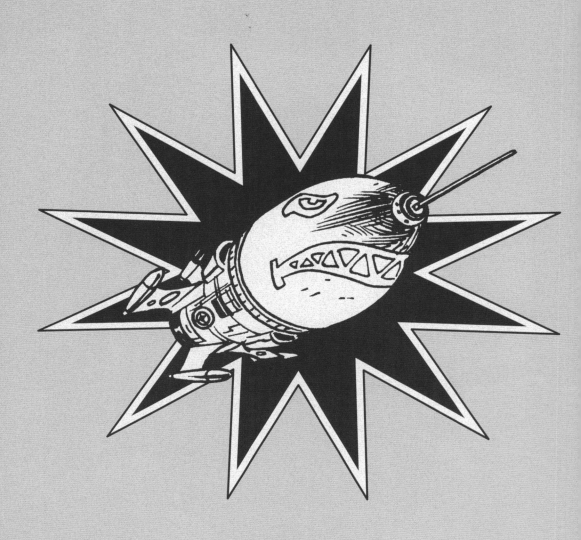

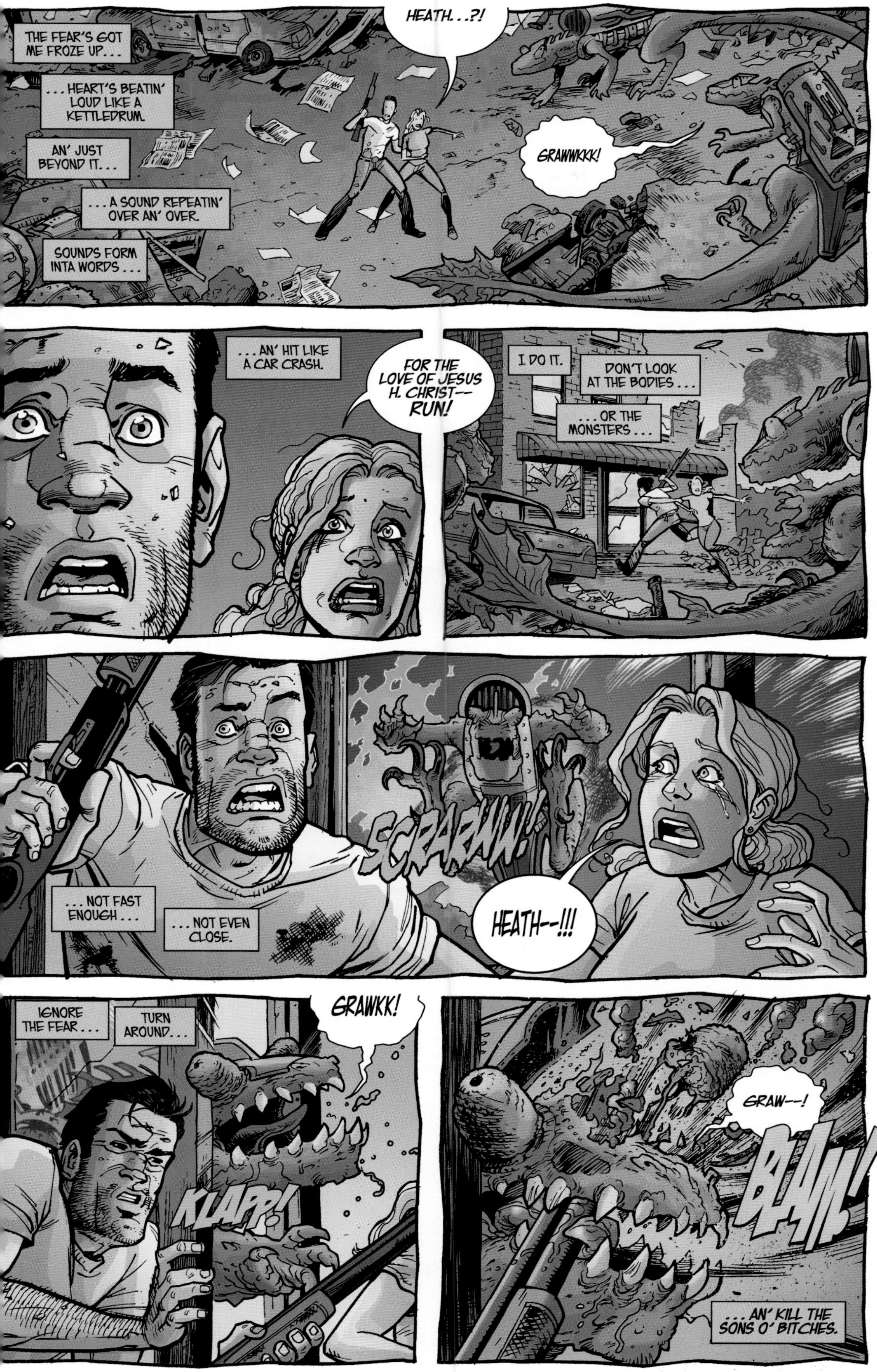
THE FEAR'S GOT ME FROZE UP...
...HEART'S BEATIN' LOUD LIKE A KETTLEDRUM.
AN' JUST BEYOND IT...
...A SOUND REPEATIN' OVER AN' OVER.
SOUNDS FORM INTA WORDS...
HEATH...?!
GRAWWKKK!
...AN' HIT LIKE A CAR CRASH.
FOR THE LOVE OF JESUS H. CHRIST-- RUN!
I DO IT.
DON'T LOOK AT THE BODIES...
...OR THE MONSTERS...
SCRRAWW!
...NOT FAST ENOUGH...
...NOT EVEN CLOSE.
HEATH--!!!
IGNORE THE FEAR...
TURN AROUND...
GRAWKK!
KLAPP!
GRAW--!
BLAM!
...AN' KILL THE SONS O' BITCHES.

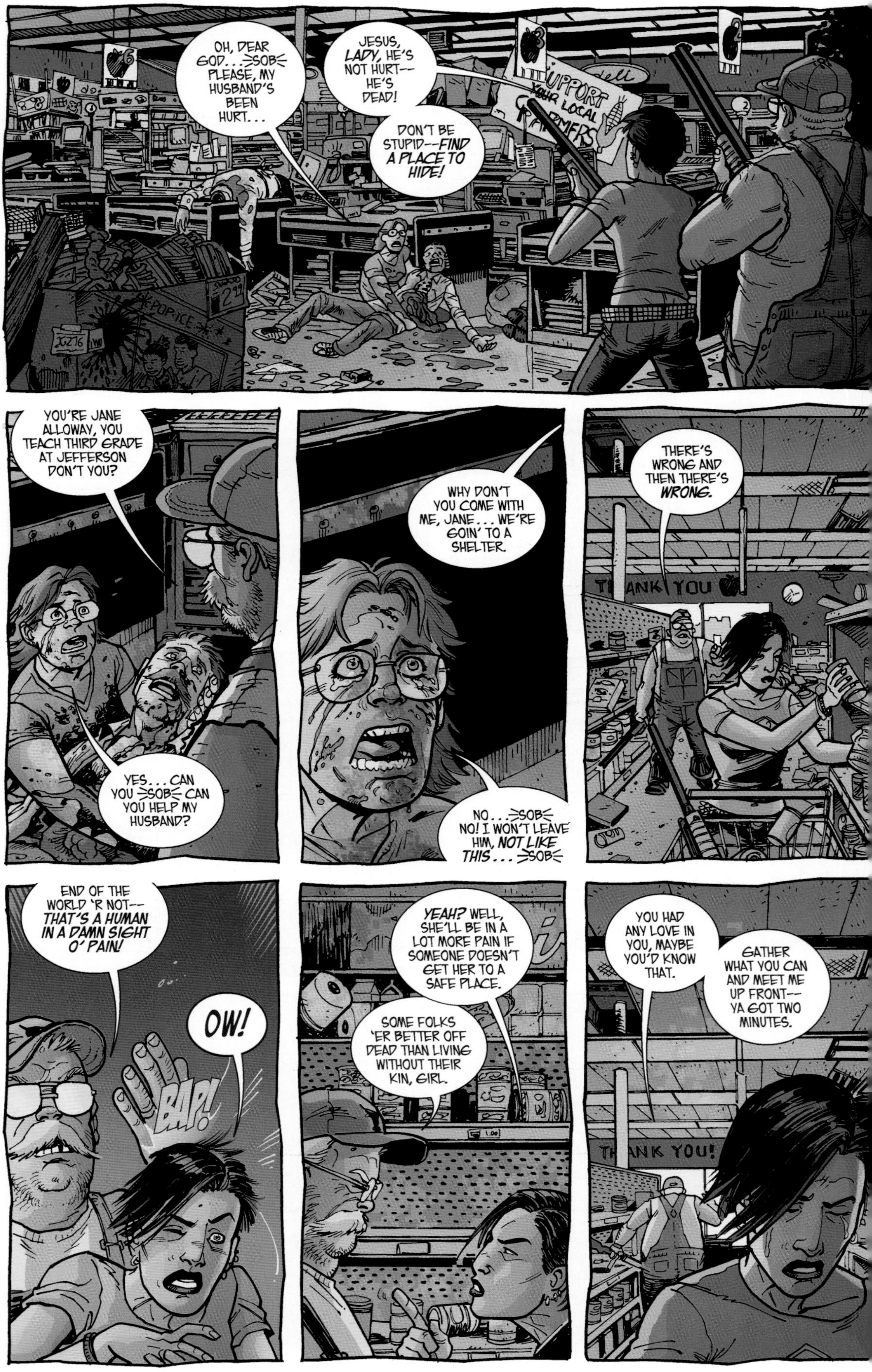
OH, DEAR GOD... ⋝SOB⋜ PLEASE, MY HUSBAND'S BEEN HURT...
JESUS, LADY, HE'S NOT HURT-- HE'S DEAD!
DON'T BE STUPID--FIND A PLACE TO HIDE!
SUPPORT YOUR LOCAL FARMERS
YOU'RE JANE ALLOWAY, YOU TEACH THIRD GRADE AT JEFFERSON DON'T YOU?
YES... CAN YOU ⋝SOB⋜ CAN YOU HELP MY HUSBAND?
WHY DON'T YOU COME WITH ME, JANE... WE'RE GOIN' TO A SHELTER.
NO... ⋝SOB⋜ NO! I WON'T LEAVE HIM, NOT LIKE THIS... ⋝SOB⋜
THERE'S WRONG AND THEN THERE'S WRONG.
THANK YOU
END OF THE WORLD 'R NOT-- THAT'S A HUMAN IN A DAMN SIGHT O' PAIN!
BAP!
OW!
YEAH? WELL, SHE'LL BE IN A LOT MORE PAIN IF SOMEONE DOESN'T GET HER TO A SAFE PLACE.
SOME FOLKS 'ER BETTER OFF DEAD THAN LIVING WITHOUT THEIR KIN, GIRL.
YOU HAD ANY LOVE IN YOU, MAYBE YOU'D KNOW THAT.
GATHER WHAT YOU CAN AND MEET ME UP FRONT-- YA GOT TWO MINUTES.
THANK YOU!

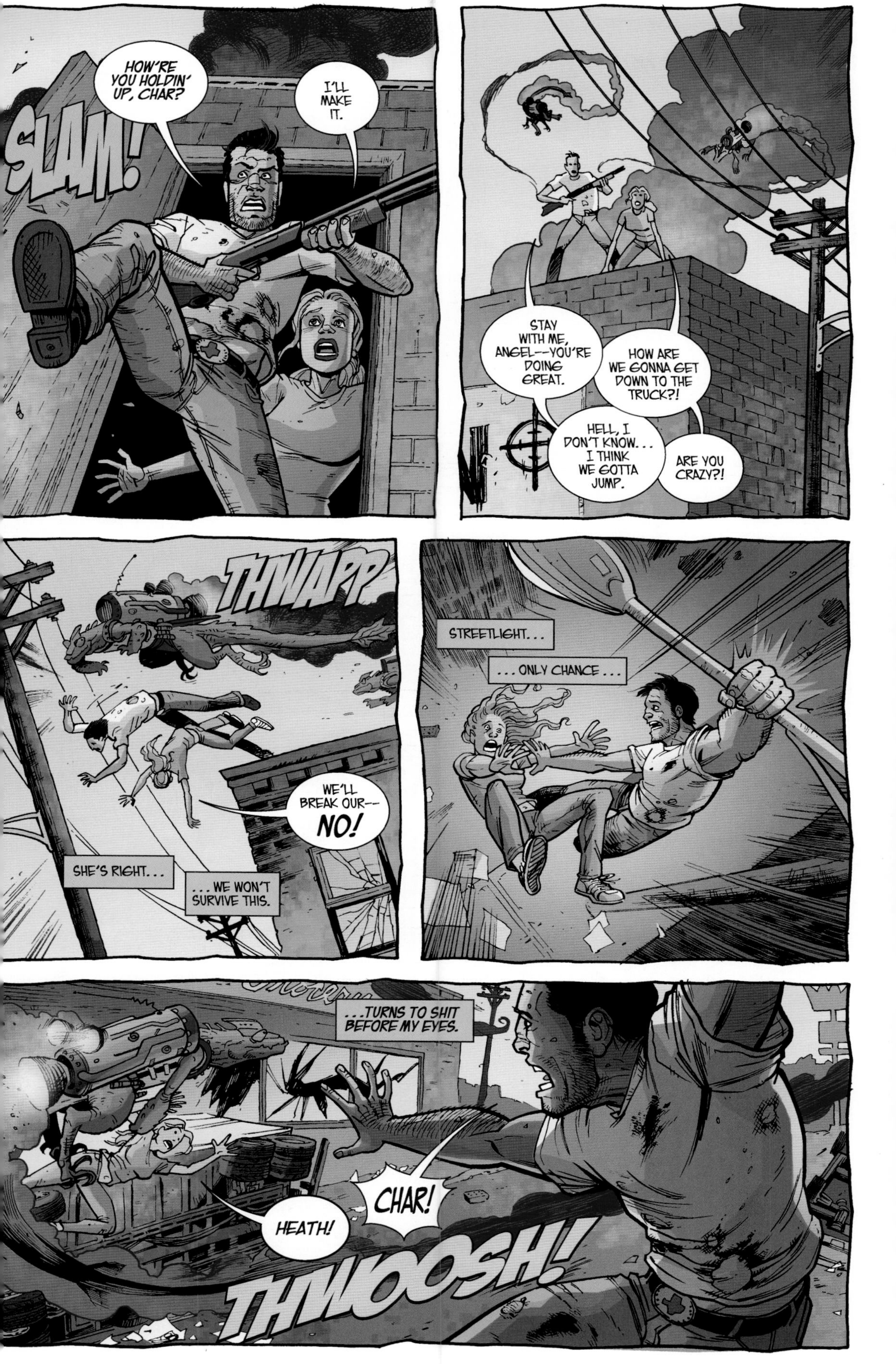
SLAM!
HOW'RE YOU HOLDIN' UP, CHAR?
I'LL MAKE IT.
STAY WITH ME, ANGEL--YOU'RE DOING GREAT.
HOW ARE WE GONNA GET DOWN TO THE TRUCK?!
HELL, I DON'T KNOW... I THINK WE GOTTA JUMP.
ARE YOU CRAZY?!
THWAPP
WE'LL BREAK OUR-- NO!
SHE'S RIGHT...
...WE WON'T SURVIVE THIS.
STREETLIGHT...
...ONLY CHANCE...
...TURNS TO SHIT BEFORE MY EYES.
CHAR!
HEATH!
THWOOSH!

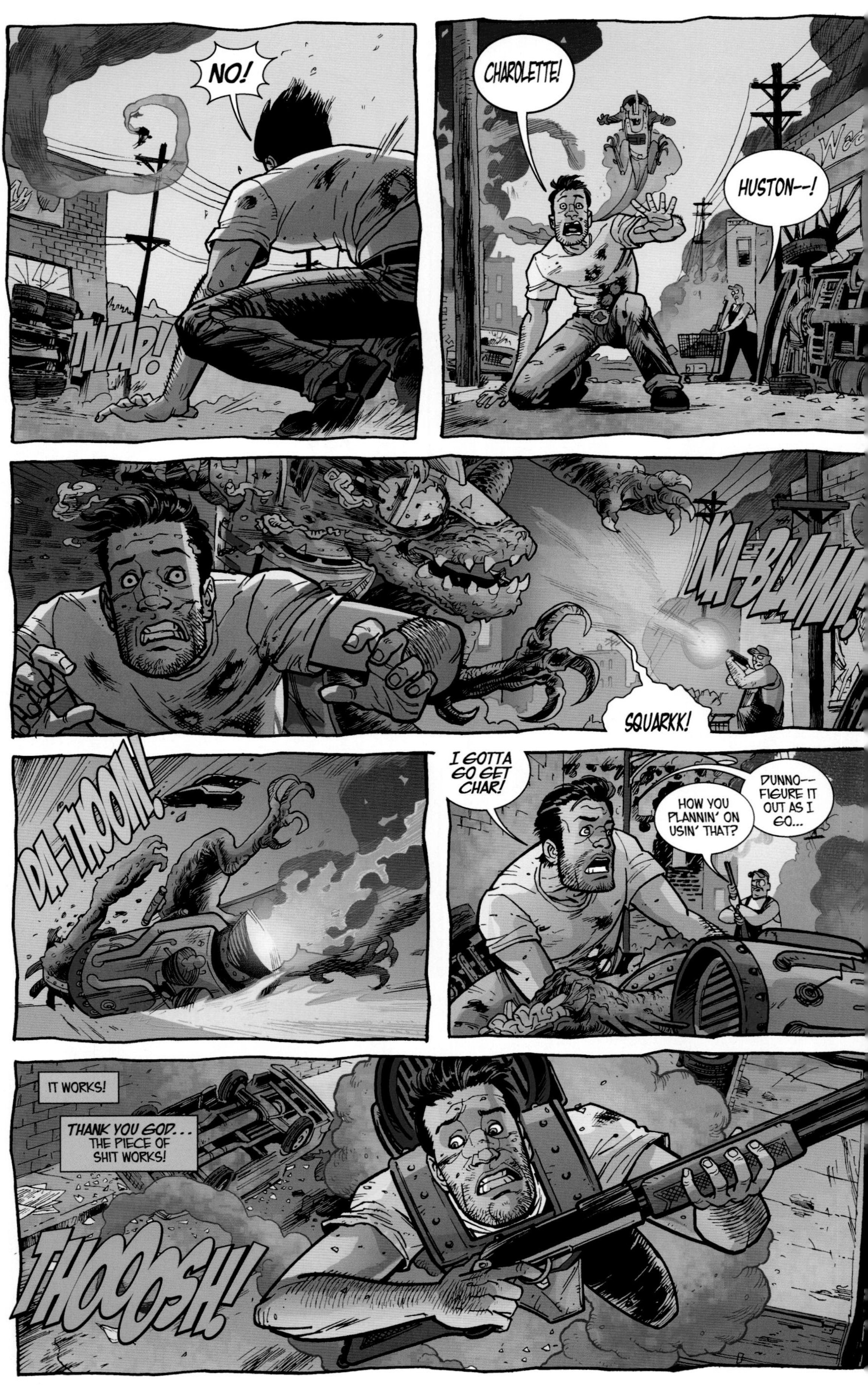
NO!
TWAP!
CHAROLETTE!
HUSTON--!
KA-BLAMM
SQUARKK!
DA-THOOM!
I GOTTA GO GET CHAR!
HOW YOU PLANNIN' ON USIN' THAT?
DUNNO--FIGURE IT OUT AS I GO...
IT WORKS!
THANK YOU GOD... THE PIECE OF SHIT WORKS!
THOOOSH!

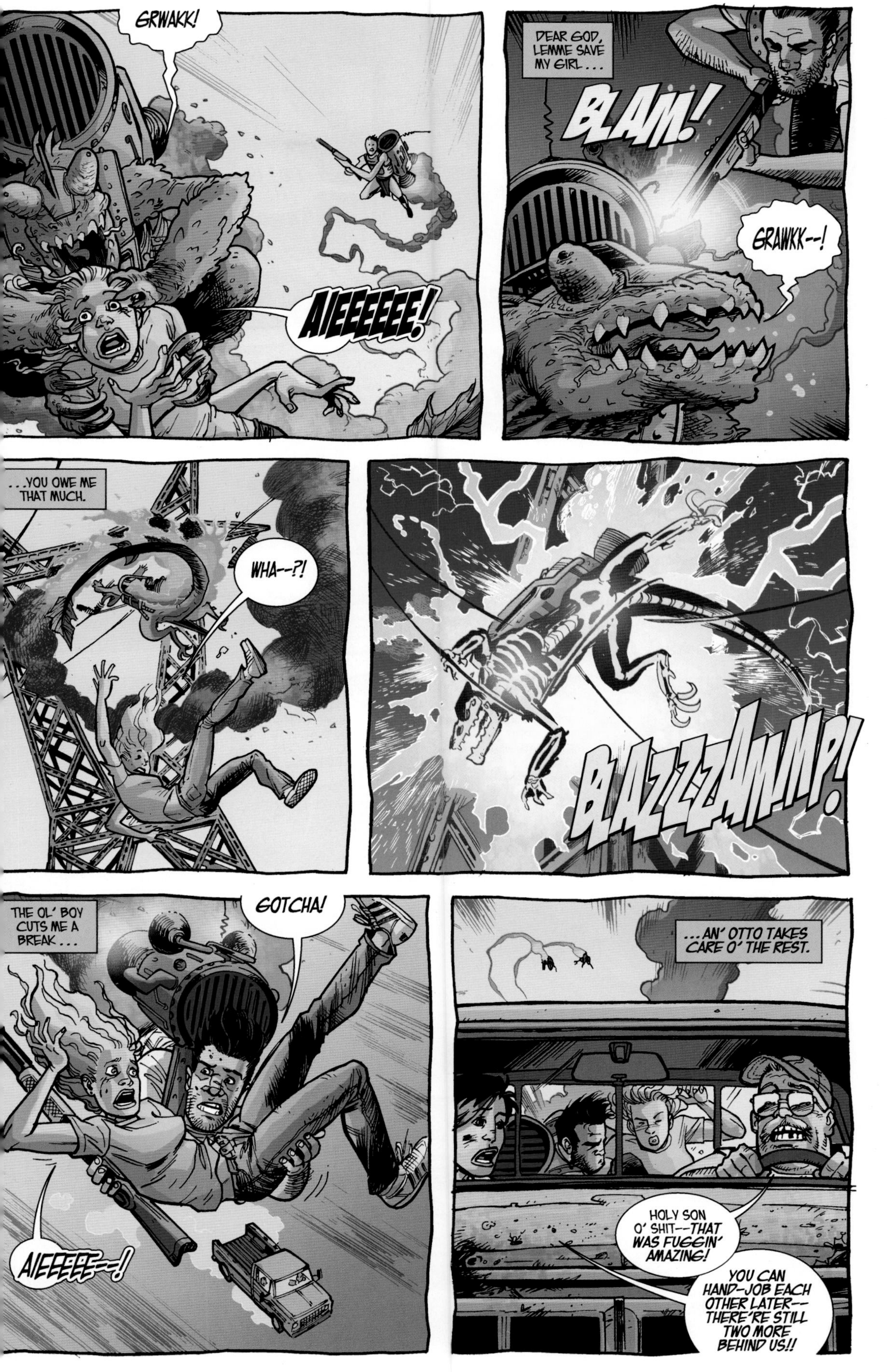
GRWAKK!
AIEEEEEE!
DEAR GOD, LEMME SAVE MY GIRL . . .
BLAM!
GRAWKK--!
. . .YOU OWE ME THAT MUCH.
WHA--?!
BLAZZZAMMP!
THE OL' BOY CUTS ME A BREAK . . .
GOTCHA!
AIEEEEE--!
. . .AN' OTTO TAKES CARE O' THE REST.
HOLY SON O' SHIT--THAT WAS FUGGIN' AMAZING!
YOU CAN HAND-JOB EACH OTHER LATER-- THERE'RE STILL TWO MORE BEHIND US!!

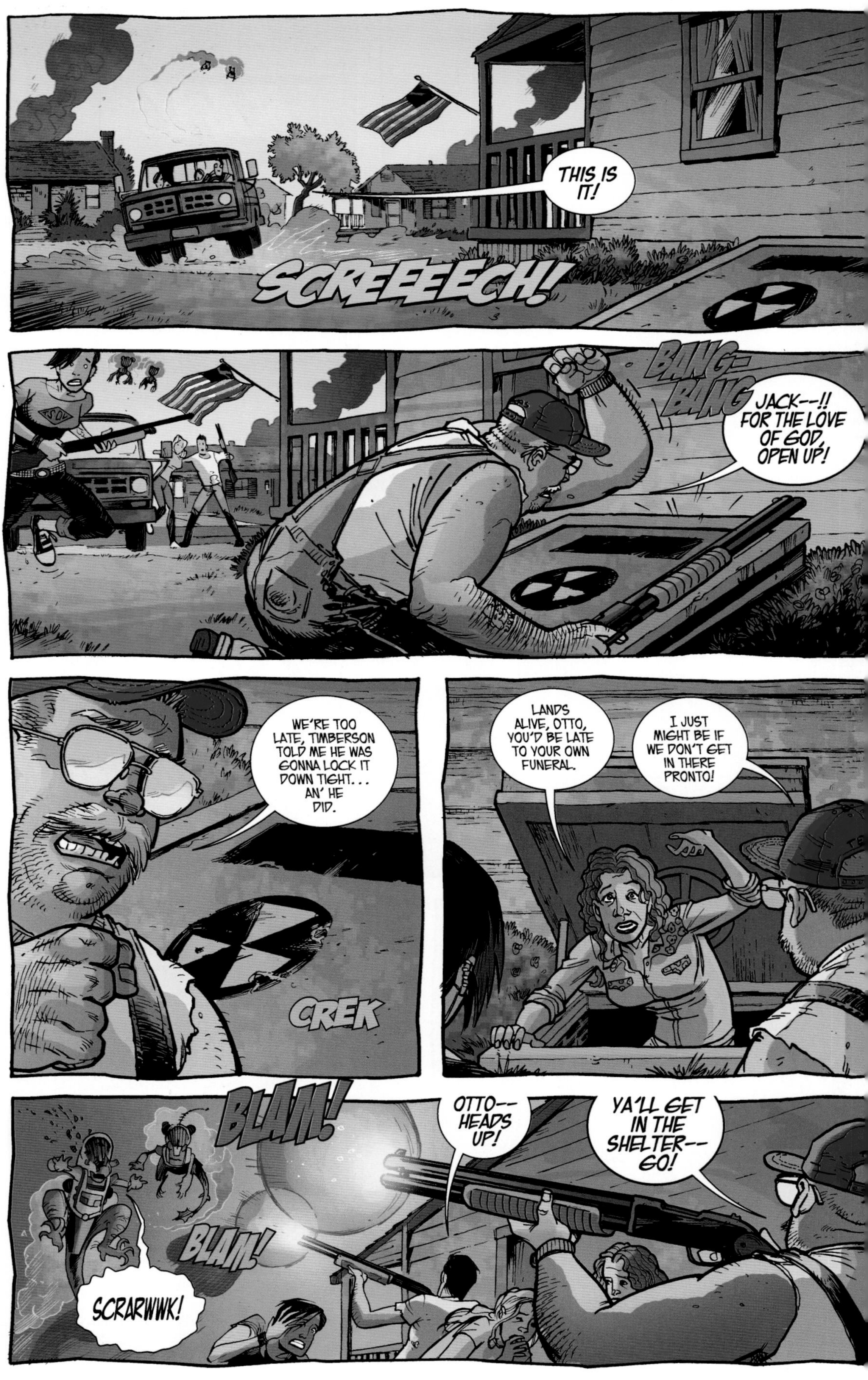
THIS IS IT!
SCREEEEECH!
BANG-BANG
JACK--!! FOR THE LOVE OF GOD, OPEN UP!
WE'RE TOO LATE, TIMBERSON TOLD ME HE WAS GONNA LOCK IT DOWN TIGHT. . . AN' HE DID.
CREK
LANDS ALIVE, OTTO, YOU'D BE LATE TO YOUR OWN FUNERAL.
I JUST MIGHT BE IF WE DON'T GET IN THERE PRONTO!
BLAM!
OTTO-- HEADS UP!
YA'LL GET IN THE SHELTER-- GO!
BLAM!
SCRARWWK!

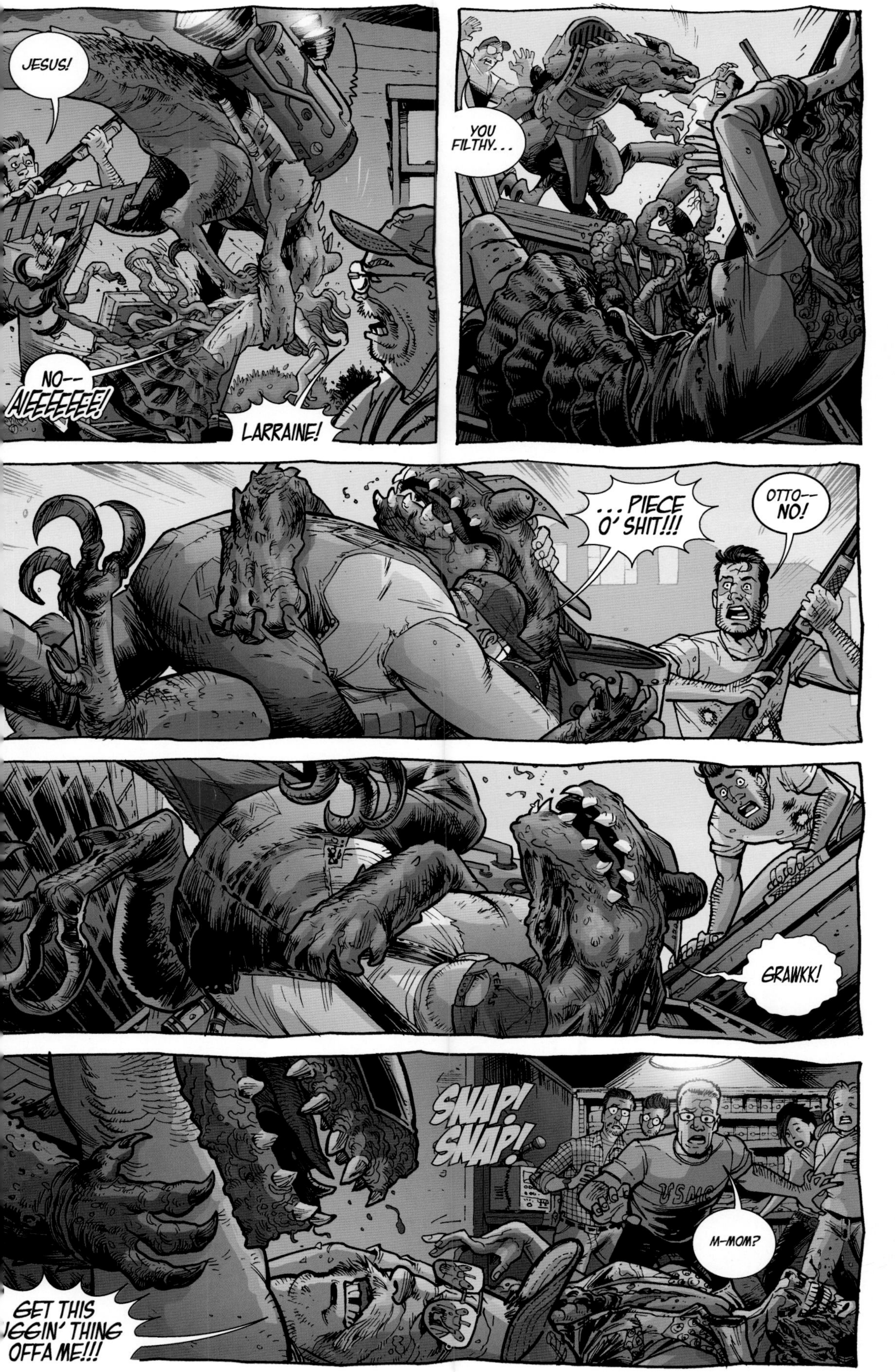
JESUS!
HRETT!
NO--
AIEEEEEEE!
LARRAINE!
YOU FILTHY...
...PIECE O' SHIT!!!
OTTO-- NO!
GRAWKK!
SNAP! SNAP!
M-MOM?
GET THIS
UGGIN' THING
OFFA ME!!!

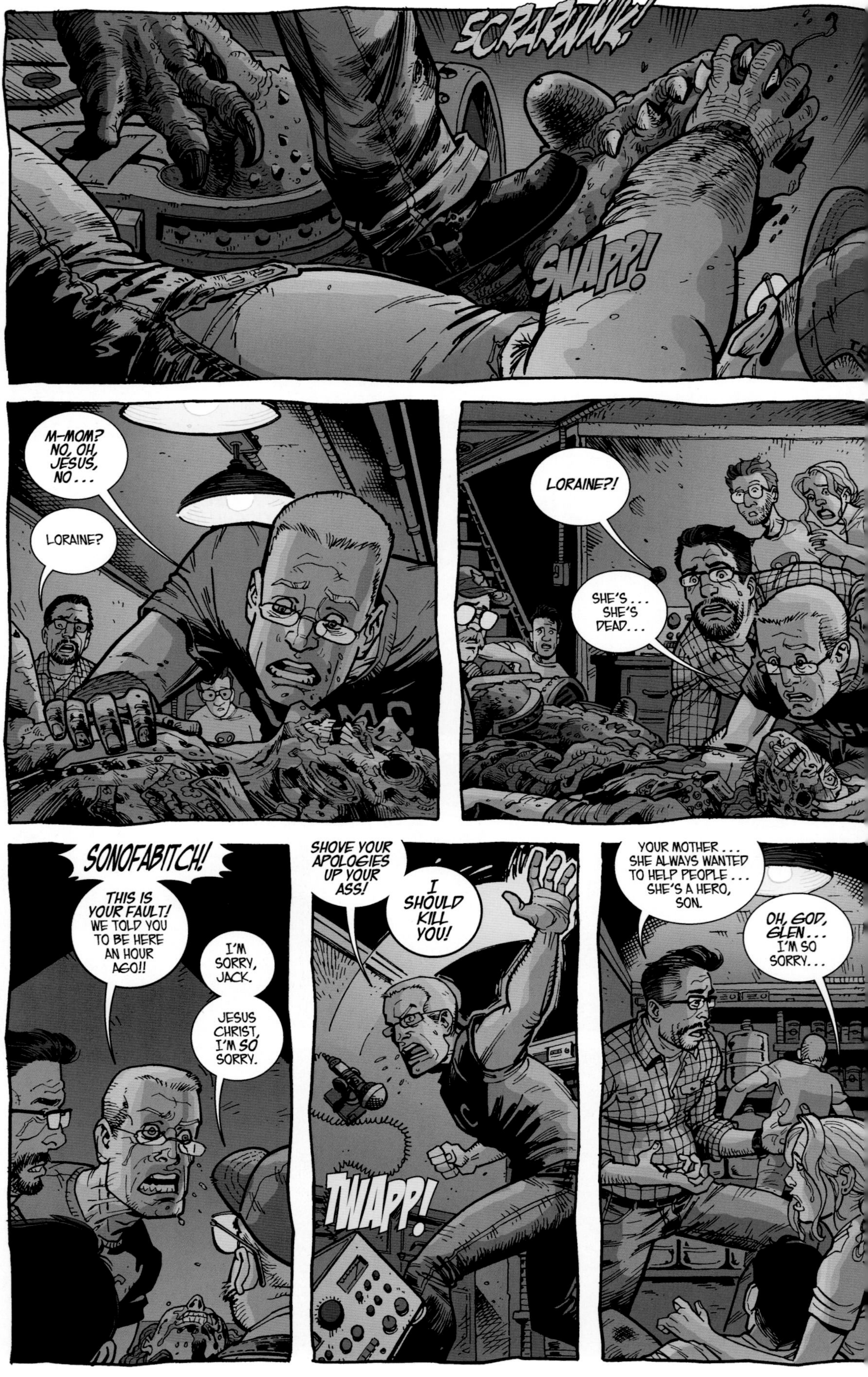
SCRAAWK!
SNAPP!
M-MOM? NO, OH, JESUS, NO . . .
LORAINE?
LORAINE?!
SHE'S . . . SHE'S DEAD . . .
SONOFABITCH!
THIS IS YOUR FAULT! WE TOLD YOU TO BE HERE AN HOUR AGO!!
I'M SORRY, JACK.
JESUS CHRIST, I'M SO SORRY.
SHOVE YOUR APOLOGIES UP YOUR ASS!
I SHOULD KILL YOU!
TWAPP!
YOUR MOTHER . . . SHE ALWAYS WANTED TO HELP PEOPLE . . . SHE'S A HERO, SON.
OH, GOD, GLEN . . . I'M SO SORRY . . .

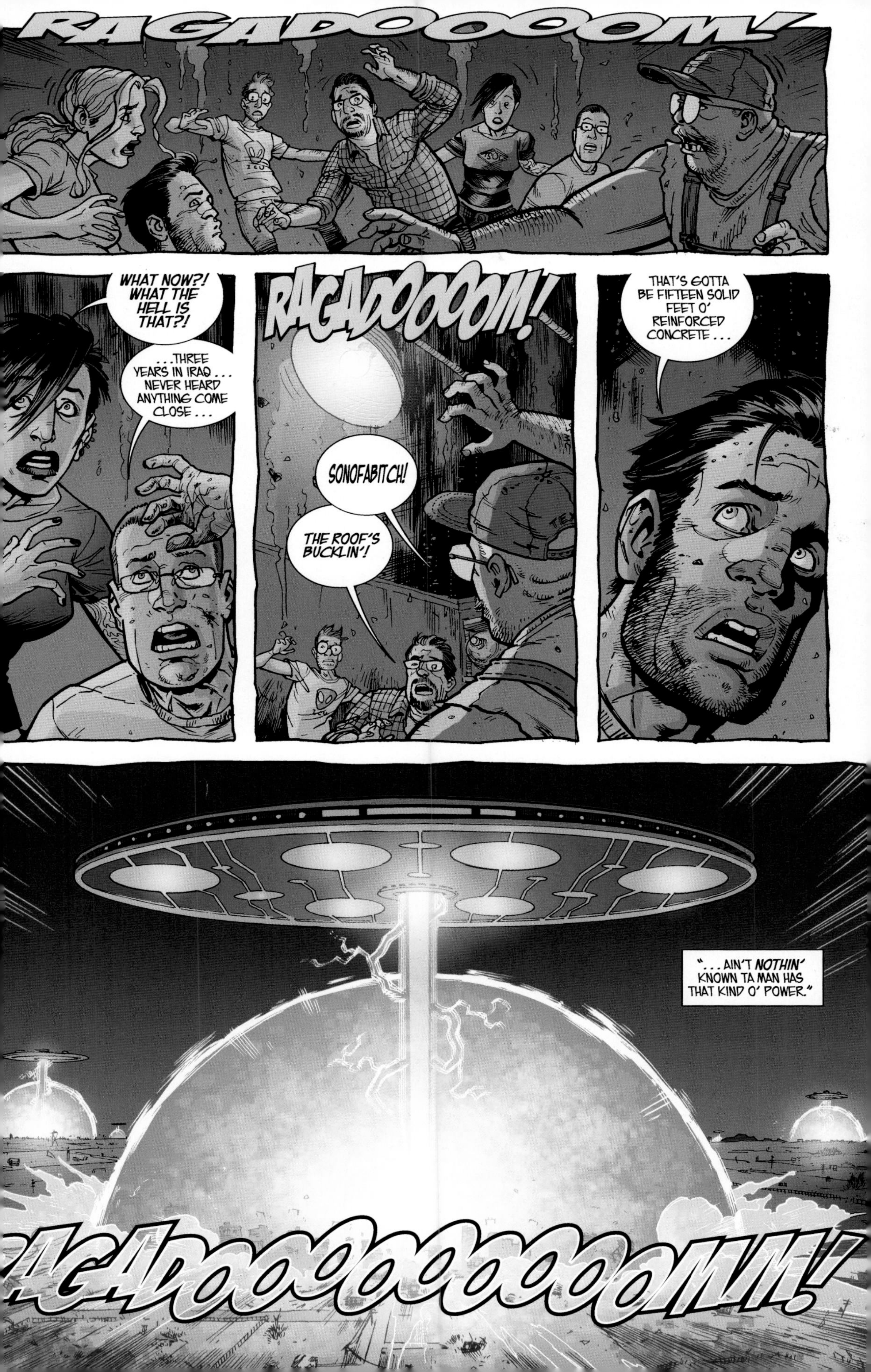
RAGADOOOOOM!
WHAT NOW?! WHAT THE HELL IS THAT?!
. . . THREE YEARS IN IRAQ . . . NEVER HEARD ANYTHING COME CLOSE . . .
RAGADOOOOOM!
SONOFABITCH!
THE ROOF'S BUCKLIN'!
THAT'S GOTTA BE FIFTEEN SOLID FEET O' REINFORCED CONCRETE . . .
". . . AIN'T NOTHIN' KNOWN TA MAN HAS THAT KIND O' POWER."
AGADOOOOOOOOOM!

Three months pass . . .

IT'S THIS PIECE HERE-- THIS IS WHAT WE NEED TO REPLACE TO GET THE RADIO WORKING?

IF WE ONLY HAD A SOLDERING GUN...

HELL, IF I HAD A SOLDER GUN I COULD JUST ABOUT BUILD ONE FROM SCRATCH.

SO THE REPTILE MEN, THE ZERIN YOU CALLED THEM, THEY'RE JUST SCAVENGERS WHO FOLLOW THESE OTHER TWO RACES AROUND EATING UP THE POOR SUCKERS CAUGHT IN THE MIDDLE?

YES, THAT'S RIGHT!

I'VE BEEN PERSECUTED MY ENTIRE LIFE FOR MY STUDIES OF ALIEN CONSPIRACY... YOU HAVE NO IDEA HOW GOOD IT FEELS TO BE PROVEN RIGHT-- TO FINALLY HAVE PEOPLE LISTEN TO ME!

YEAH, SO ALIEN INVASION AN' THE EXECUTION OF YOUR RACE IS JUST A SMALL PRICE TA PAY FER BRAGGIN' RIGHTS, HUH?

IF THEY'D LISTENED WE COULD HAVE STOPPED IT!

THE U.S. AND MANY OTHER NATIONS KNEW WE WERE PRECARIOUSLY SET BETWEEN THE TETALDIAN AND DRESSITE BORDERS FOR YEARS, BUT THE FOOLS CHOSE TO KEEP IT QUIET.

DECADES AGO, REPRESENTATIVES FROM THE UNITED SYSTEMS CAME AND WARNED OUR LEADERS THAT THE AVERAGE HUMAN MONKEY WOULD GO CRAZY AT PROOF OF EXTRATERRESTRIAL LIFE... IT DISPROVES NEARLY ALL OUR ARCHAIC RELIGIONS.

THEY MADE A DEAL WITH THE EMPIRES FOR EARTH TO REMAIN NEUTRAL... IN EXCHANGE FOR A PROMISE THAT WE'D BE LEFT ALONE.

BUT ANYONE WHO KNEW ANYTHING ABOUT THE TETALDIANS KNEW IT COULDN'T LAST.

TETALDIANS MUST HAVE STARTED THE FIGHT BECAUSE THEY KNEW THE DRESSITES WERE HERE, UNDERCOVER, IN HUMAN SKINS.

I MEAN-- IT'S COMMON KNOWLEDGE THEY'VE BEEN SLOWLY TAKING US OVER FOR YEARS!

LOOK HOW EVIL AND CORRUPT OUR GOVERNMENTS HAD BECOME!

I GUESS IT DIDN'T MATTER IF WE HUMANS WERE IN CAHOOTS OR NOT...

ENOUGH!

LISTEN, MILKSOP--I'VE BEEN LISTENING TO YOU RAMBLE ON ABOUT THIS SHIT FER THREE MONTHS NOW...WE ALL HAVE.

'LESS THIS LEADS TA TRAVELIN' BACK IN TIME TA SAVE MY OLD MAN AN' MY BOY-- THEN PACK IT IN!

TIME TRAVEL IS IMPOSSIBLE...

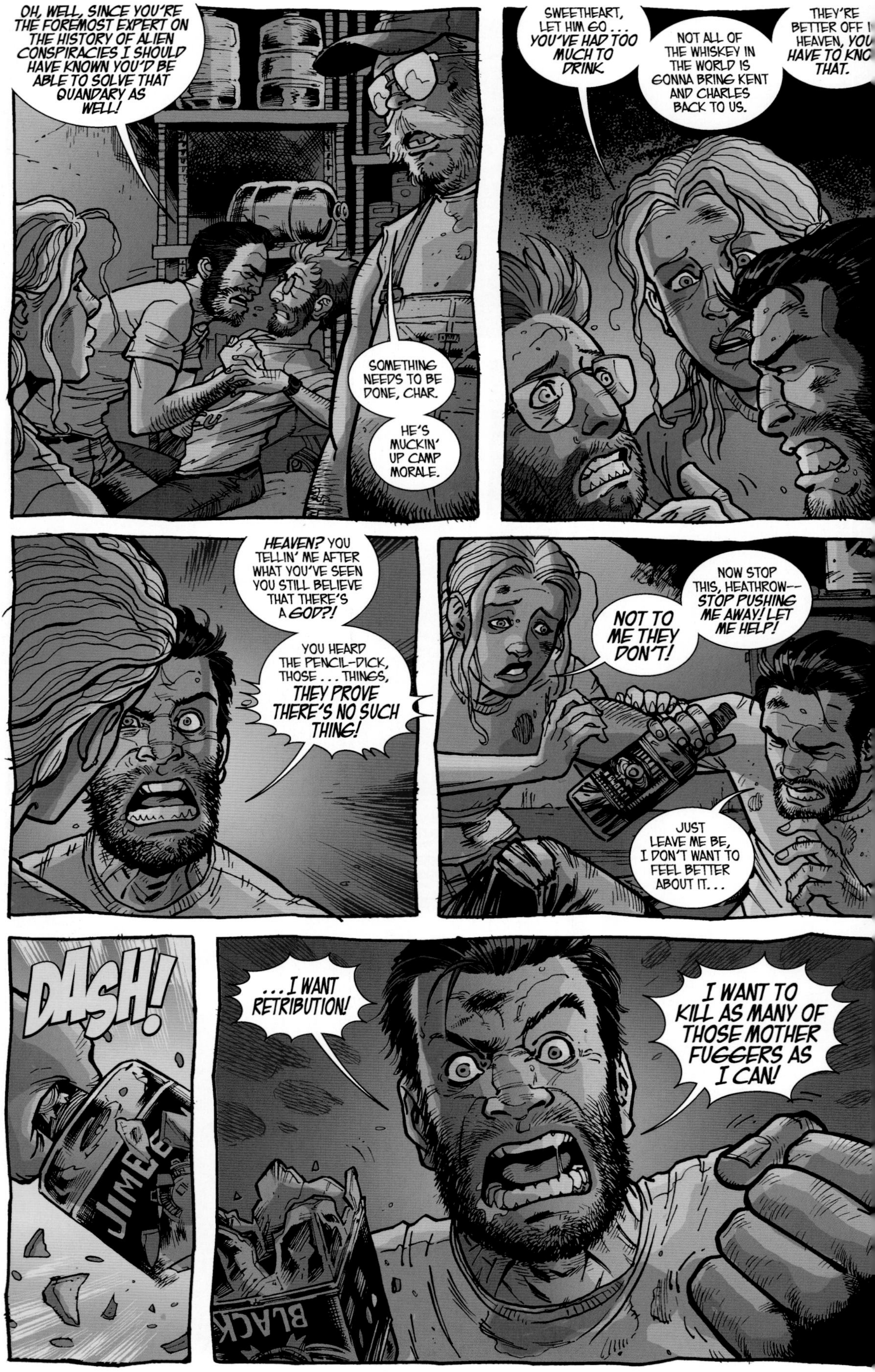
OH, WELL, SINCE YOU'RE THE FOREMOST EXPERT ON THE HISTORY OF ALIEN CONSPIRACIES I SHOULD HAVE KNOWN YOU'D BE ABLE TO SOLVE THAT QUANDARY AS WELL!
SOMETHING NEEDS TO BE DONE, CHAR.
HE'S MUCKIN' UP CAMP MORALE.
SWEETHEART, LET HIM GO . . . YOU'VE HAD TOO MUCH TO DRINK.
NOT ALL OF THE WHISKEY IN THE WORLD IS GONNA BRING KENT AND CHARLES BACK TO US.
THEY'RE BETTER OFF I HEAVEN, YOU HAVE TO KNO THAT.
HEAVEN? YOU TELLIN' ME AFTER WHAT YOU'VE SEEN YOU STILL BELIEVE THAT THERE'S A GOD?!
YOU HEARD THE PENCIL-DICK, THOSE . . . THINGS, THEY PROVE THERE'S NO SUCH THING!
NOT TO ME THEY DON'T!
NOW STOP THIS, HEATHROW-- STOP PUSHING ME AWAY! LET ME HELP!
JUST LEAVE ME BE, I DON'T WANT TO FEEL BETTER ABOUT IT . . .
DASH!
. . . I WANT RETRIBUTION!
I WANT TO KILL AS MANY OF THOSE MOTHER FUGGERS AS I CAN!

I CAN'T SIT IN THIS BOX-- NOT FOR ONE MORE HOUR!

BRING IT DOWN A NOTCH, HUSTON...THIS HERE IS COUNTER-PRODUCTIVE.

I DON'T CARE IF IT'S RADIOACTIVE OUT THERE OR NOT.

I HAVE TO GET OUT OF THIS COFFIN!

OOF--!

ANGEL, YOU GOTTA GET A HOLD O' YOURSELF!

FOR WHAT?!

SO I CAN SIT HERE STARVING TO DEATH ENDURING THE UNBEARABLE ROTTING SMELL FROM THOSE CORPSES?

YOU CARELESS SON OF A BITCH!

THAT SMELL IS MY MOTHER-- AND SHE'D STILL BE ALIVE IF IT WEREN'T FOR YOU!

BUT SHE'S NOT ALIVE, AND NEITHER IS MY KIN.

THEY'RE DEAD AN' WE'RE ALIVE...

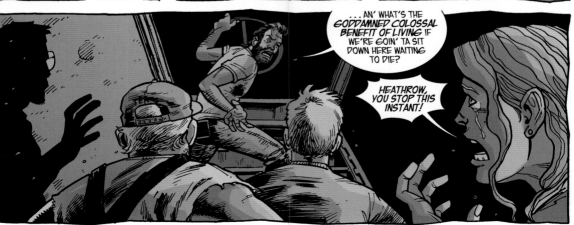

...AN' WHAT'S THE GODDAMNED COLOSSAL BENEFIT OF LIVING IF WE'RE GOIN' TA SIT DOWN HERE WAITING TO DIE?

HEATHROW, YOU STOP THIS INSTANT!

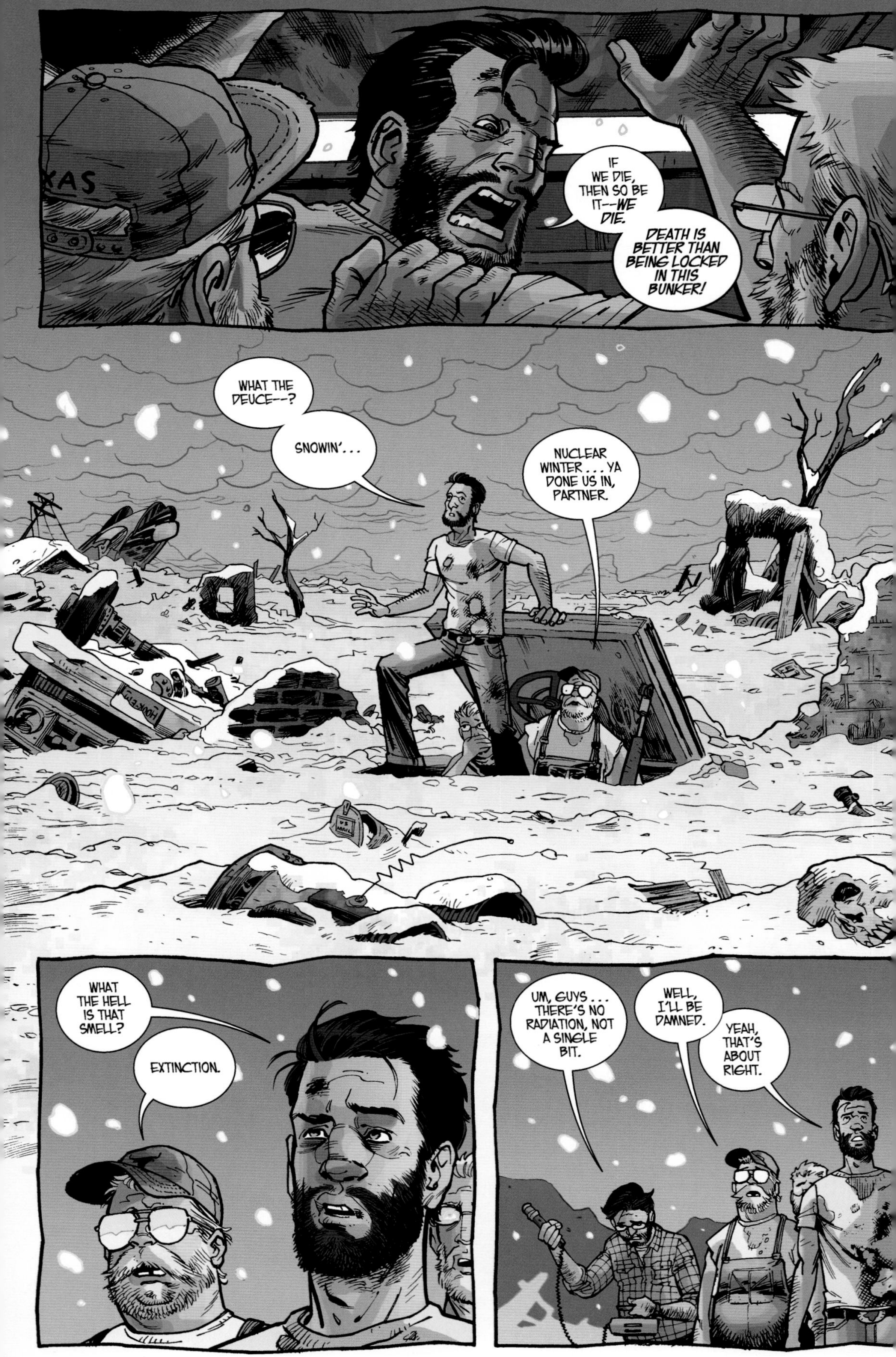

IF WE DIE, THEN SO BE IT--WE DIE.
DEATH IS BETTER THAN BEING LOCKED IN THIS BUNKER!
WHAT THE DEUCE--?
SNOWIN'. . .
NUCLEAR WINTER . . . YA DONE US IN, PARTNER.
WHAT THE HELL IS THAT SMELL?
EXTINCTION.
UM, GUYS . . . THERE'S NO RADIATION, NOT A SINGLE BIT.
WELL, I'LL BE DAMNED.
YEAH, THAT'S ABOUT RIGHT.

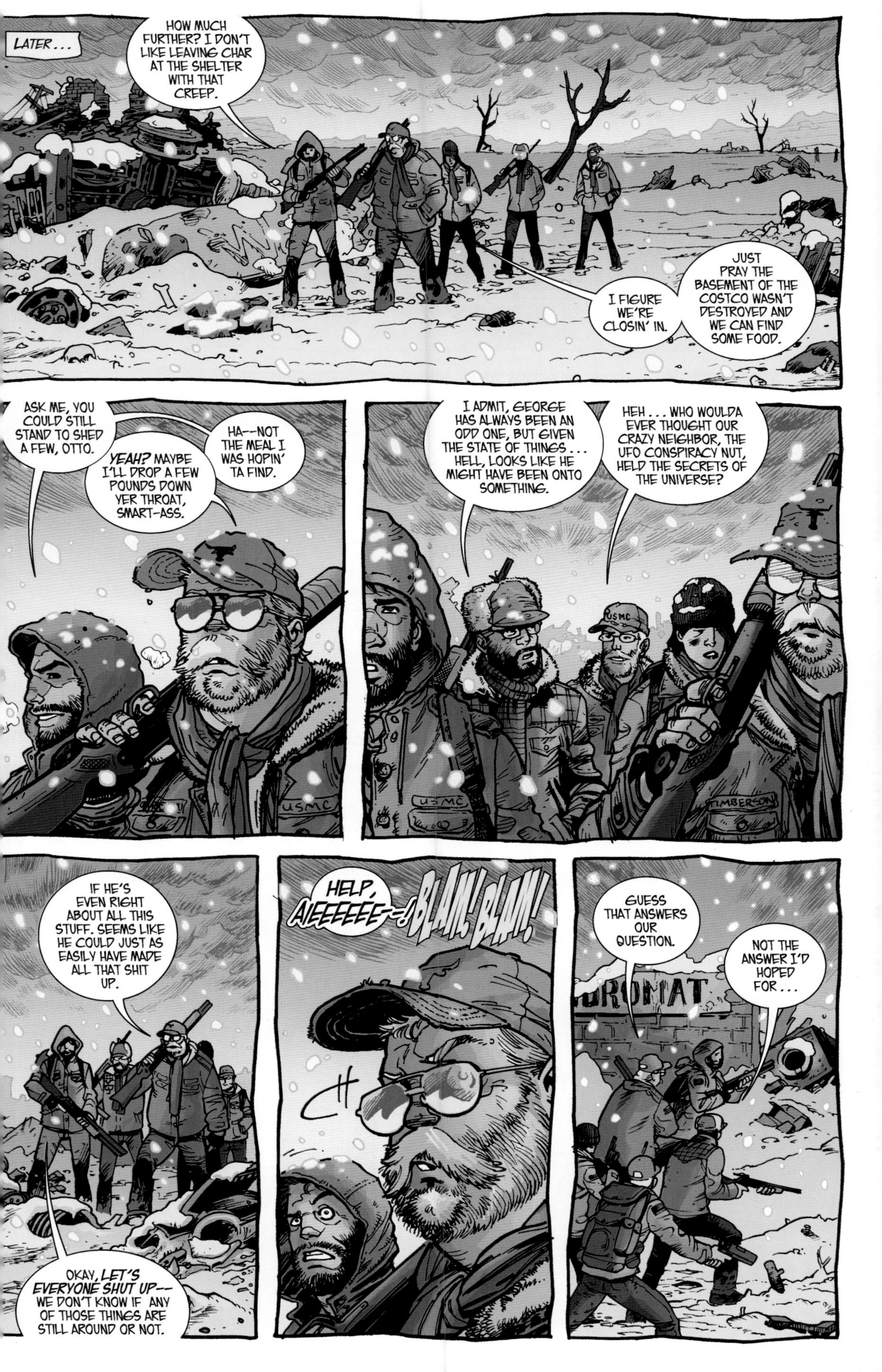
LATER...
HOW MUCH FURTHER? I DON'T LIKE LEAVING CHAR AT THE SHELTER WITH THAT CREEP.
I FIGURE WE'RE CLOSIN' IN.
JUST PRAY THE BASEMENT OF THE COSTCO WASN'T DESTROYED AND WE CAN FIND SOME FOOD.
HA--NOT THE MEAL I WAS HOPIN' TA FIND.
ASK ME, YOU COULD STILL STAND TO SHED A FEW, OTTO.
YEAH? MAYBE I'LL DROP A FEW POUNDS DOWN YER THROAT, SMART-ASS.
I ADMIT, GEORGE HAS ALWAYS BEEN AN ODD ONE, BUT GIVEN THE STATE OF THINGS... HELL, LOOKS LIKE HE MIGHT HAVE BEEN ONTO SOMETHING.
HEH... WHO WOULDA EVER THOUGHT OUR CRAZY NEIGHBOR, THE UFO CONSPIRACY NUT, HELD THE SECRETS OF THE UNIVERSE?
IF HE'S EVEN RIGHT ABOUT ALL THIS STUFF. SEEMS LIKE HE COULD JUST AS EASILY HAVE MADE ALL THAT SHIT UP.
OKAY, LET'S EVERYONE SHUT UP-- WE DON'T KNOW IF ANY OF THOSE THINGS ARE STILL AROUND OR NOT.
HELP, AIEEEEEE--!
BLAM! BLAM!
GUESS THAT ANSWERS OUR QUESTION.
NOT THE ANSWER I'D HOPED FOR...

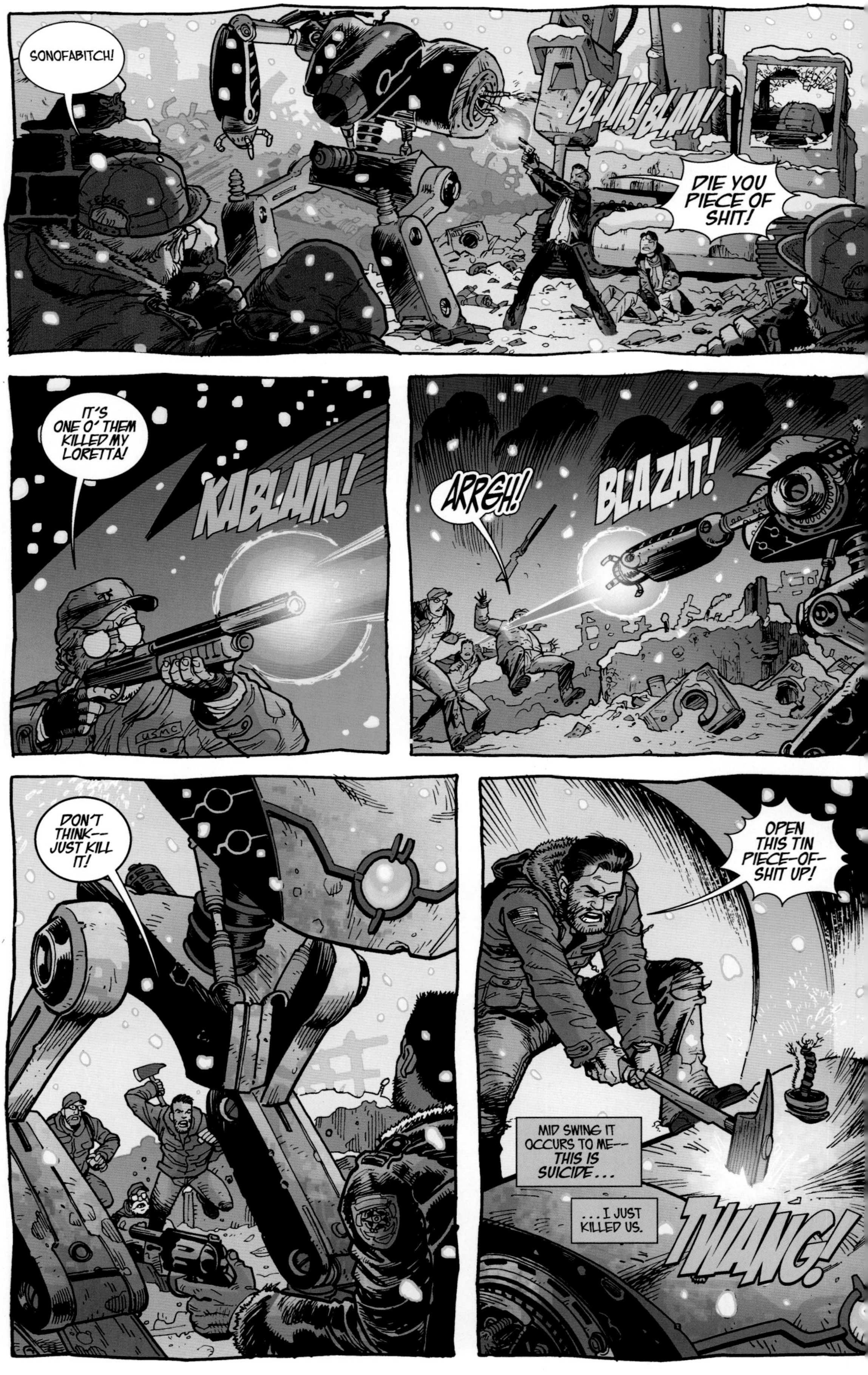
SONOFABITCH!
BLAM! BLAM!
DIE YOU PIECE OF SHIT!
IT'S ONE O' THEM KILLED MY LORETTA!
KABLAM!
ARRGH!
BLAZAT!
DON'T THINK-- JUST KILL IT!
OPEN THIS TIN PIECE-OF-SHIT UP!
MID SWING IT OCCURS TO ME-- THIS IS SUICIDE . . .
. . . I JUST KILLED US.
TWANG!

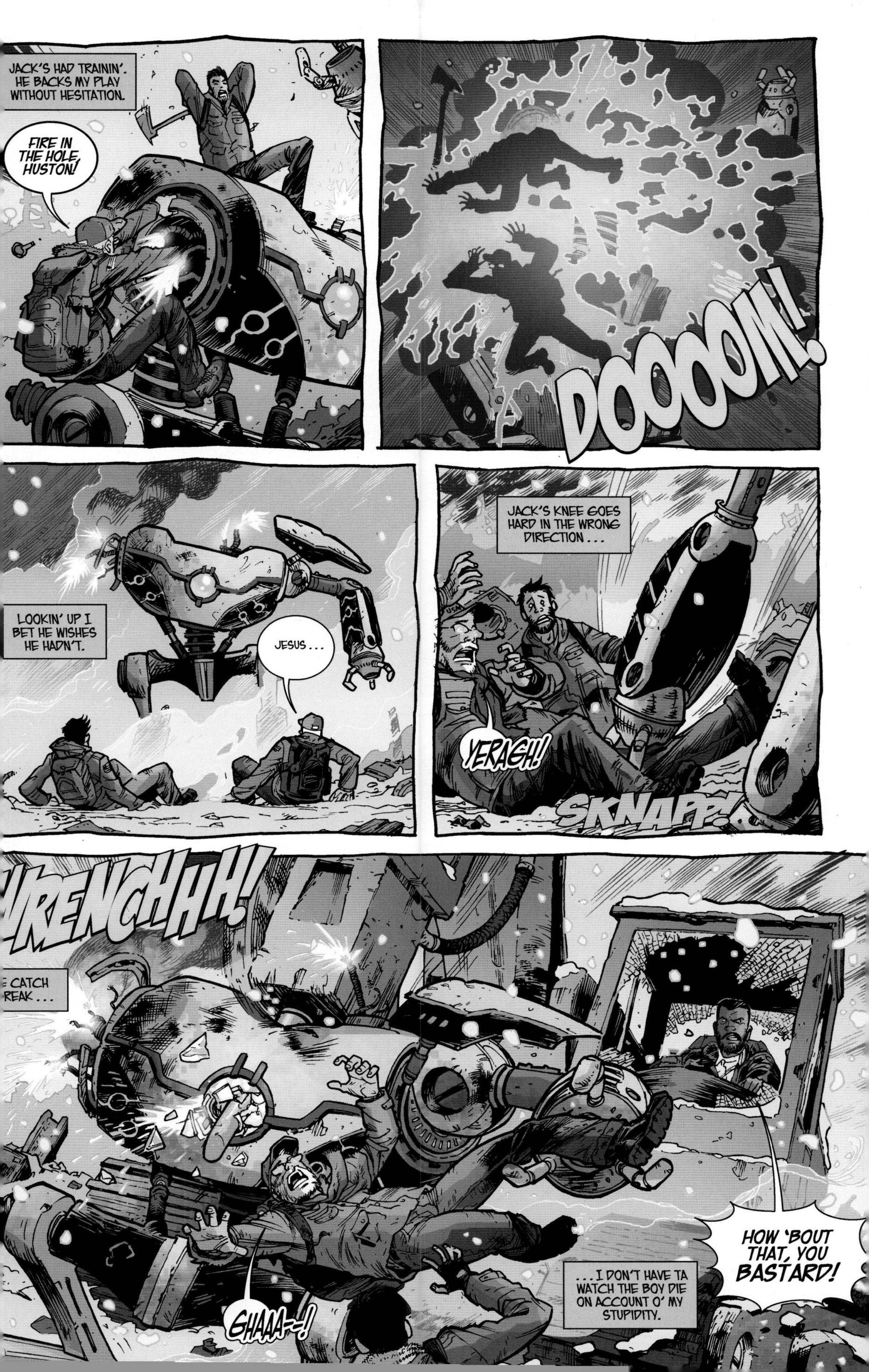
JACK'S HAD TRAININ'. HE BACKS MY PLAY WITHOUT HESITATION.
FIRE IN THE HOLE, HUSTON!
DOOOOOM!
LOOKIN' UP I BET HE WISHES HE HADN'T.
JESUS . . .
JACK'S KNEE GOES HARD IN THE WRONG DIRECTION . . .
YERAGH!
SKNAPP!
CRENCHHH!
E CATCH
REAK . . .
HOW 'BOUT THAT, YOU BASTARD!
. . . I DON'T HAVE TA WATCH THE BOY DIE ON ACCOUNT O' MY STUPIDITY.
GHAAA--!

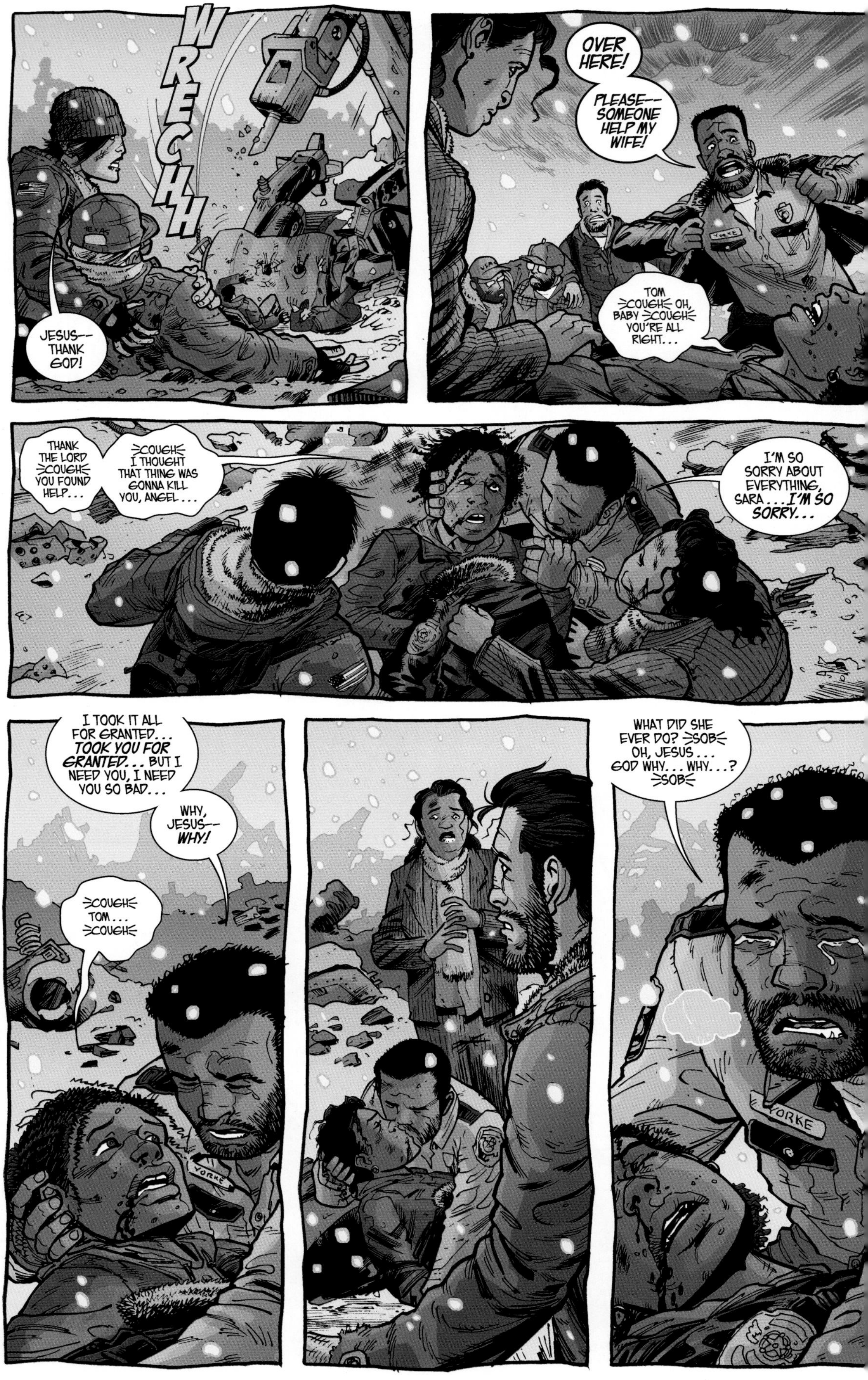
WRECHHH
JESUS-- THANK GOD!
OVER HERE!
PLEASE-- SOMEONE HELP MY WIFE!
TOM *COUGH* OH, BABY *COUGH* YOU'RE ALL RIGHT...
THANK THE LORD *COUGH* YOU FOUND HELP...
COUGH I THOUGHT THAT THING WAS GONNA KILL YOU, ANGEL...
I'M SO SORRY ABOUT EVERYTHING, SARA... I'M SO SORRY...
I TOOK IT ALL FOR GRANTED... TOOK YOU FOR GRANTED... BUT I NEED YOU, I NEED YOU SO BAD...
WHY, JESUS-- WHY!
COUGH TOM... *COUGH*
WHAT DID SHE EVER DO? *SOB* OH, JESUS... GOD WHY... WHY...? *SOB*

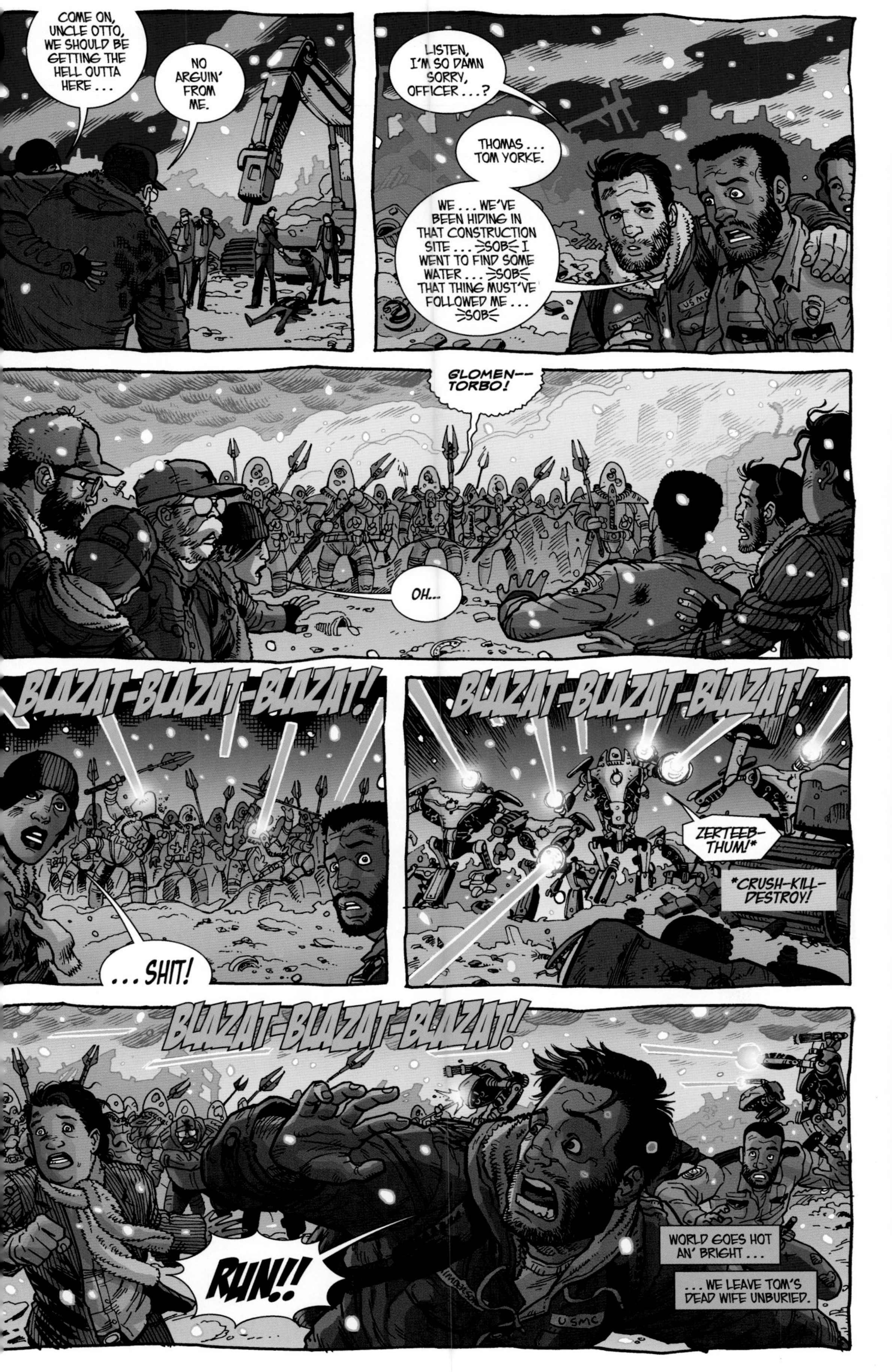
COME ON, UNCLE OTTO, WE SHOULD BE GETTING THE HELL OUTTA HERE . . .
NO ARGUIN' FROM ME.
LISTEN, I'M SO DAMN SORRY, OFFICER . . . ?
THOMAS . . . TOM YORKE.
WE . . . WE'VE BEEN HIDING IN THAT CONSTRUCTION SITE . . . SOB I WENT TO FIND SOME WATER . . . SOB THAT THING MUST'VE FOLLOWED ME . . . SOB
GLOMEN--TORBO!
OH...
BLAZAT-BLAZAT-BLAZAT!
. . . SHIT!
BLAZAT-BLAZAT-BLAZAT!
ZERTEEB-THUM!*
*CRUSH-KILL-DESTROY!
BLAZAT-BLAZAT-BLAZAT!
RUN!!
WORLD GOES HOT AN' BRIGHT . . .
. . . WE LEAVE TOM'S DEAD WIFE UNBURIED.

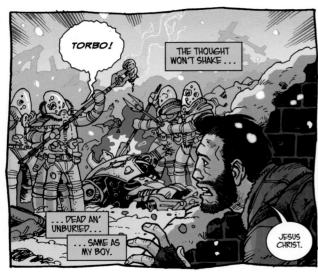

TORBO!

THE THOUGHT WON'T SHAKE...

...DEAD AN' UNBURIED...

...SAME AS MY BOY.

JESUS CHRIST.

GLORORB!

DAD, LOOK OUT--!

TOR--

GHEARGH!

BLAM!

SONOFABITCH!

YERAGH-- GET IT OFFA ME!

JESUS CHRIST, DAD-- IT HURTS SO BAD!

I GOTCHA JACK!

HE'S GONE, GLEN-- WE HAVE TO GO!

NO, PLEASE GOD...

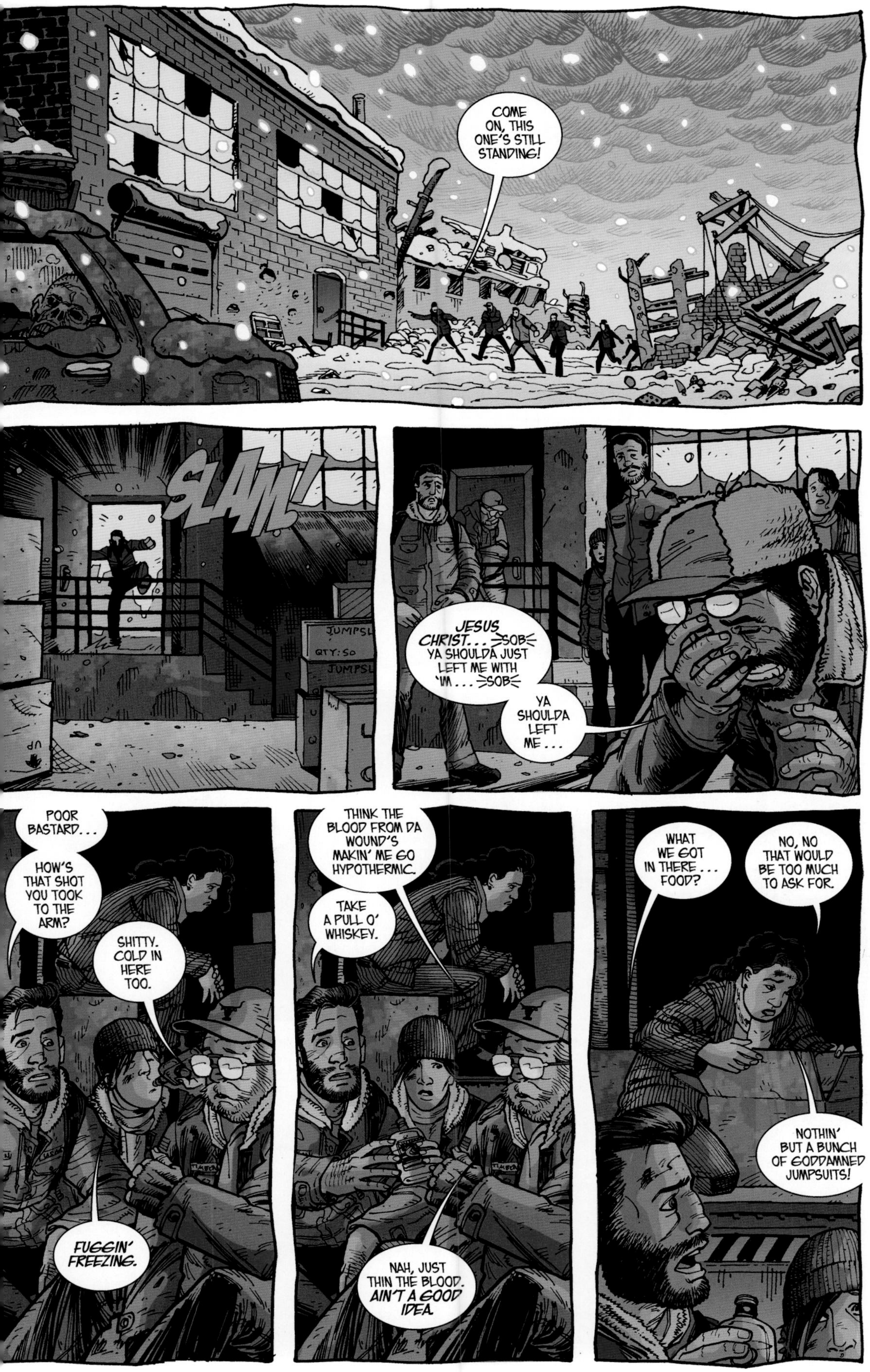
COME ON, THIS ONE'S STILL STANDING!
SLAM!
JUMPSU
QTY: 50
JUMPSU
UP
JESUS CHRIST... ≶SOB≷ YA SHOULDA JUST LEFT ME WITH 'IM... ≶SOB≷
YA SHOULDA LEFT ME...
POOR BASTARD...
HOW'S THAT SHOT YOU TOOK TO THE ARM?
SHITTY. COLD IN HERE TOO.
FUGGIN' FREEZING.
THINK THE BLOOD FROM DA WOUND'S MAKIN' ME GO HYPOTHERMIC.
TAKE A PULL O' WHISKEY.
NAH, JUST THIN THE BLOOD. AIN'T A GOOD IDEA.
WHAT WE GOT IN THERE... FOOD?
NO, NO THAT WOULD BE TOO MUCH TO ASK FOR.
NOTHIN' BUT A BUNCH OF GODDAMNED JUMPSUITS!

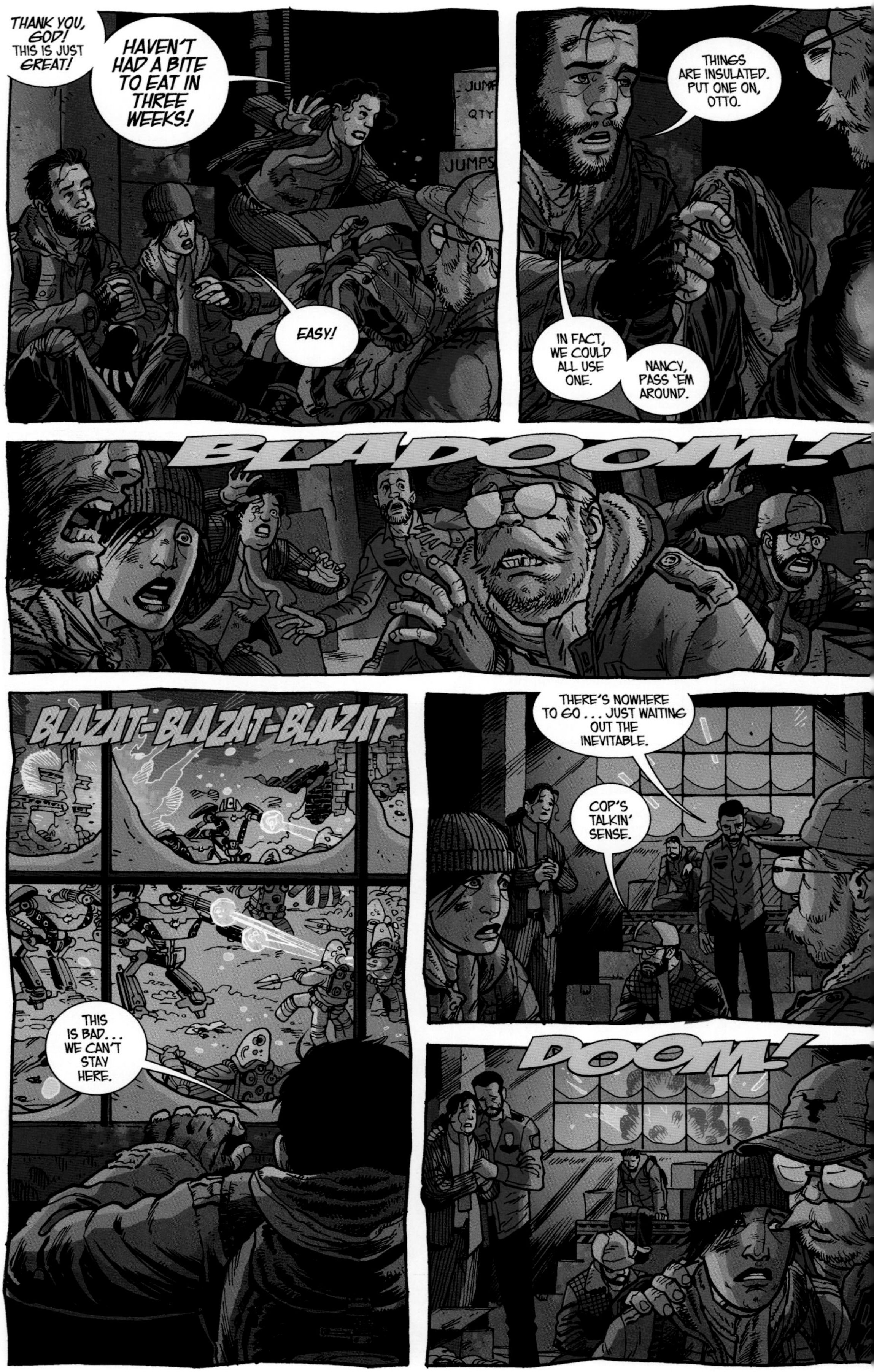
THANK YOU, GOD! THIS IS JUST GREAT!
HAVEN'T HAD A BITE TO EAT IN THREE WEEKS!
EASY!
THINGS ARE INSULATED. PUT ONE ON, OTTO.
IN FACT, WE COULD ALL USE ONE.
NANCY, PASS 'EM AROUND.
BLADOOM!
BLAZAT-BLAZAT-BLAZAT
THIS IS BAD... WE CAN'T STAY HERE.
THERE'S NOWHERE TO GO... JUST WAITING OUT THE INEVITABLE.
COP'S TALKIN' SENSE.
DOOM!

NO, I'M NOT GIVING UP. WE'RE NOT GOING TO DIE HERE IN THIS COLD WAREHOUSE.

WE ALL LOST KIN, BUT MY CHARLOTTE'S HIDING IN THAT BUNKER COUNTIN' ON ME TA MAKE IT BACK AN LOOK OUT FER 'ER...AN' I BET THERE ARE PLENTY MORE STILL HIDING TOO.

WE AIN'T GIVIN' UP.

NO.

WE'RE GONNA MARCH RIGHT THE HELL OUTTA HERE. THEY WON'T FOLLOW.

THESE THINGS, THEY'RE WARIN' WITH EACH OTHER--THEY AIN'T AFRAID OF US.

WE'RE COLLATERAL DAMAGE, IS ALL.

THESE SONSABITCHES DON'T FIGURE THEY HAD A THING TA FEAR FROM US...

...BUT BY GOD THEY'RE GONNA!

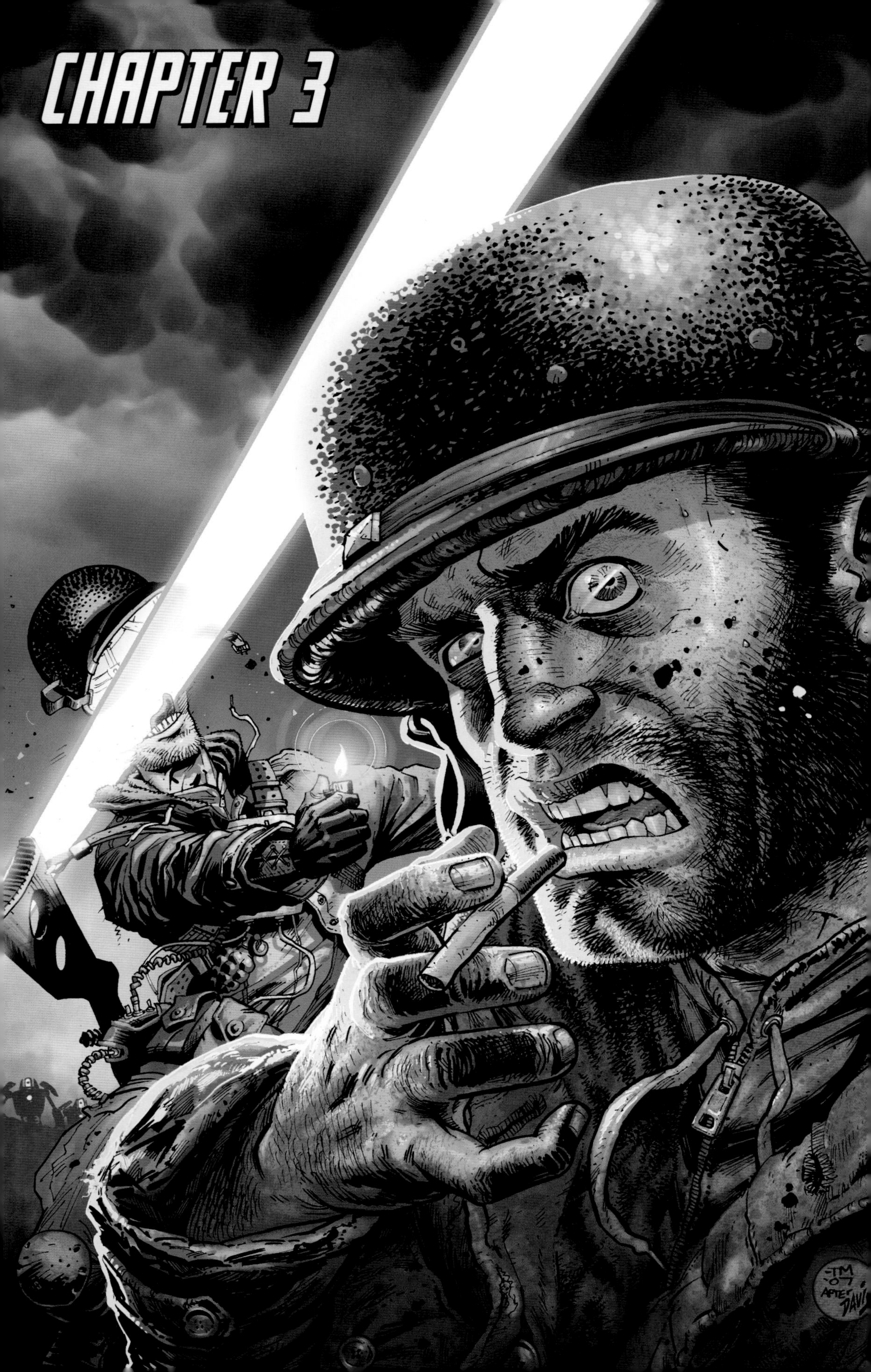
CHAPTER 3

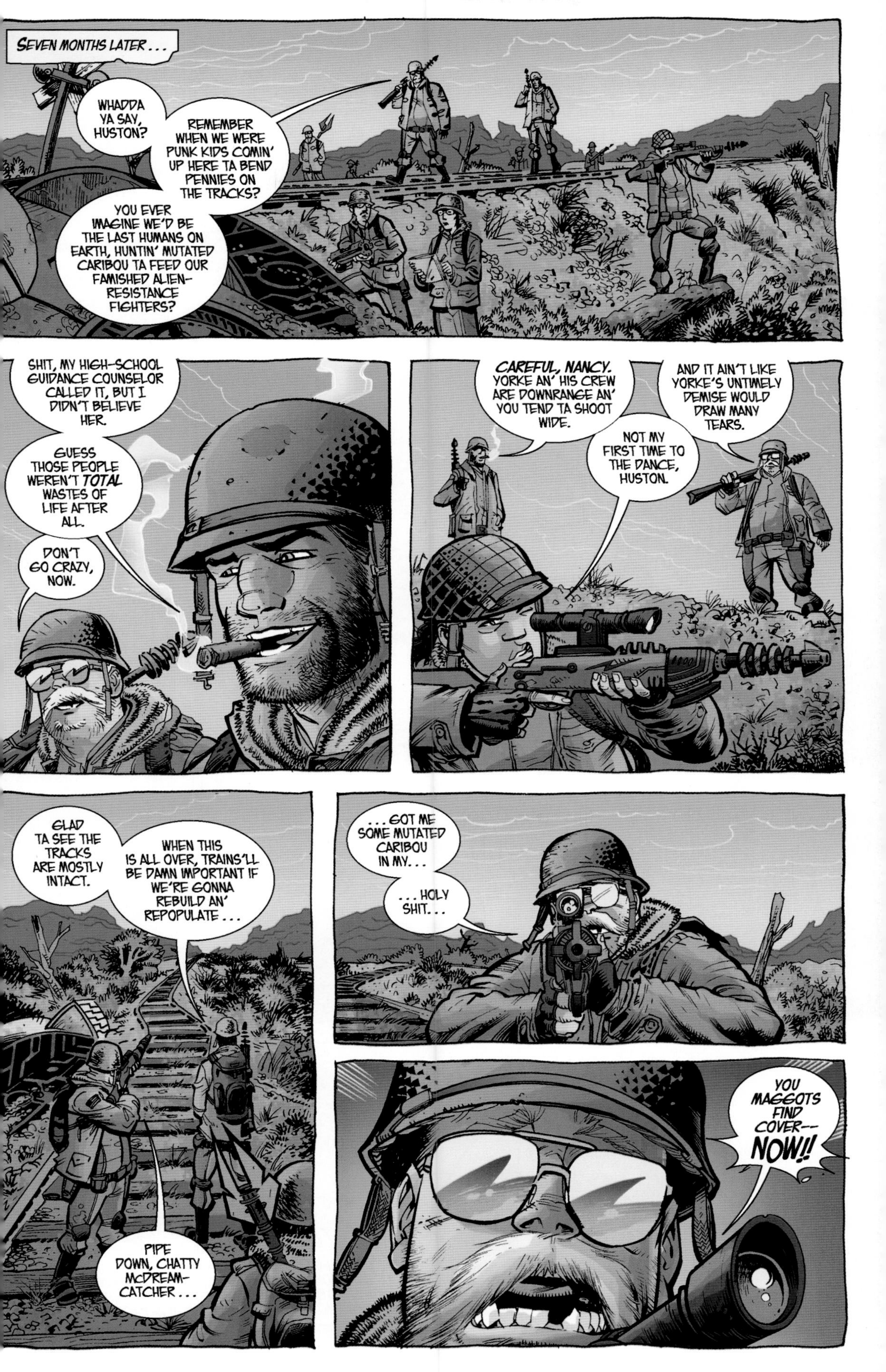
SEVEN MONTHS LATER . . .
WHADDA YA SAY, HUSTON?
REMEMBER WHEN WE WERE PUNK KIDS COMIN' UP HERE TA BEND PENNIES ON THE TRACKS?
YOU EVER IMAGINE WE'D BE THE LAST HUMANS ON EARTH, HUNTIN' MUTATED CARIBOU TA FEED OUR FAMISHED ALIEN-RESISTANCE FIGHTERS?
SHIT, MY HIGH-SCHOOL GUIDANCE COUNSELOR CALLED IT, BUT I DIDN'T BELIEVE HER.
GUESS THOSE PEOPLE WEREN'T TOTAL WASTES OF LIFE AFTER ALL.
DON'T GO CRAZY, NOW.
CAREFUL, NANCY. YORKE AN' HIS CREW ARE DOWNRANGE AN' YOU TEND TA SHOOT WIDE.
NOT MY FIRST TIME TO THE DANCE, HUSTON.
AND IT AIN'T LIKE YORKE'S UNTIMELY DEMISE WOULD DRAW MANY TEARS.
GLAD TA SEE THE TRACKS ARE MOSTLY INTACT.
WHEN THIS IS ALL OVER, TRAINS'LL BE DAMN IMPORTANT IF WE'RE GONNA REBUILD AN' REPOPULATE . . .
PIPE DOWN, CHATTY McDREAM-CATCHER . . .
. . . GOT ME SOME MUTATED CARIBOU IN MY . . .
. . . HOLY SHIT . . .
YOU MAGGOTS FIND COVER-- NOW!!

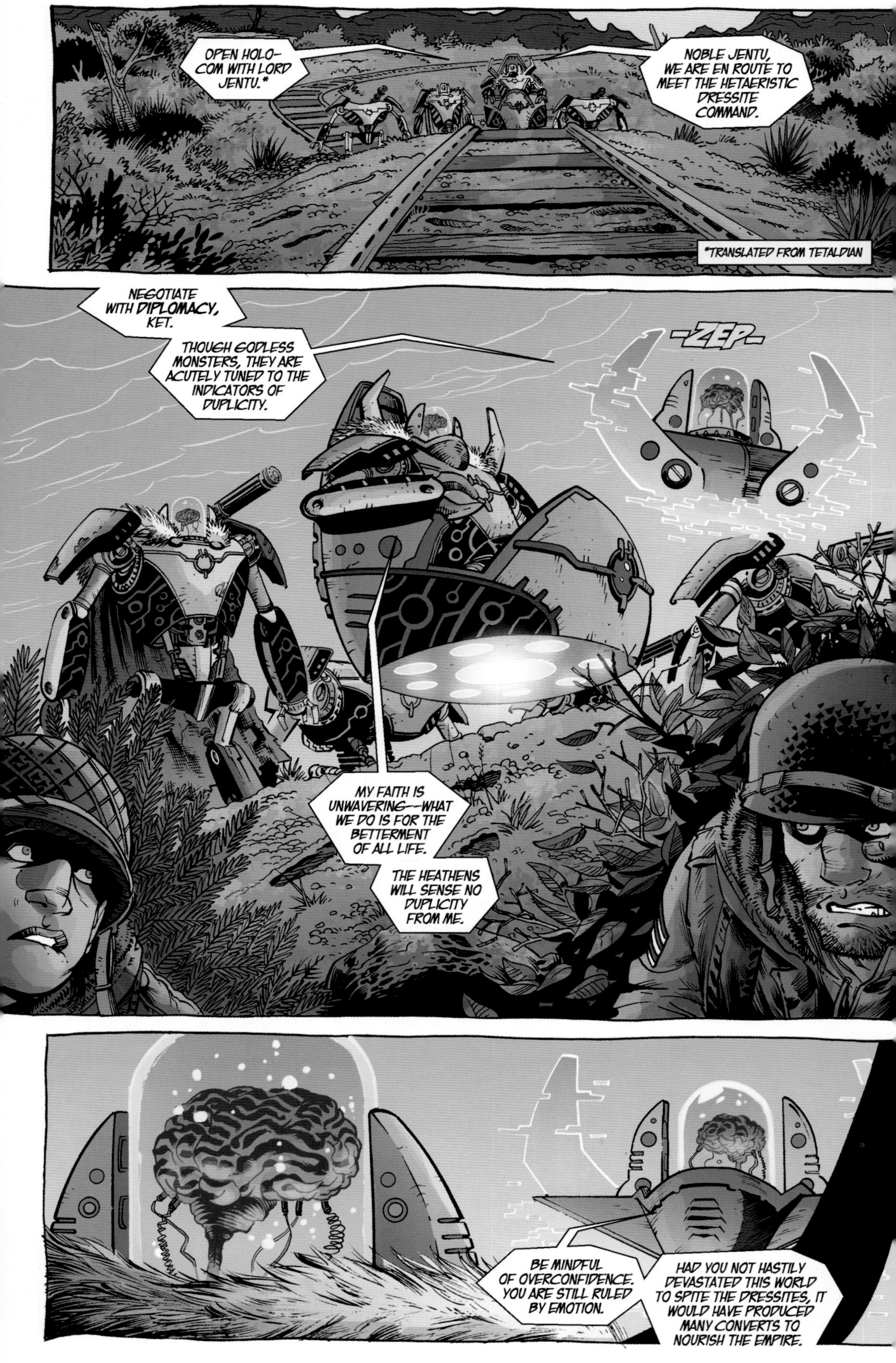
OPEN HOLO-COM WITH LORD JENTU.*
NOBLE JENTU, WE ARE EN ROUTE TO MEET THE HETAERISTIC DRESSITE COMMAND.
*TRANSLATED FROM TETALDIAN
NEGOTIATE WITH DIPLOMACY, KET.
THOUGH GODLESS MONSTERS, THEY ARE ACUTELY TUNED TO THE INDICATORS OF DUPLICITY.
-ZEP-
MY FAITH IS UNWAVERING--WHAT WE DO IS FOR THE BETTERMENT OF ALL LIFE.
THE HEATHENS WILL SENSE NO DUPLICITY FROM ME.
BE MINDFUL OF OVERCONFIDENCE. YOU ARE STILL RULED BY EMOTION.
HAD YOU NOT HASTILY DEVASTATED THIS WORLD TO SPITE THE DRESSITES, IT WOULD HAVE PRODUCED MANY CONVERTS TO NOURISH THE EMPIRE.

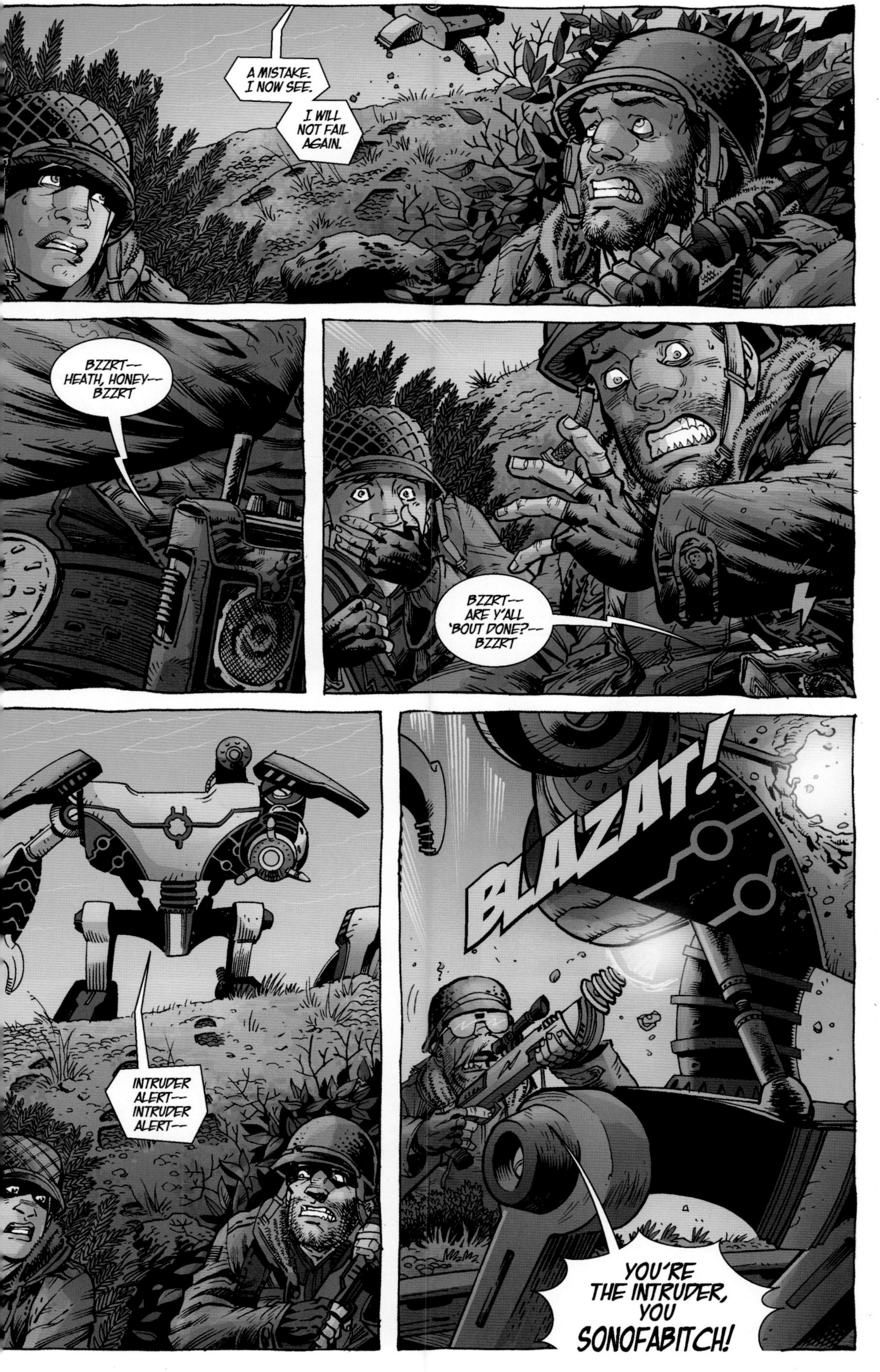
A MISTAKE. I NOW SEE.
I WILL NOT FAIL AGAIN.
BZZRT-- HEATH, HONEY-- BZZRT
BZZRT-- ARE Y'ALL 'BOUT DONE?-- BZZRT
INTRUDER ALERT-- INTRUDER ALERT--
BLAZAT!
YOU'RE THE INTRUDER, YOU SONOFABITCH!

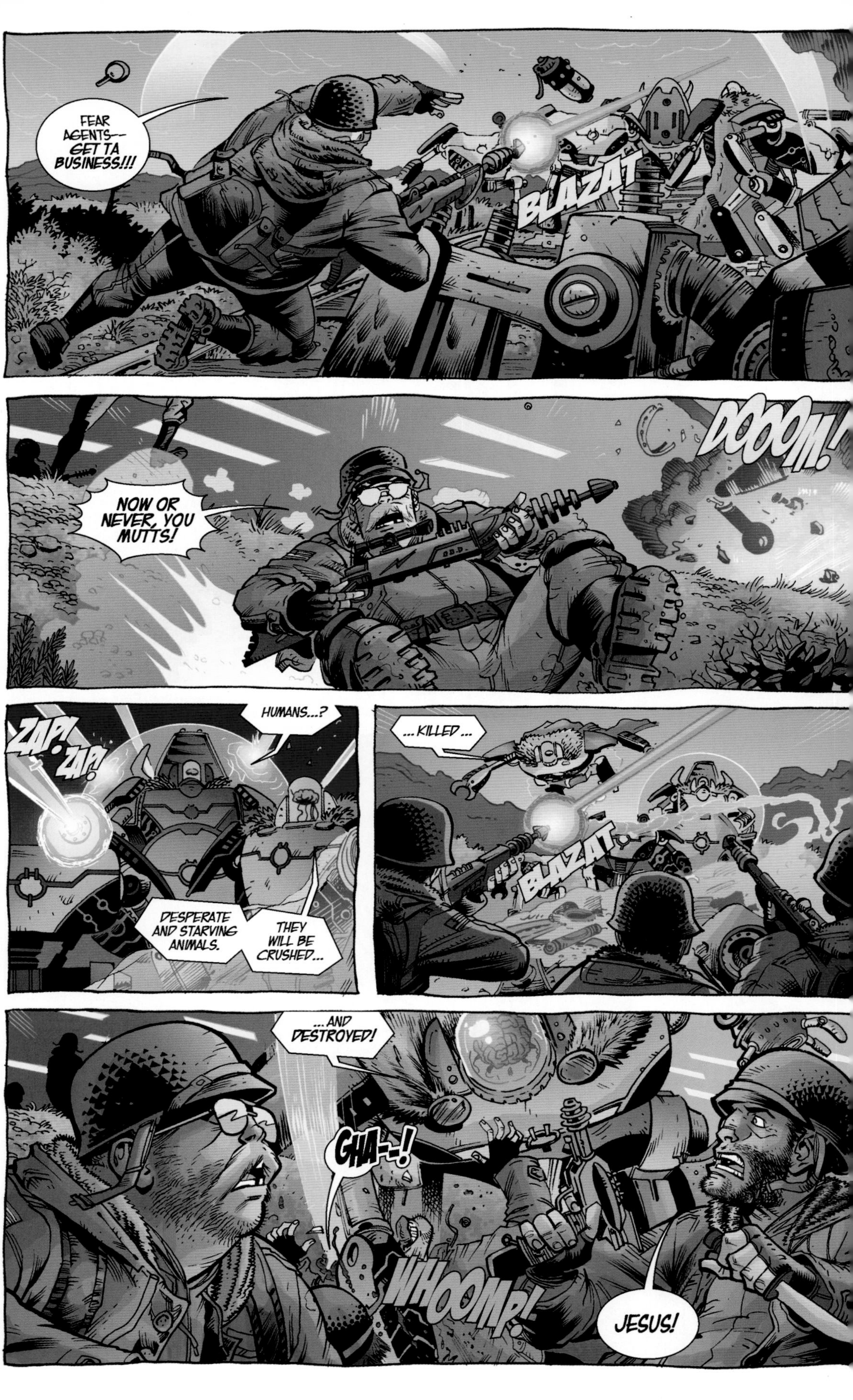
FEAR AGENTS-- GET TA BUSINESS!!!
BLAZAT
NOW OR NEVER, YOU MUTTS!
DOOOM!
ZAP! ZAP!
HUMANS...?
DESPERATE AND STARVING ANIMALS.
THEY WILL BE CRUSHED...
...KILLED...
BLAZAT
...AND DESTROYED!
GHA--!
WHOOMP!
JESUS!

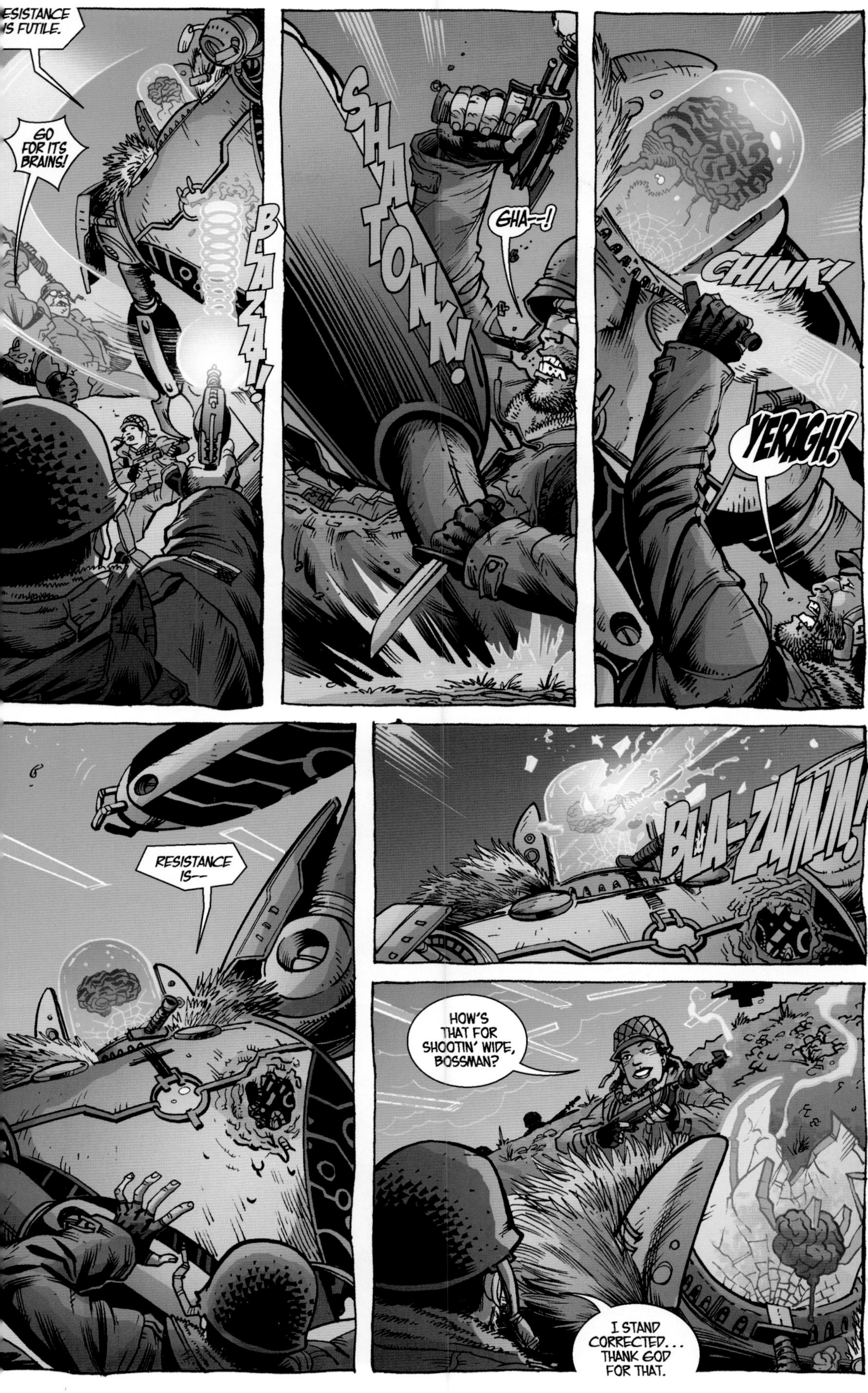
RESISTANCE IS FUTILE.
GO FOR ITS BRAINS!
BLAZAT!
SHATONK!
GHA--!
CHINK!
YERAGH!
RESISTANCE IS--
BLA-ZAMM!
HOW'S THAT FOR SHOOTIN' WIDE, BOSSMAN?
I STAND CORRECTED... THANK GOD FOR THAT.

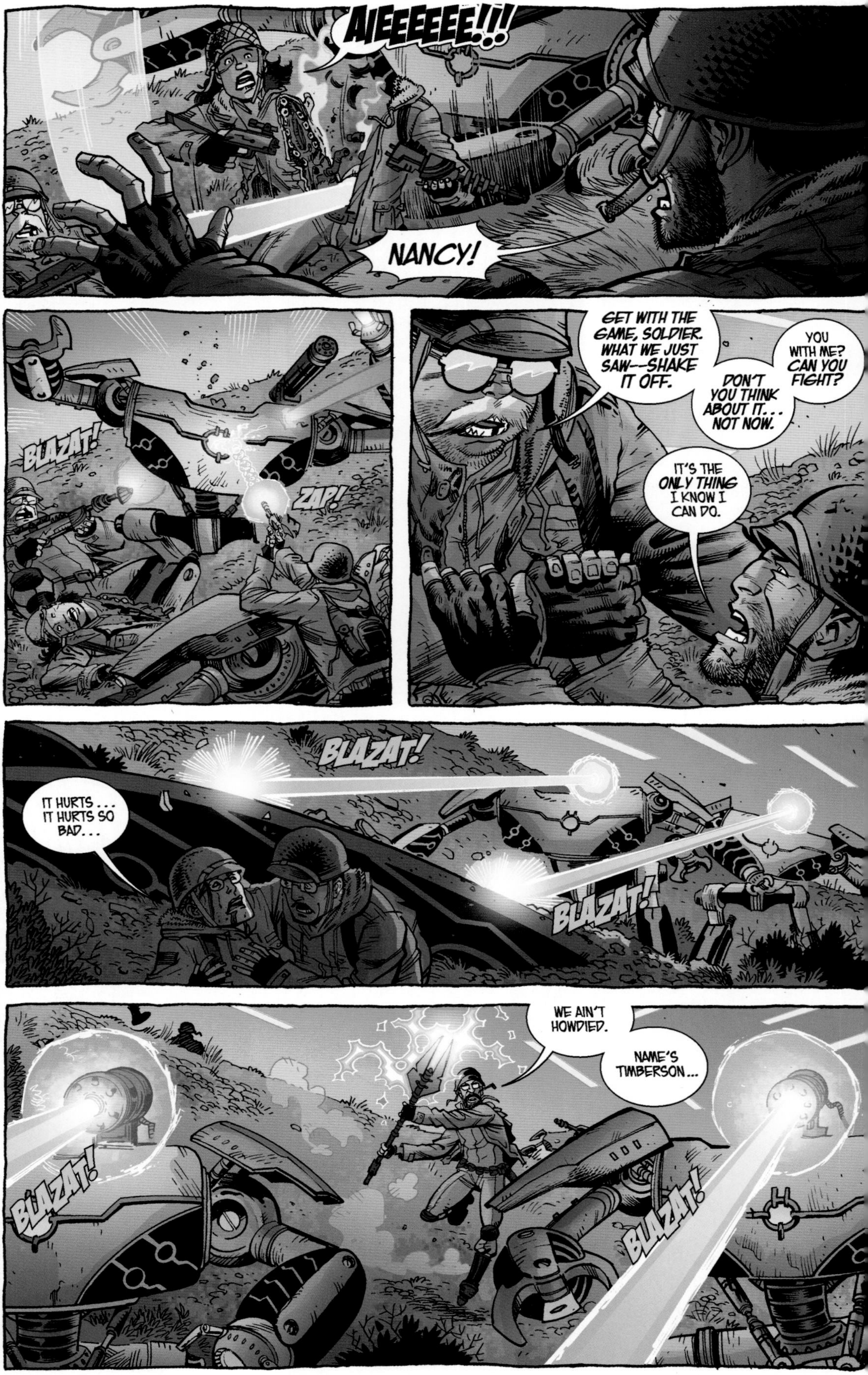
AIEEEEEE!!!
NANCY!
BLAZAT!
ZAP!
GET WITH THE GAME, SOLDIER. WHAT WE JUST SAW--SHAKE IT OFF.
DON'T YOU THINK ABOUT IT... NOT NOW.
YOU WITH ME? CAN YOU FIGHT?
IT'S THE ONLY THING I KNOW I CAN DO.
BLAZAT!
IT HURTS... IT HURTS SO BAD...
BLAZAT!
WE AIN'T HOWDIED.
NAME'S TIMBERSON...
BLAZAT!
BLAZAT!

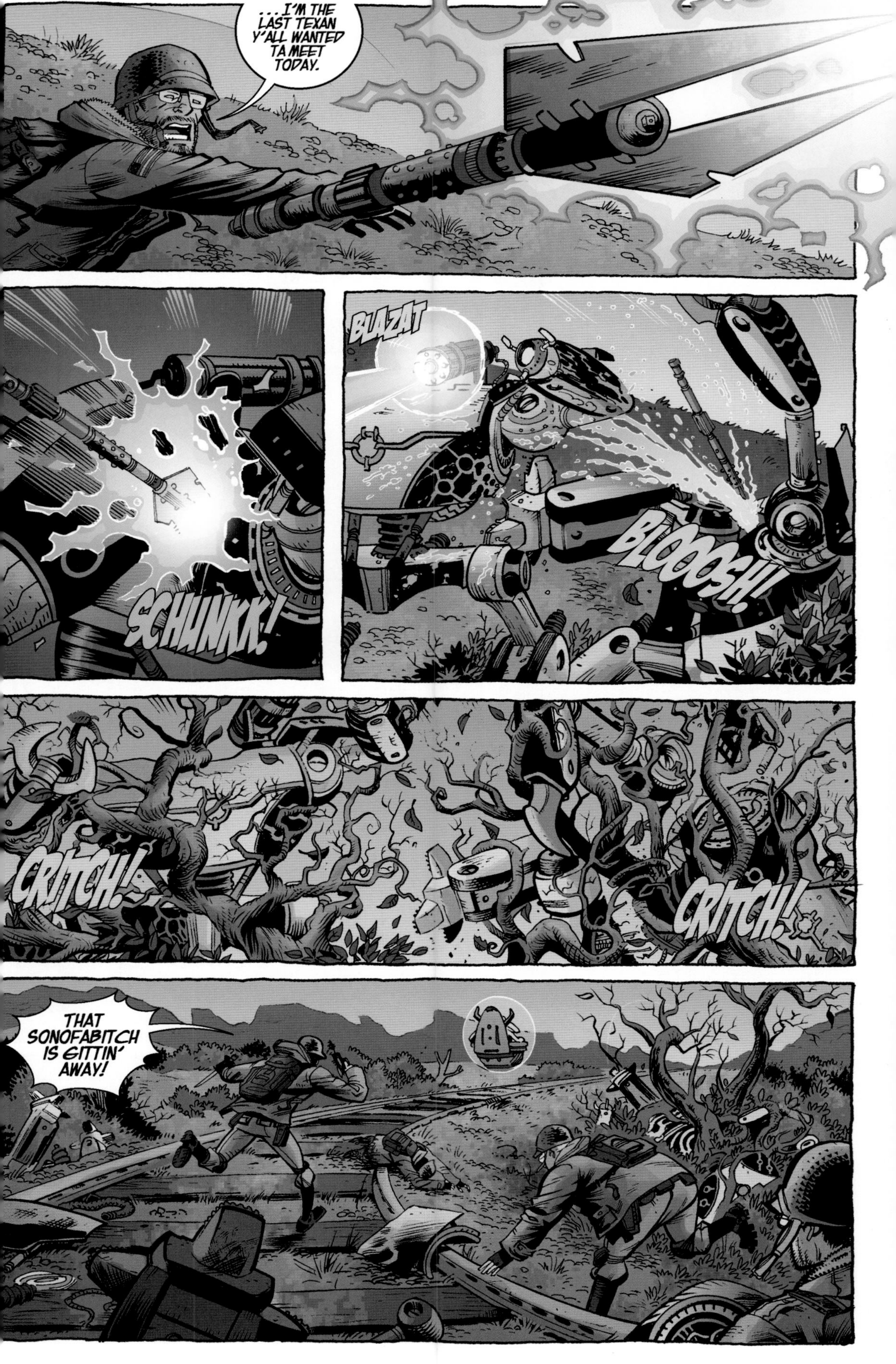
. . . I'M THE LAST TEXAN Y'ALL WANTED TA MEET TODAY.
SCHUNKK!
BLAZAT
BLOOOSH!
CRITCH!
CRITCH!
THAT SONOFABITCH IS GITTIN' AWAY!

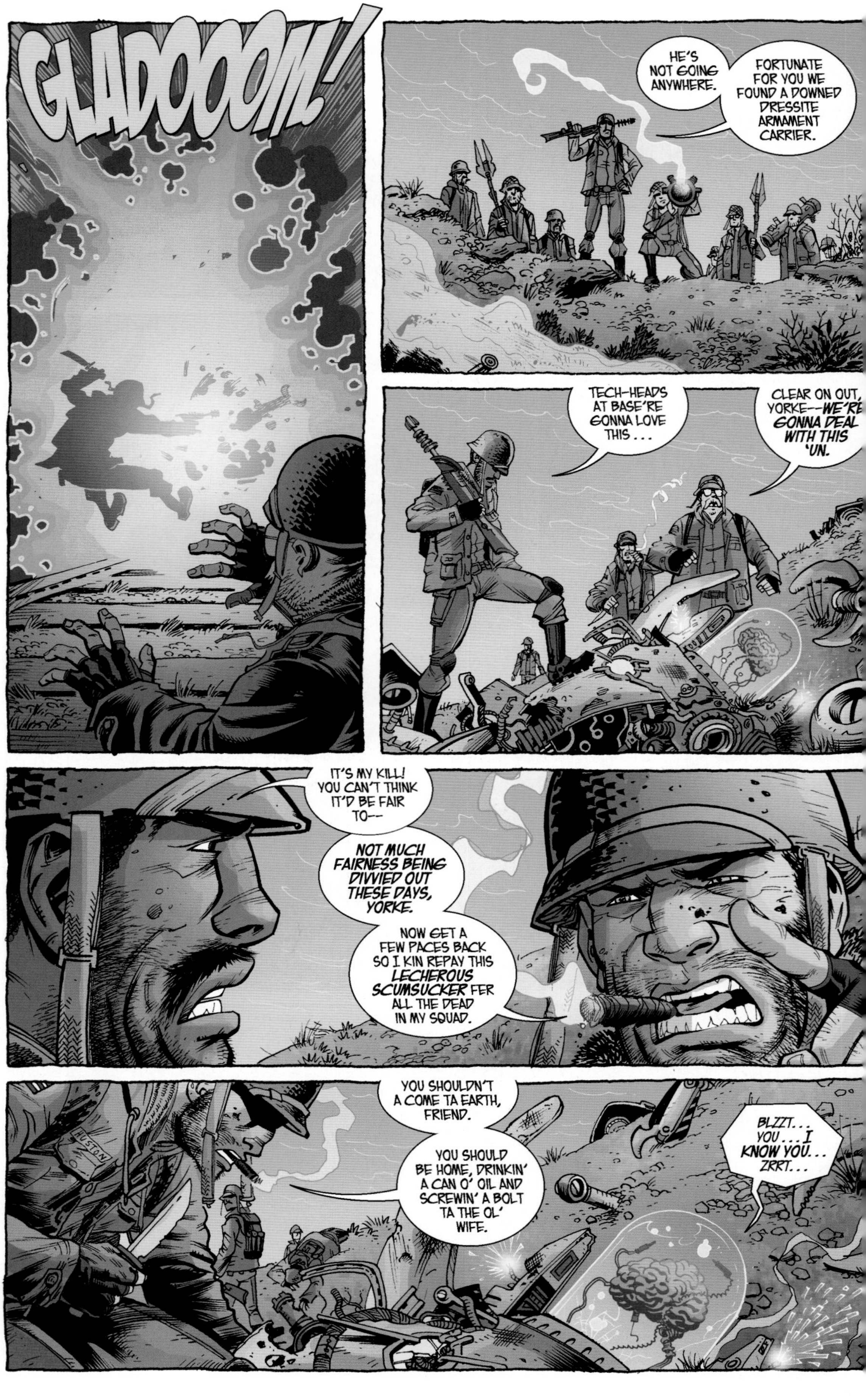
GLADOOOM!
HE'S NOT GOING ANYWHERE.
FORTUNATE FOR YOU WE FOUND A DOWNED DRESSITE ARMAMENT CARRIER.
TECH-HEADS AT BASE'RE GONNA LOVE THIS . . .
CLEAR ON OUT, YORKE--WE'RE GONNA DEAL WITH THIS 'UN.
IT'S MY KILL! YOU CAN'T THINK IT'D BE FAIR TO--
NOT MUCH FAIRNESS BEING DIVVIED OUT THESE DAYS, YORKE.
NOW GET A FEW PACES BACK SO I KIN REPAY THIS LECHEROUS SCUMSUCKER FER ALL THE DEAD IN MY SQUAD.
YOU SHOULDN'T A COME TA EARTH, FRIEND.
YOU SHOULD BE HOME, DRINKIN' A CAN O' OIL AND SCREWIN' A BOLT TA THE OL' WIFE.
BLZZT. . . YOU . . . I KNOW YOU. . . ZRRT. . .

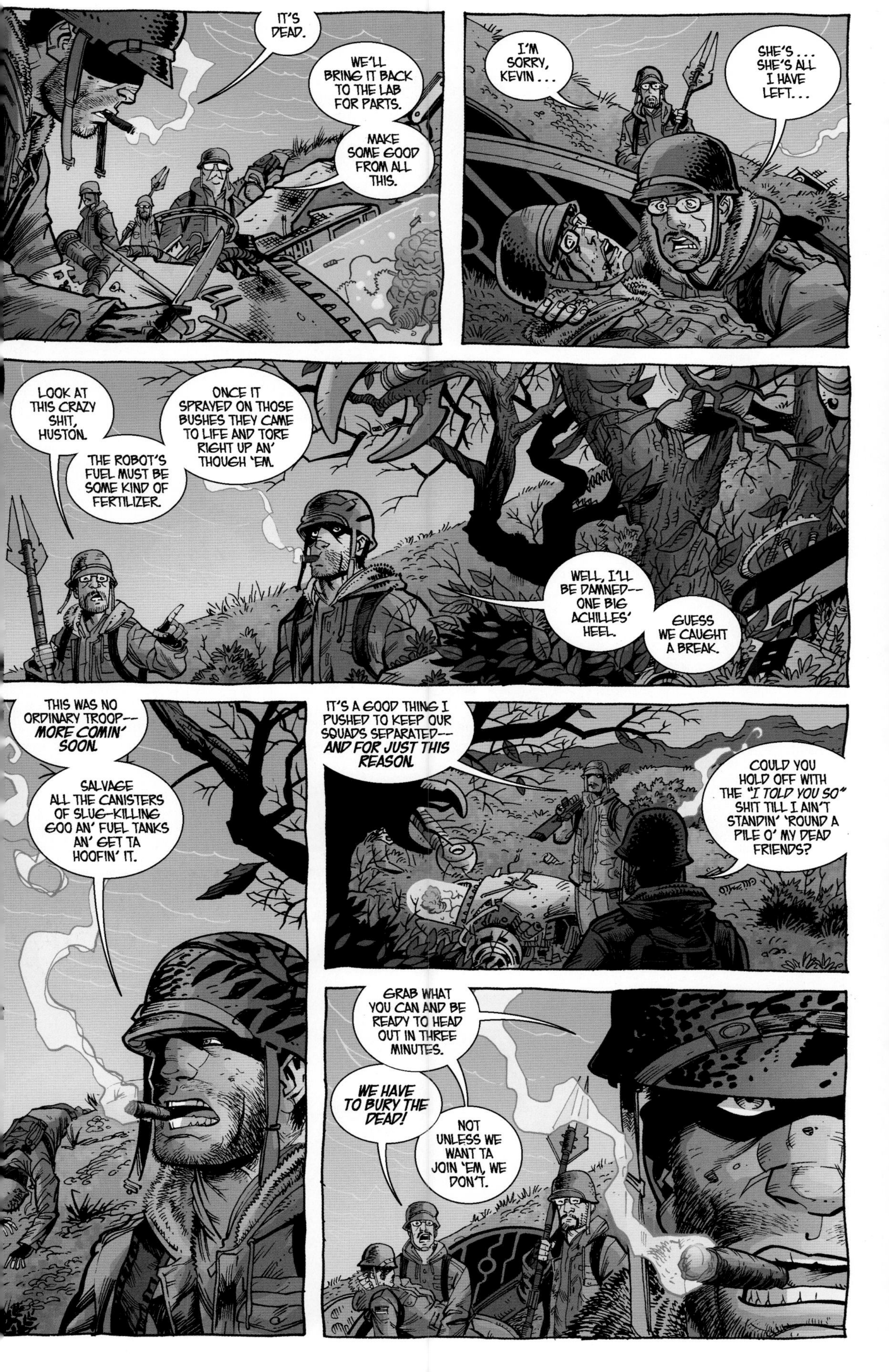
IT'S DEAD.
WE'LL BRING IT BACK TO THE LAB FOR PARTS.
MAKE SOME GOOD FROM ALL THIS.
I'M SORRY, KEVIN . . .
SHE'S . . . SHE'S ALL I HAVE LEFT. . .
LOOK AT THIS CRAZY SHIT, HUSTON.
THE ROBOT'S FUEL MUST BE SOME KIND OF FERTILIZER.
ONCE IT SPRAYED ON THOSE BUSHES THEY CAME TO LIFE AND TORE RIGHT UP AN' THOUGH 'EM.
WELL, I'LL BE DAMNED-- ONE BIG ACHILLES' HEEL.
GUESS WE CAUGHT A BREAK.
THIS WAS NO ORDINARY TROOP-- MORE COMIN' SOON.
SALVAGE ALL THE CANISTERS OF SLUG-KILLING GOO AN' FUEL TANKS AN' GET TA HOOFIN' IT.
IT'S A GOOD THING I PUSHED TO KEEP OUR SQUADS SEPARATED-- AND FOR JUST THIS REASON.
COULD YOU HOLD OFF WITH THE "I TOLD YOU SO" SHIT TILL I AIN'T STANDIN' 'ROUND A PILE O' MY DEAD FRIENDS?
GRAB WHAT YOU CAN AND BE READY TO HEAD OUT IN THREE MINUTES.
WE HAVE TO BURY THE DEAD!
NOT UNLESS WE WANT TA JOIN 'EM, WE DON'T.

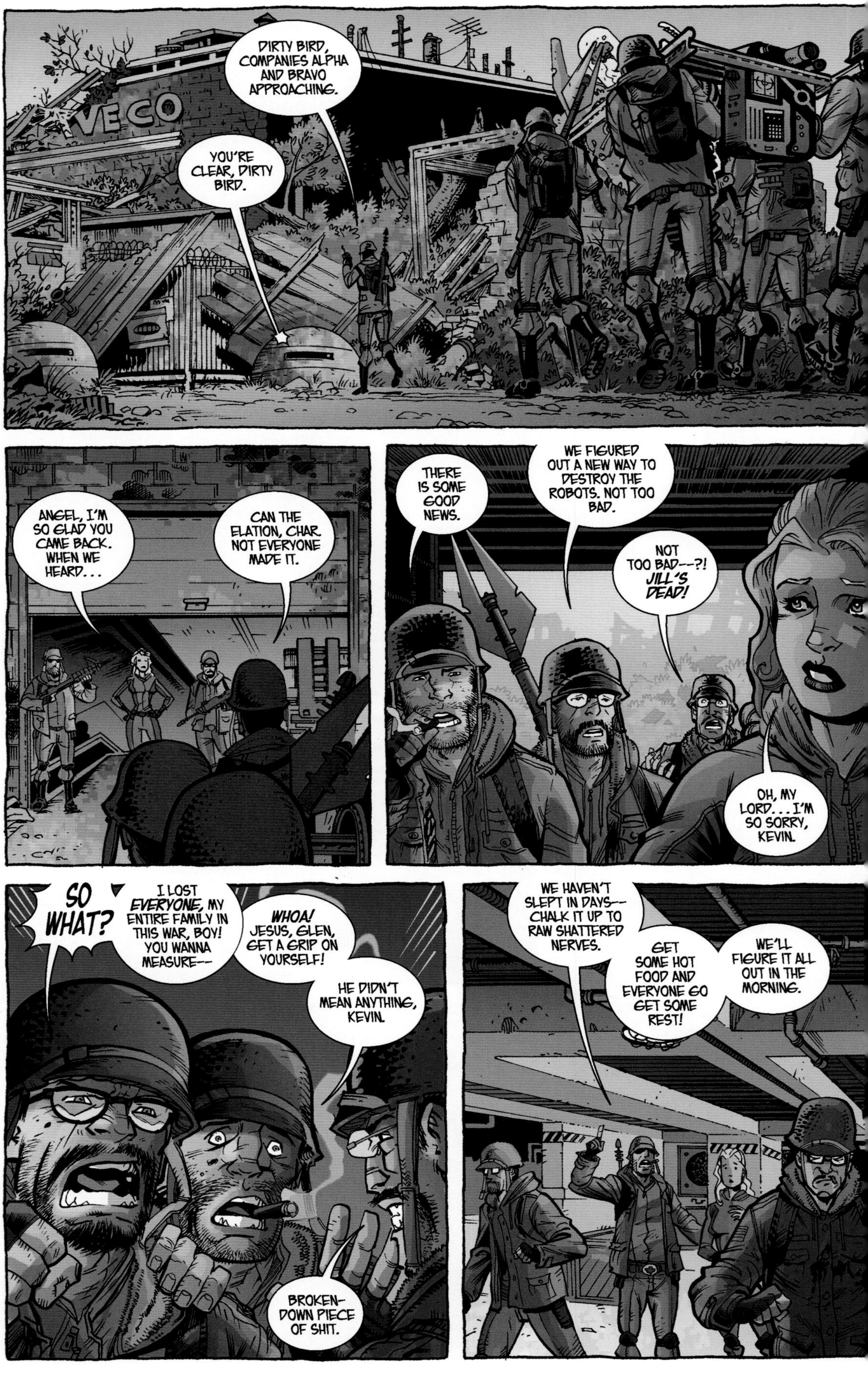
DIRTY BIRD, COMPANIES ALPHA AND BRAVO APPROACHING.
YOU'RE CLEAR, DIRTY BIRD.
VECO
ANGEL, I'M SO GLAD YOU CAME BACK. WHEN WE HEARD...
CAN THE ELATION, CHAR NOT EVERYONE MADE IT.
THERE IS SOME GOOD NEWS.
WE FIGURED OUT A NEW WAY TO DESTROY THE ROBOTS. NOT TOO BAD.
NOT TOO BAD--?! JILL'S DEAD!
OH, MY LORD... I'M SO SORRY, KEVIN.
SO WHAT?
I LOST EVERYONE, MY ENTIRE FAMILY IN THIS WAR, BOY! YOU WANNA MEASURE--
WHOA! JESUS, GLEN, GET A GRIP ON YOURSELF!
HE DIDN'T MEAN ANYTHING, KEVIN.
BROKEN-DOWN PIECE OF SHIT.
WE HAVEN'T SLEPT IN DAYS-- CHALK IT UP TO RAW SHATTERED NERVES.
GET SOME HOT FOOD AND EVERYONE GO GET SOME REST!
WE'LL FIGURE IT ALL OUT IN THE MORNING.

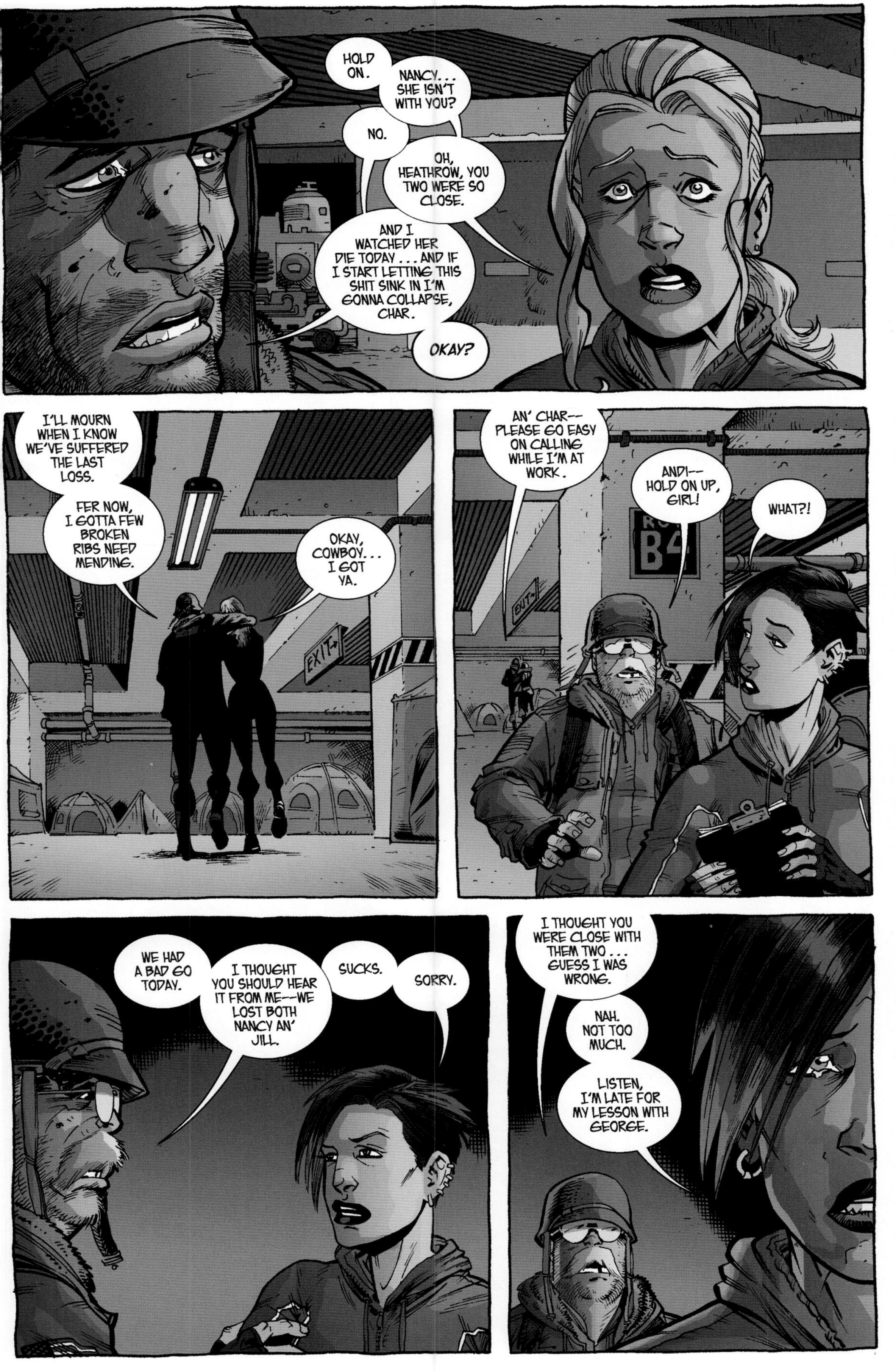
HOLD ON.
NANCY... SHE ISN'T WITH YOU?
NO.
OH, HEATHROW, YOU TWO WERE SO CLOSE.
AND I WATCHED HER DIE TODAY... AND IF I START LETTING THIS SHIT SINK IN I'M GONNA COLLAPSE, CHAR.
OKAY?
I'LL MOURN WHEN I KNOW WE'VE SUFFERED THE LAST LOSS.
FER NOW, I GOTTA FEW BROKEN RIBS NEED MENDING.
OKAY, COWBOY... I GOT YA.
EXIT
AN' CHAR-- PLEASE GO EASY ON CALLING WHILE I'M AT WORK.
ANDI-- HOLD ON UP, GIRL!
WHAT?!
B4
EXIT
WE HAD A BAD GO TODAY.
I THOUGHT YOU SHOULD HEAR IT FROM ME--WE LOST BOTH NANCY AN' JILL.
SUCKS.
SORRY.
I THOUGHT YOU WERE CLOSE WITH THEM TWO... GUESS I WAS WRONG.
NAH. NOT TOO MUCH.
LISTEN, I'M LATE FOR MY LESSON WITH GEORGE.

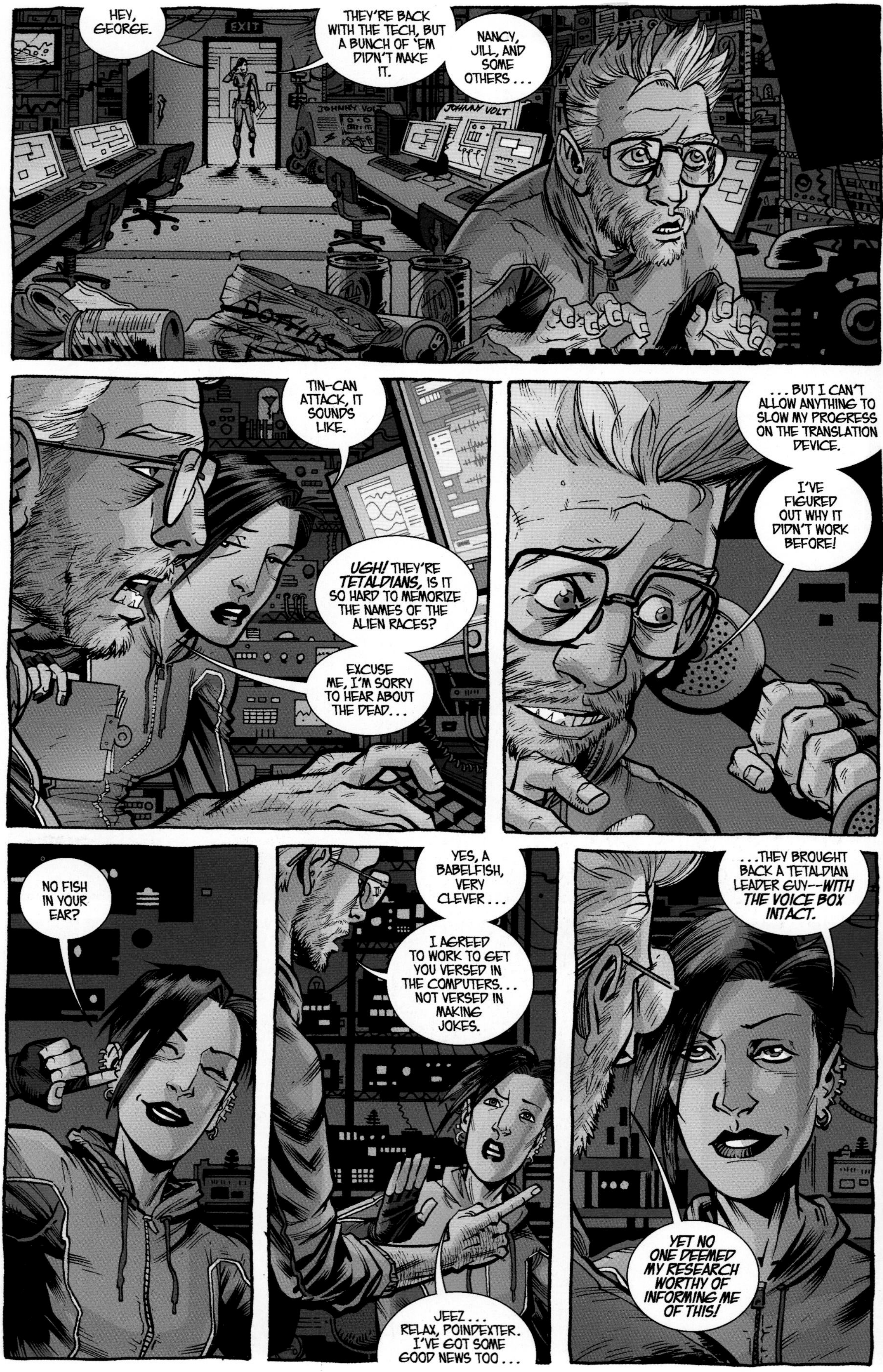
HEY, GEORGE.
THEY'RE BACK WITH THE TECH, BUT A BUNCH OF 'EM DIDN'T MAKE IT.
NANCY, JILL, AND SOME OTHERS . . .
EXIT
JOHNNY VOLT
JOHNNY VOLT
TIN-CAN ATTACK, IT SOUNDS LIKE.
UGH! THEY'RE TETALDIANS, IS IT SO HARD TO MEMORIZE THE NAMES OF THE ALIEN RACES?
EXCUSE ME, I'M SORRY TO HEAR ABOUT THE DEAD . . .
. . . BUT I CAN'T ALLOW ANYTHING TO SLOW MY PROGRESS ON THE TRANSLATION DEVICE.
I'VE FIGURED OUT WHY IT DIDN'T WORK BEFORE!
NO FISH IN YOUR EAR?
YES, A BABELFISH, VERY CLEVER . . .
I AGREED TO WORK TO GET YOU VERSED IN THE COMPUTERS . . . NOT VERSED IN MAKING JOKES.
JEEZ . . . RELAX, POINDEXTER. I'VE GOT SOME GOOD NEWS TOO . . .
. . . THEY BROUGHT BACK A TETALDIAN LEADER GUY-- WITH THE VOICE BOX INTACT.
YET NO ONE DEEMED MY RESEARCH WORTHY OF INFORMING ME OF THIS!

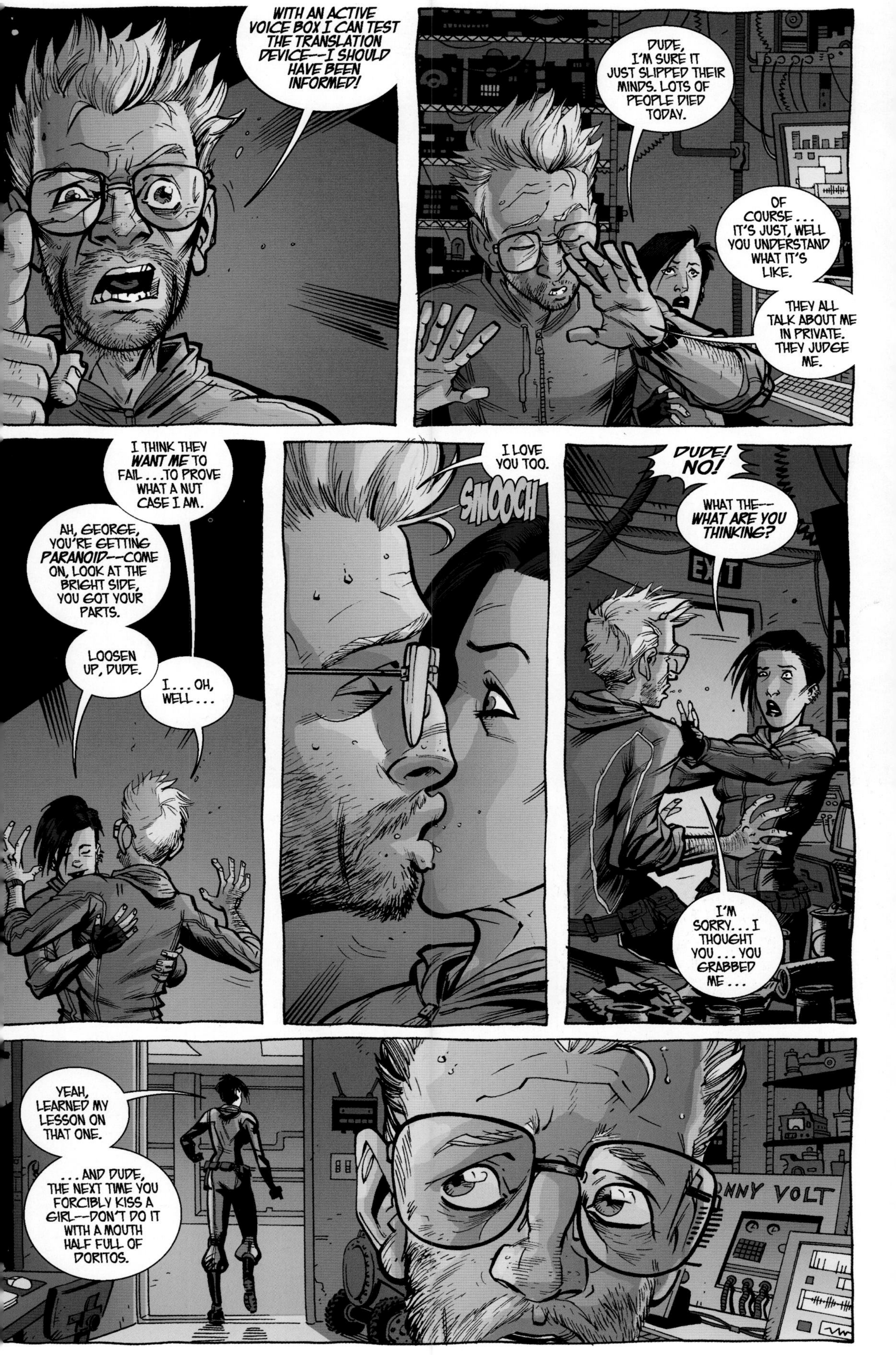

WITH AN ACTIVE VOICE BOX I CAN TEST THE TRANSLATION DEVICE--I SHOULD HAVE BEEN INFORMED!
DUDE, I'M SURE IT JUST SLIPPED THEIR MINDS. LOTS OF PEOPLE DIED TODAY.
OF COURSE . . . IT'S JUST, WELL YOU UNDERSTAND WHAT IT'S LIKE.
THEY ALL TALK ABOUT ME IN PRIVATE. THEY JUDGE ME.
I THINK THEY WANT ME TO FAIL . . . TO PROVE WHAT A NUT CASE I AM.
AH, GEORGE, YOU'RE GETTING PARANOID--COME ON, LOOK AT THE BRIGHT SIDE, YOU GOT YOUR PARTS.
LOOSEN UP, DUDE.
I . . . OH, WELL . . .
I LOVE YOU TOO.
SMOOCH
DUDE! NO!
WHAT THE-- WHAT ARE YOU THINKING?
EXIT
I'M SORRY. . . I THOUGHT YOU . . . YOU GRABBED ME . . .
YEAH, LEARNED MY LESSON ON THAT ONE.
. . . AND DUDE, THE NEXT TIME YOU FORCIBLY KISS A GIRL--DON'T DO IT WITH A MOUTH HALF FULL OF DORITOS.
NNY VOLT

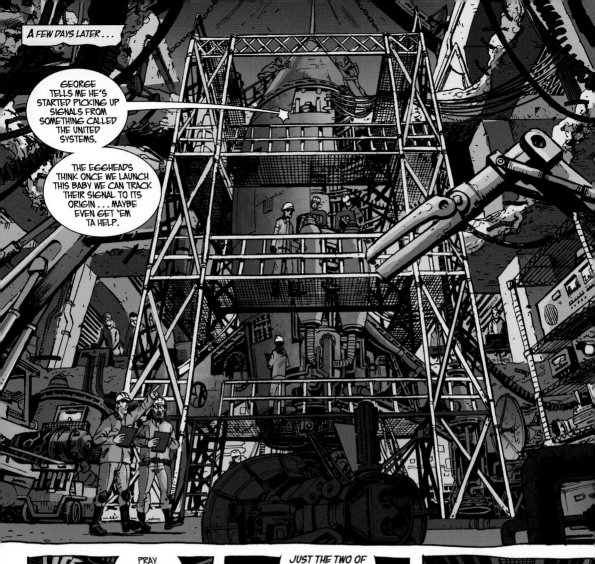

A FEW DAYS LATER...

GEORGE TELLS ME HE'S STARTED PICKING UP SIGNALS FROM SOMETHING CALLED THE UNITED SYSTEMS.

THE EGGHEADS THINK ONCE WE LAUNCH THIS BABY WE CAN TRACK THEIR SIGNAL TO ITS ORIGIN... MAYBE EVEN GET 'EM TA HELP.

PRAY TA THE LORD THEY AREN'T ALL BAD.

I CAN'T BELIEVE GOD WOULD MAKE HUMANITY HIS ONLY SENSIBLE CREATION.

YOU KNOW WHAT WOULD BE SENSIBLE... IF WE JUST TOOK THIS BEAUTY UP AN' MAKE A NEW LIFE IN THE STARS.

JUST THE TWO OF US... FIND A SHINY NEW PLANET AND PLAY AT ADAM AND EVE.

HAVE TA ENGAGE IN TWENTY-FOUR-HOUR-A-DAY LOVE MAKIN' TA ENSURE SUCCESS.

UGH... EXCUSE ME.

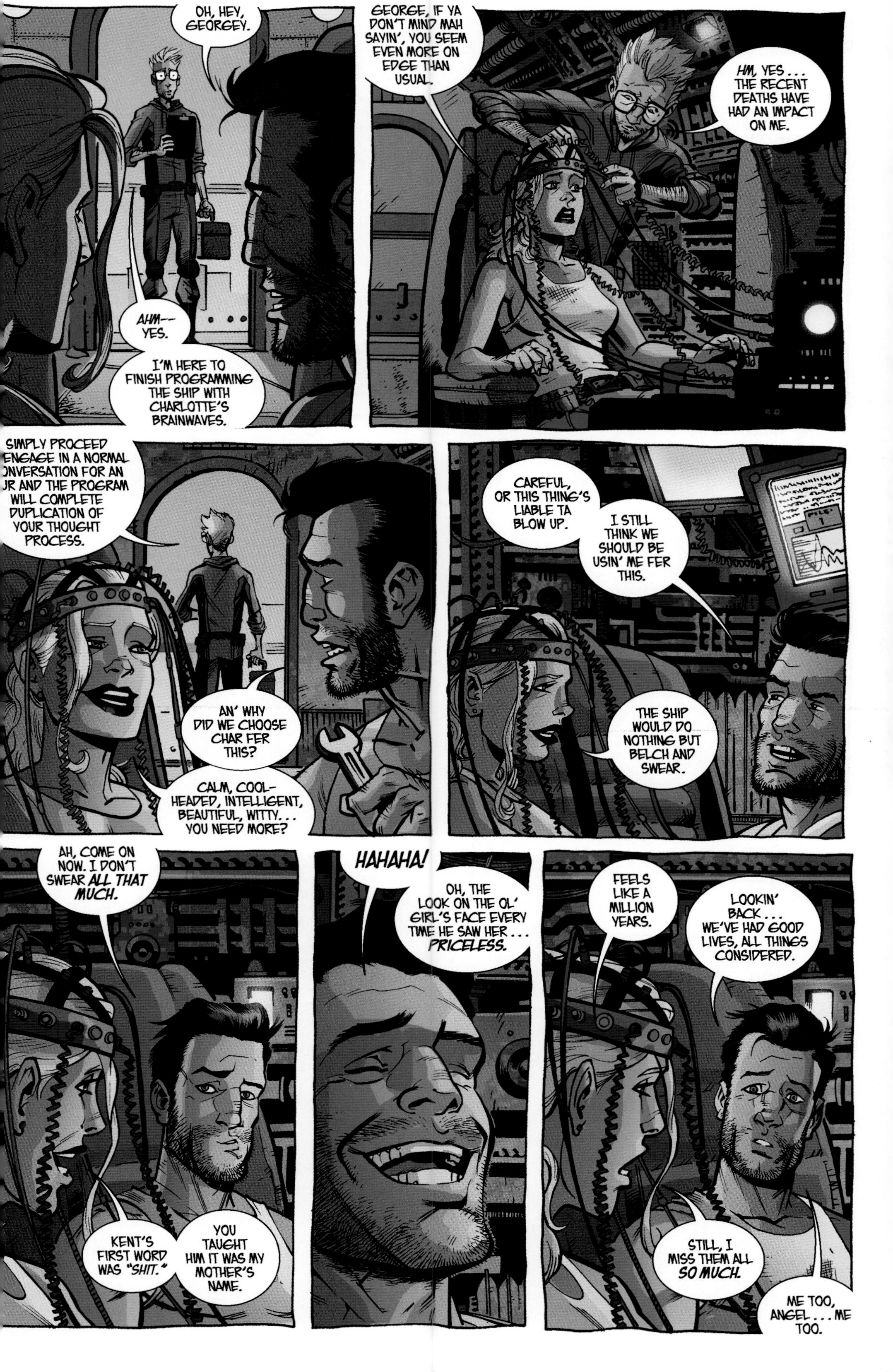
OH, HEY, GEORGEY.
AHM-- YES.
I'M HERE TO FINISH PROGRAMMING THE SHIP WITH CHARLOTTE'S BRAINWAVES.
GEORGE, IF YA DON'T MIND MAH SAYIN', YOU SEEM EVEN MORE ON EDGE THAN USUAL.
HM, YES... THE RECENT DEATHS HAVE HAD AN IMPACT ON ME.
SIMPLY PROCEED ENGAGE IN A NORMAL ONVERSATION FOR AN UR AND THE PROGRAM WILL COMPLETE DUPLICATION OF YOUR THOUGHT PROCESS.
AN' WHY DID WE CHOOSE CHAR FER THIS?
CALM, COOL-HEADED, INTELLIGENT, BEAUTIFUL, WITTY... YOU NEED MORE?
CAREFUL, OR THIS THING'S LIABLE TA BLOW UP.
I STILL THINK WE SHOULD BE USIN' ME FER THIS.
THE SHIP WOULD DO NOTHING BUT BELCH AND SWEAR.
AH, COME ON NOW. I DON'T SWEAR ALL THAT MUCH.
KENT'S FIRST WORD WAS "SHIT."
YOU TAUGHT HIM IT WAS MY MOTHER'S NAME.
HAHAHA!
OH, THE LOOK ON THE OL' GIRL'S FACE EVERY TIME HE SAW HER... PRICELESS.
FEELS LIKE A MILLION YEARS.
LOOKIN' BACK... WE'VE HAD GOOD LIVES, ALL THINGS CONSIDERED.
STILL, I MISS THEM ALL SO MUCH.
ME TOO, ANGEL... ME TOO.

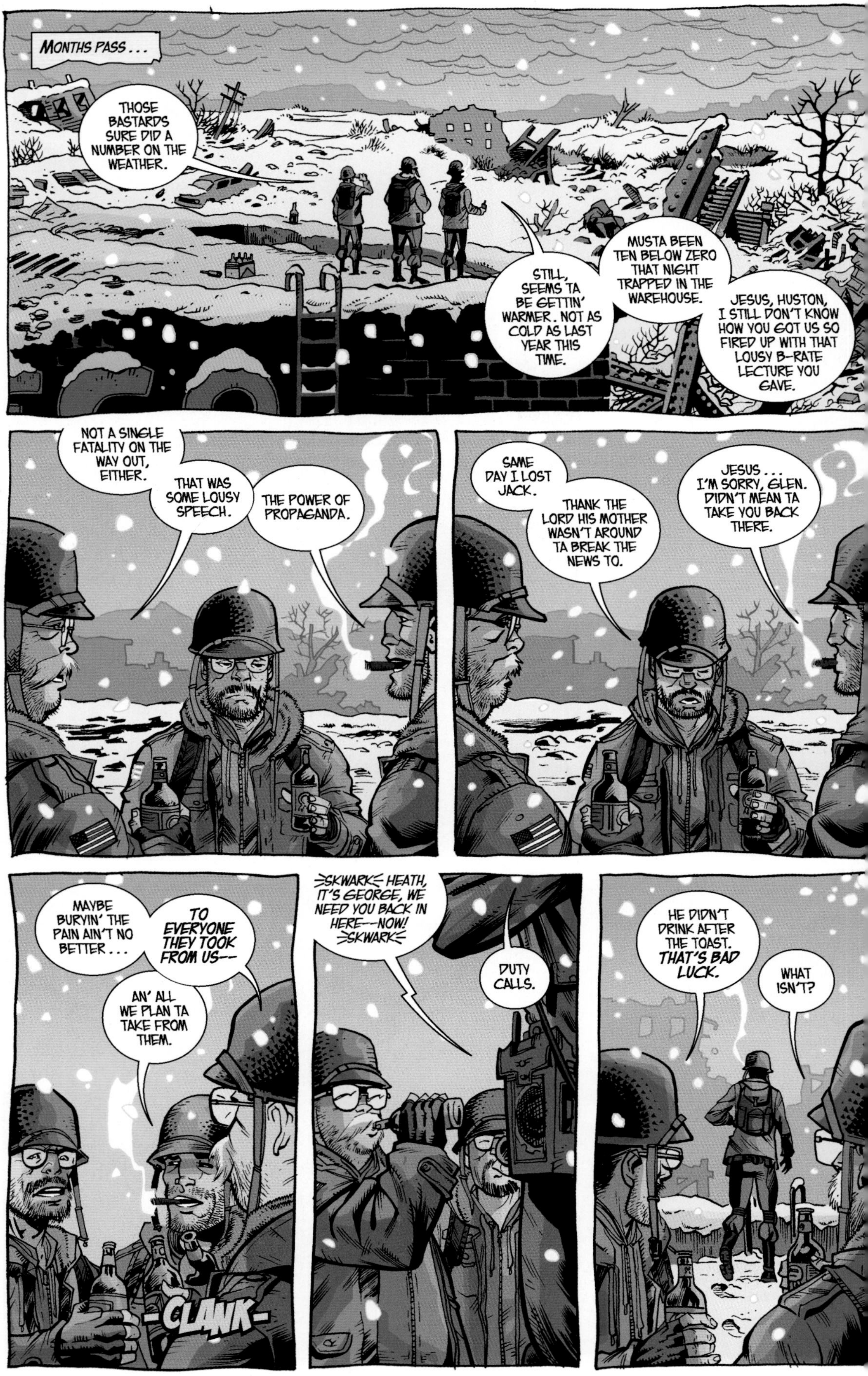
MONTHS PASS . . .
THOSE BASTARDS SURE DID A NUMBER ON THE WEATHER.
STILL, SEEMS TA BE GETTIN' WARMER. NOT AS COLD AS LAST YEAR THIS TIME.
MUSTA BEEN TEN BELOW ZERO THAT NIGHT TRAPPED IN THE WAREHOUSE.
JESUS, HUSTON, I STILL DON'T KNOW HOW YOU GOT US SO FIRED UP WITH THAT LOUSY B-RATE LECTURE YOU GAVE.
NOT A SINGLE FATALITY ON THE WAY OUT, EITHER.
THAT WAS SOME LOUSY SPEECH.
THE POWER OF PROPAGANDA.
SAME DAY I LOST JACK.
THANK THE LORD HIS MOTHER WASN'T AROUND TA BREAK THE NEWS TO.
JESUS . . . I'M SORRY, GLEN. DIDN'T MEAN TA TAKE YOU BACK THERE.
MAYBE BURYIN' THE PAIN AIN'T NO BETTER . . .
TO EVERYONE THEY TOOK FROM US--
AN' ALL WE PLAN TA TAKE FROM THEM.
-CLANK-
SKWARK HEATH, IT'S GEORGE, WE NEED YOU BACK IN HERE--NOW! SKWARK
DUTY CALLS.
HE DIDN'T DRINK AFTER THE TOAST. THAT'S BAD LUCK.
WHAT ISN'T?

WHAT'S SO GAL DARN IMPORTANT?

WE NEEDED A TEST OF THE SPACE SUITS BEFORE SENDING A TEAM OUT IN THE ROCKET.

YORKE VOLUNTEERED TO TAKE HIS TEAM THROUGH THE ZERIN PORTAL TO THE MOON...

WE'RE IN BAD TROUBLE, HUSTON.

THE DRESSITES ARE BUILDING A *GIANT GODDAMNED GUN* ON THE MOON...

...POINTED RIGHT AT EARTH.

ON THE MOON?

HOW'S THAT *POSSIBLE*-- WOULDN'T THE TETALDIANS SEE IT? HELL, WOULDN'T *WE* FER THAT MATTER?

CLOAKING DEVICE. NO VISUAL ON THE THING TILL ABOUT A QUARTER MILE AWAY.

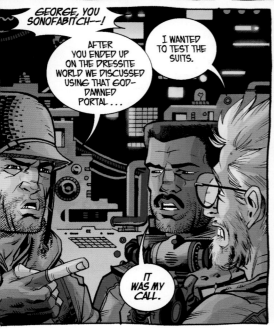

GEORGE, YOU SONOFABITCH--!

AFTER YOU ENDED UP ON THE DRESSITE WORLD WE DISCUSSED USING THAT GOD-DAMNED PORTAL...

I WANTED TO TEST THE SUITS.

IT WAS MY CALL.

AIN'T NOTHIN' YOUR CALL, YORKE!

OKAY, OKAY-- LATER, OTTO.

MORE PRESSIN' MATTERS AT HAND.

LIKE WHY'D THEY FIGHT SO HARD FER EARTH JUST TA DESTROY 'ER?

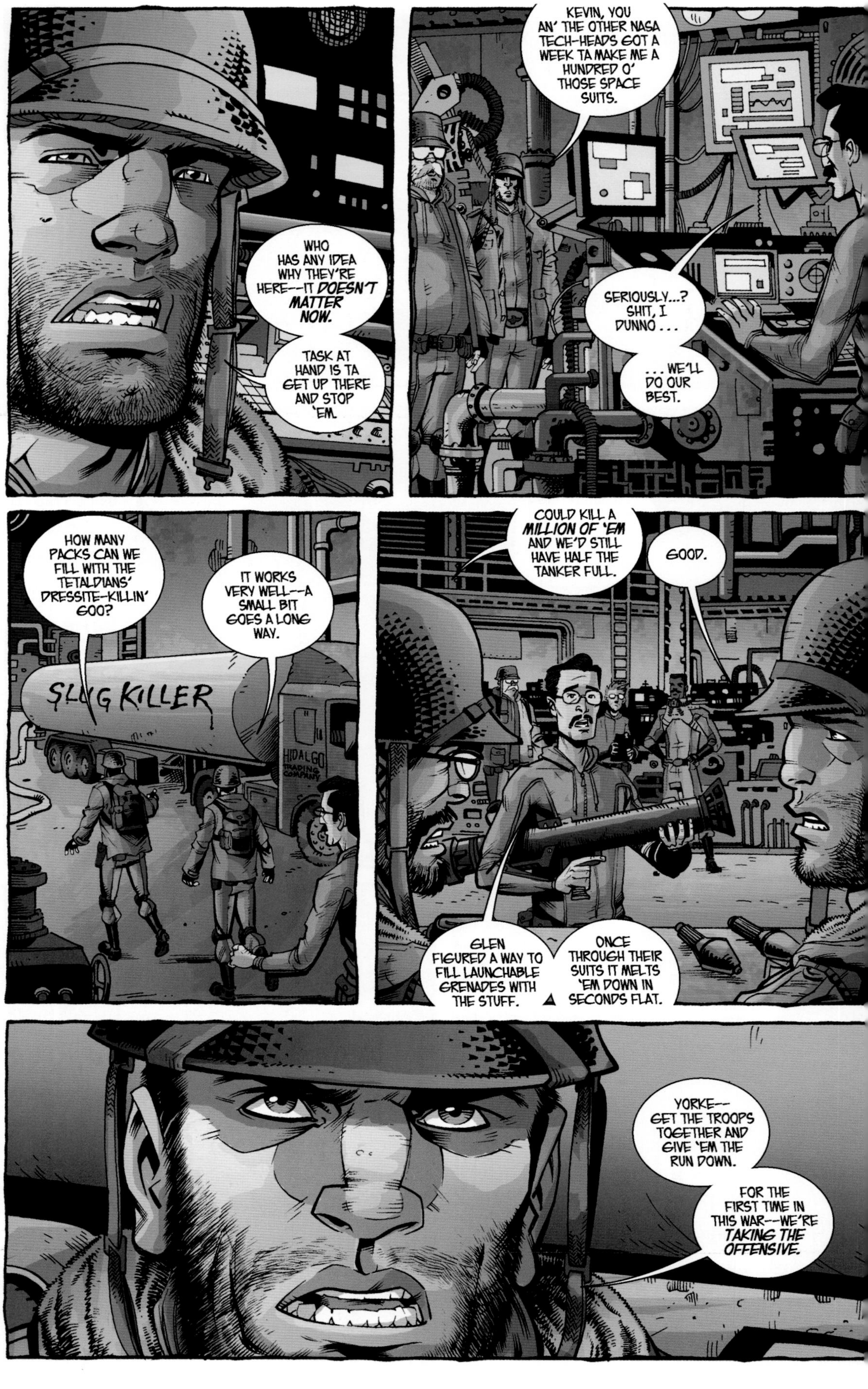
WHO HAS ANY IDEA WHY THEY'RE HERE--IT DOESN'T MATTER NOW.
TASK AT HAND IS TA GET UP THERE AND STOP 'EM.
KEVIN, YOU AN' THE OTHER NASA TECH-HEADS GOT A WEEK TA MAKE ME A HUNDRED O' THOSE SPACE SUITS.
SERIOUSLY...? SHIT, I DUNNO . . .
. . . WE'LL DO OUR BEST.
HOW MANY PACKS CAN WE FILL WITH THE TETALDIANS' DRESSITE-KILLIN' GOO?
IT WORKS VERY WELL--A SMALL BIT GOES A LONG WAY.
SLUG KILLER
HIDALGO TRADING COMPANY
COULD KILL A MILLION OF 'EM AND WE'D STILL HAVE HALF THE TANKER FULL.
GOOD.
GLEN FIGURED A WAY TO FILL LAUNCHABLE GRENADES WITH THE STUFF.
ONCE THROUGH THEIR SUITS IT MELTS 'EM DOWN IN SECONDS FLAT.
YORKE-- GET THE TROOPS TOGETHER AND GIVE 'EM THE RUN DOWN.
FOR THE FIRST TIME IN THIS WAR--WE'RE TAKING THE OFFENSIVE.

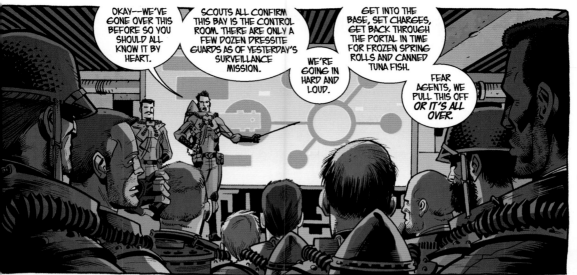

OKAY--WE'VE GONE OVER THIS BEFORE SO YOU SHOULD ALL KNOW IT BY HEART.

SCOUTS ALL CONFIRM THIS BAY IS THE CONTROL ROOM. THERE ARE ONLY A FEW DOZEN DRESSITE GUARDS AS OF YESTERDAY'S SURVEILLANCE MISSION.

WE'RE GOING IN HARD AND LOUD.

GET INTO THE BASE, SET CHARGES, GET BACK THROUGH THE PORTAL IN TIME FOR FROZEN SPRING ROLLS AND CANNED TUNA FISH.

FEAR AGENTS, WE PULL THIS OFF OR IT'S ALL OVER.

I'M READY, UNCLE OTTO.

ANDI, WHEN YOUR MOM SENT YA TA DETOX ON MY RANCH, I SWORE TA PROTECT YA.

FER THE LOVIN' MEMORY O' YOUR MOM, MY LITTLE SISTER... PLEASE, GIRL-- SIT THIS ONE OUT.

OKAY. I'LL BE HERE WAITING... YOU PROMISE ME YOU'LL COME HOME.

HONEST, I WILL.

HEATH, BABY, SOMETHING FEELS SO WRONG ABOUT ALL THIS.

DON'T GO FRETTIN', ANGEL.

EASY MISSION, THEY HAVE NO IDEA WE'RE COMING.

BE STRONG, ANGEL.

I LOVE YOU, CHAR.

WE'LL BE HOME SOON.

GOD-DAMNED RIGHT.

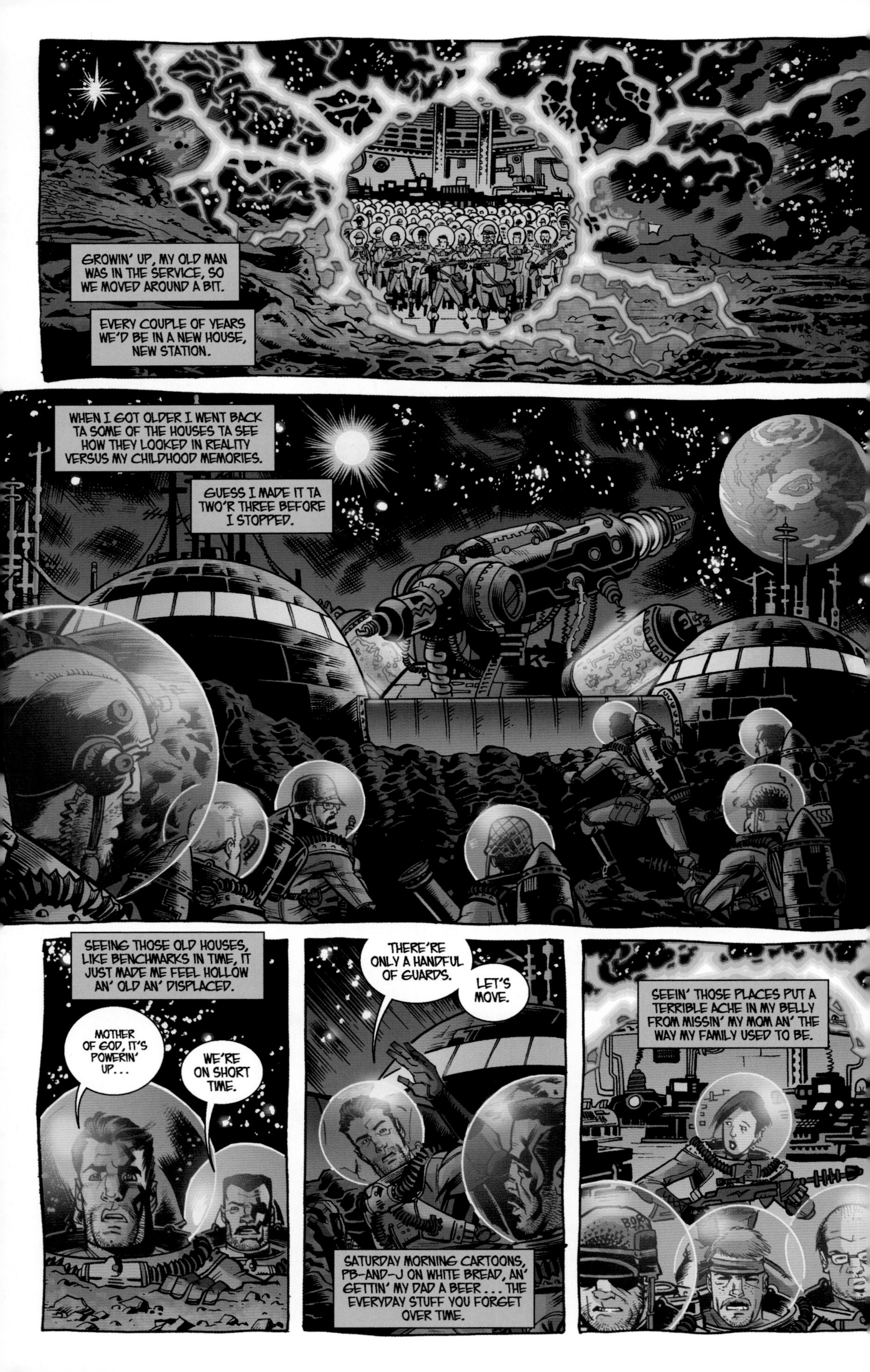
GROWIN' UP, MY OLD MAN WAS IN THE SERVICE, SO WE MOVED AROUND A BIT.
EVERY COUPLE OF YEARS WE'D BE IN A NEW HOUSE, NEW STATION.
WHEN I GOT OLDER I WENT BACK TA SOME OF THE HOUSES TA SEE HOW THEY LOOKED IN REALITY VERSUS MY CHILDHOOD MEMORIES.
GUESS I MADE IT TA TWO'R THREE BEFORE I STOPPED.
SEEING THOSE OLD HOUSES, LIKE BENCHMARKS IN TIME, IT JUST MADE ME FEEL HOLLOW AN' OLD AN' DISPLACED.
MOTHER OF GOD, IT'S POWERIN' UP...
WE'RE ON SHORT TIME.
THERE'RE ONLY A HANDFUL OF GUARDS.
LET'S MOVE.
SATURDAY MORNING CARTOONS, PB-AND-J ON WHITE BREAD, AN' GETTIN' MY DAD A BEER... THE EVERYDAY STUFF YOU FORGET OVER TIME.
SEEIN' THOSE PLACES PUT A TERRIBLE ACHE IN MY BELLY FROM MISSIN' MY MOM AN' THE WAY MY FAMILY USED TO BE.

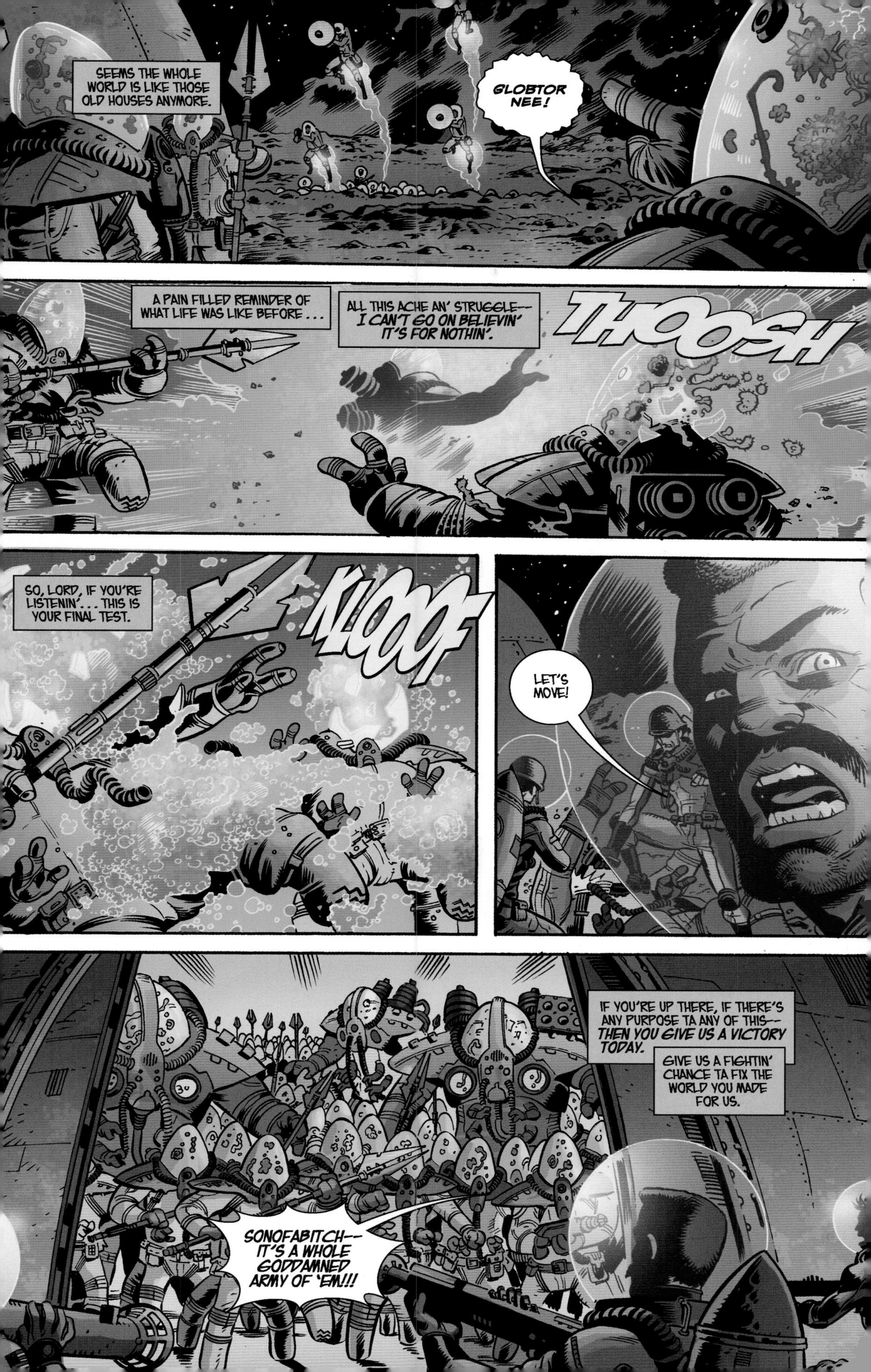
SEEMS THE WHOLE WORLD IS LIKE THOSE OLD HOUSES ANYMORE.
GLOBTOR NEE!
A PAIN FILLED REMINDER OF WHAT LIFE WAS LIKE BEFORE . . .
ALL THIS ACHE AN' STRUGGLE-- I CAN'T GO ON BELIEVIN' IT'S FOR NOTHIN'.
THOOSH
SO, LORD, IF YOU'RE LISTENIN'. . . THIS IS YOUR FINAL TEST.
KLOOOF
LET'S MOVE!
IF YOU'RE UP THERE, IF THERE'S ANY PURPOSE TA ANY OF THIS-- THEN YOU GIVE US A VICTORY TODAY.
GIVE US A FIGHTIN' CHANCE TA FIX THE WORLD YOU MADE FOR US.
SONOFABITCH-- IT'S A WHOLE GODDAMNED ARMY OF 'EM!!!

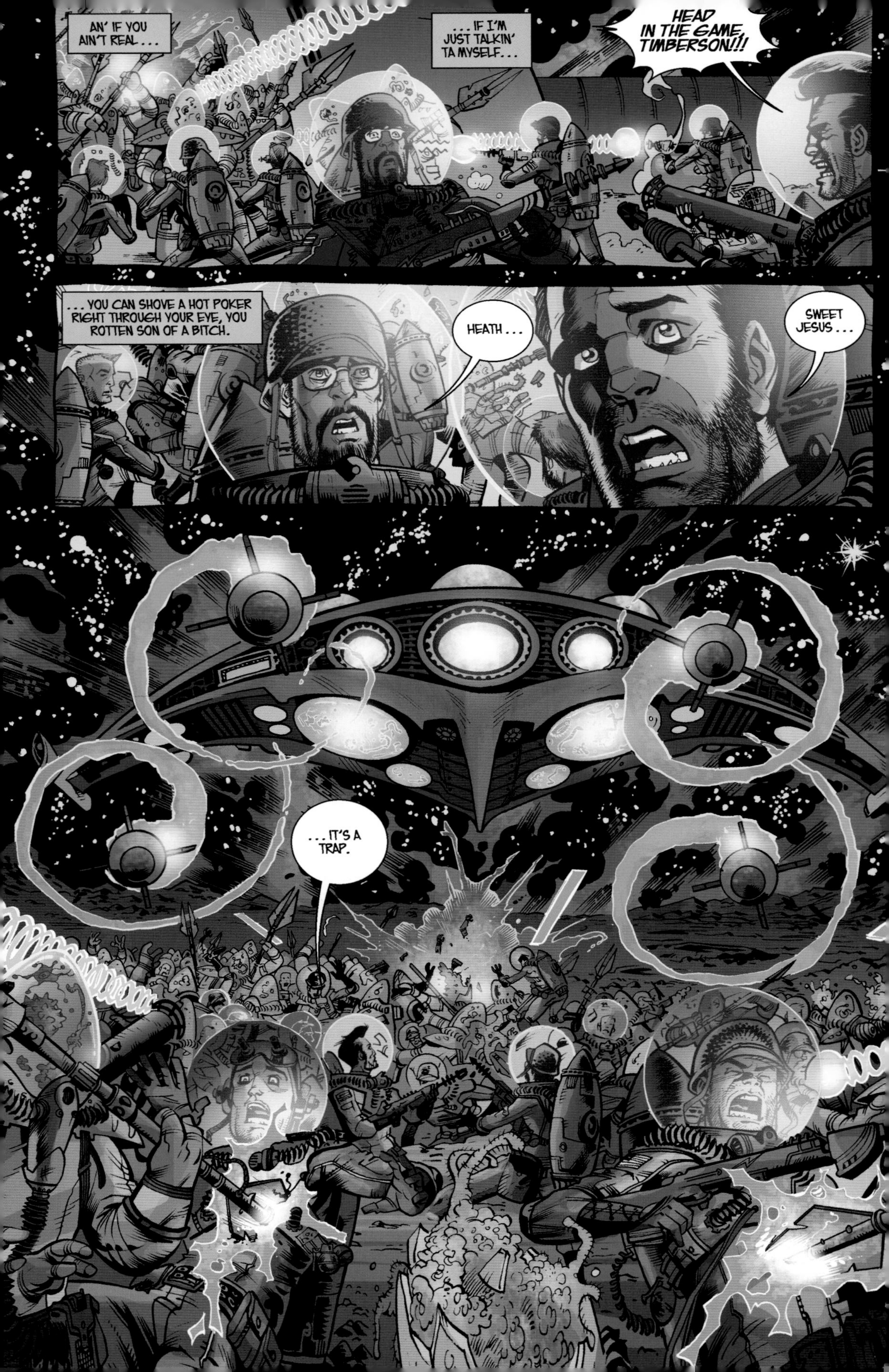

AN' IF YOU AIN'T REAL . . .
. . . IF I'M JUST TALKIN' TA MYSELF . . .
HEAD IN THE GAME, TIMBERSON!!!
. . . YOU CAN SHOVE A HOT POKER RIGHT THROUGH YOUR EYE, YOU ROTTEN SON OF A BITCH.
HEATH . . .
SWEET JESUS . . .
. . . IT'S A TRAP.

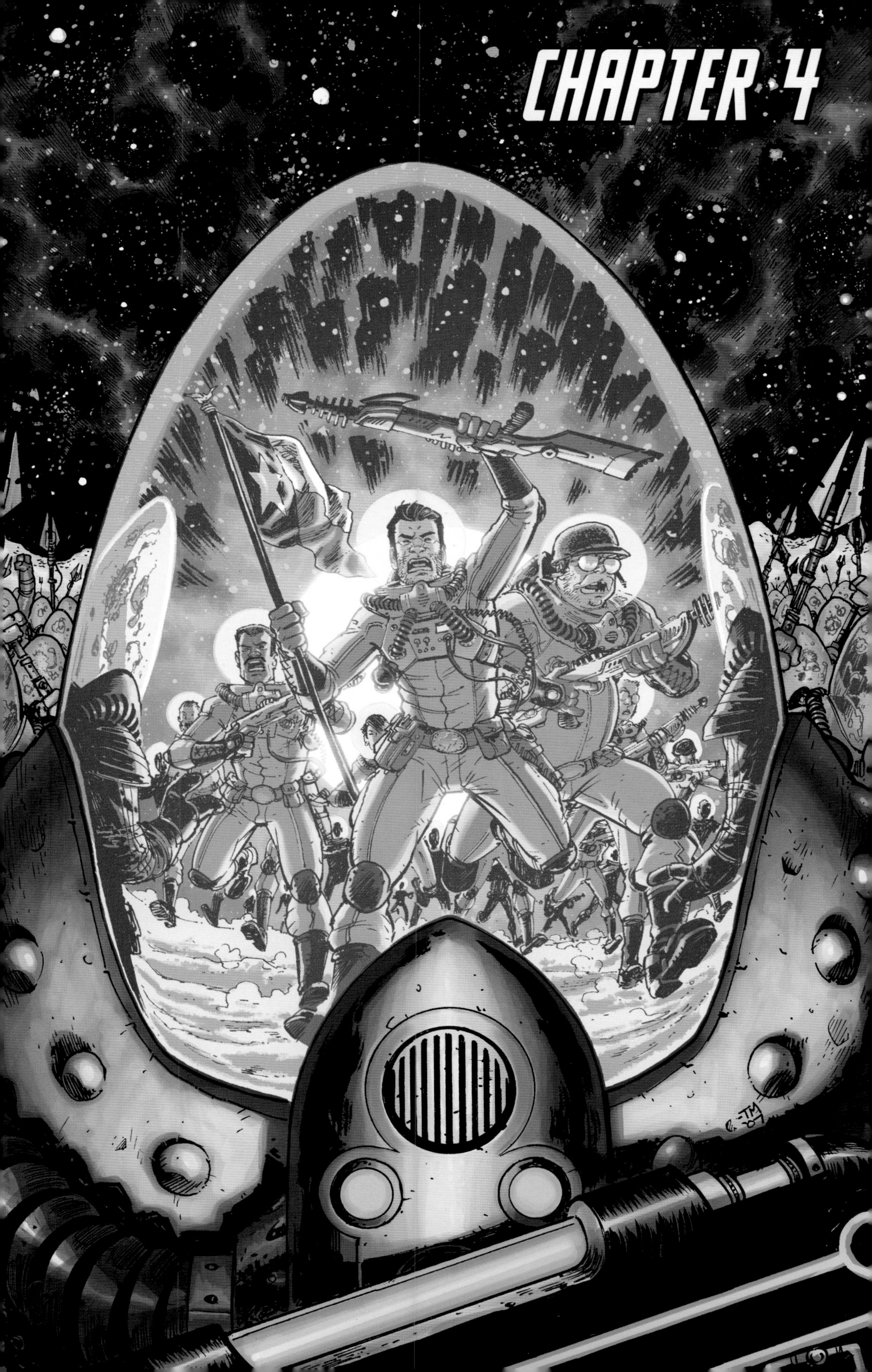
CHAPTER 4
TM '07

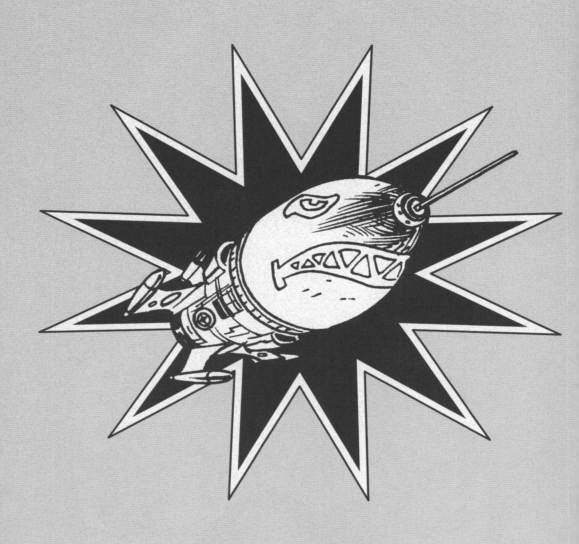

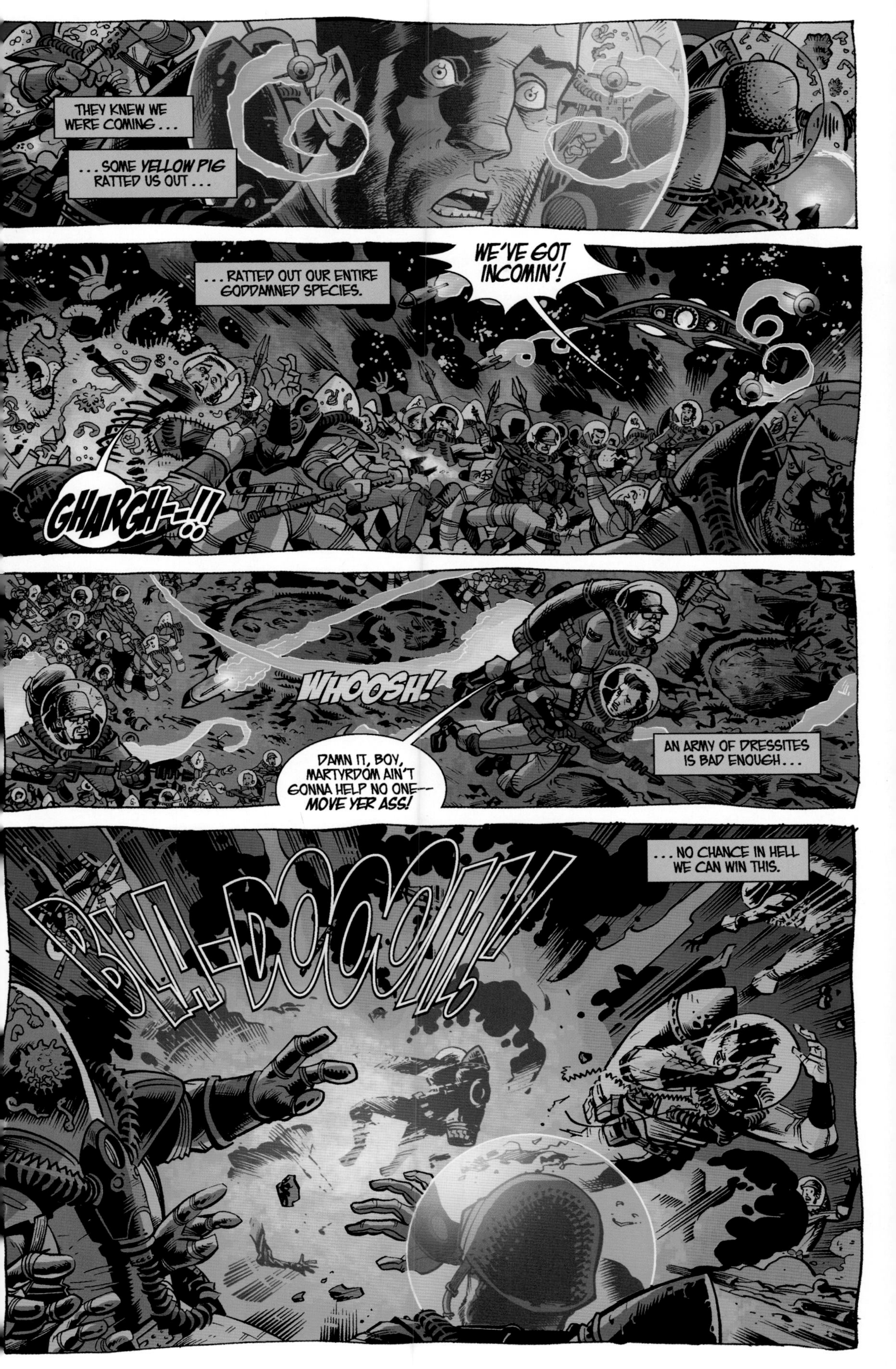

THEY KNEW WE WERE COMING . . .
. . . SOME YELLOW PIG RATTED US OUT . . .
. . . RATTED OUT OUR ENTIRE GODDAMNED SPECIES.
WE'VE GOT INCOMIN'!
GHARGH--!!
WHOOSH!
DAMN IT, BOY, MARTYRDOM AIN'T GONNA HELP NO ONE-- MOVE YER ASS!
AN ARMY OF DRESSITES IS BAD ENOUGH . . .
. . . NO CHANCE IN HELL WE CAN WIN THIS.
BLA-DOOOOM!

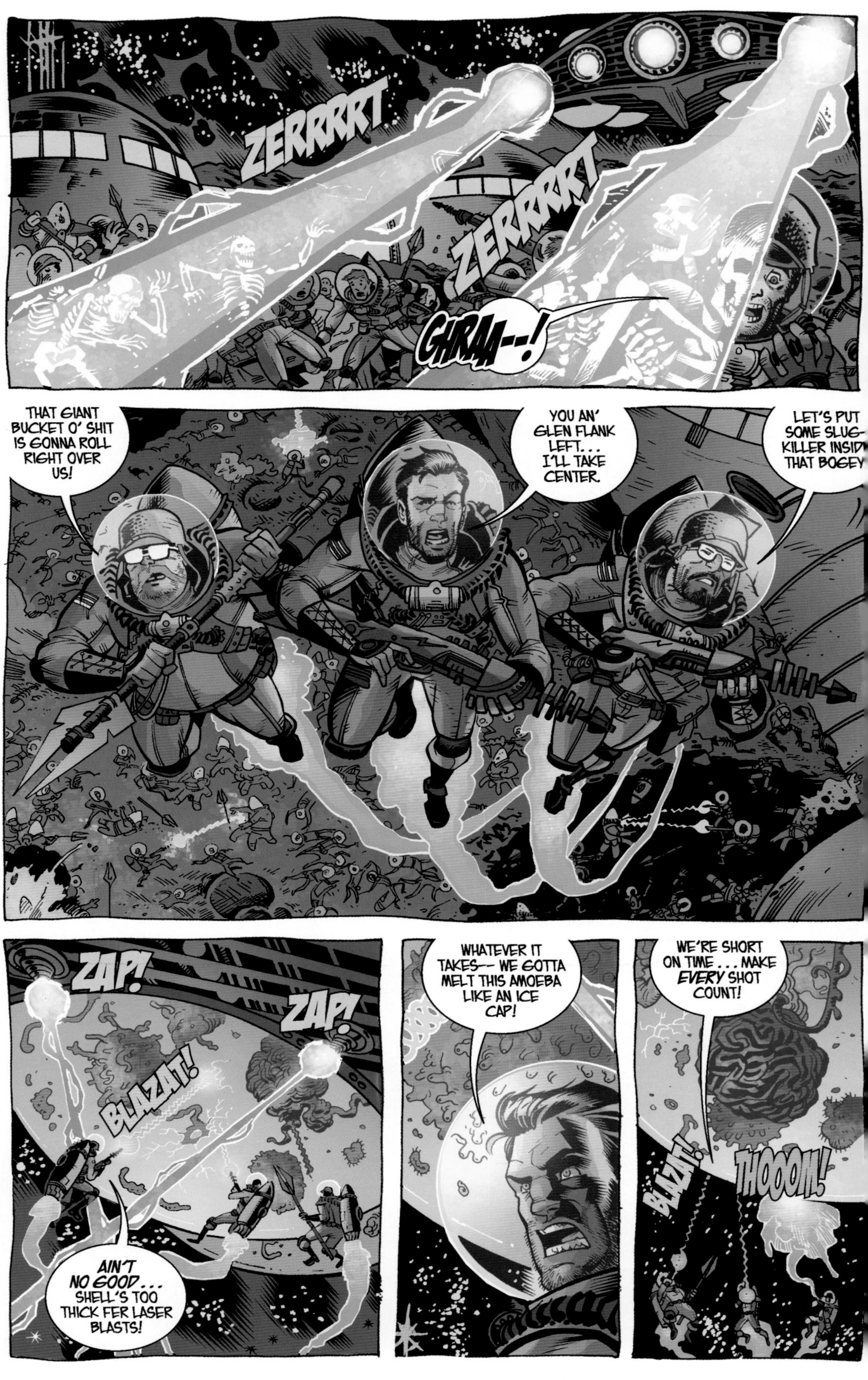
ZERRRRT
ZERRRRT
GHRAA--!
THAT GIANT BUCKET O' SHIT IS GONNA ROLL RIGHT OVER US!
YOU AN' GLEN FLANK LEFT... I'LL TAKE CENTER.
LET'S PUT SOME SLUG-KILLER INSID THAT BOGEY
ZAP!
ZAP!
BLAZAT!
AIN'T NO GOOD... SHELL'S TOO THICK FER LASER BLASTS!
WHATEVER IT TAKES-- WE GOTTA MELT THIS AMOEBA LIKE AN ICE CAP!
WE'RE SHORT ON TIME... MAKE EVERY SHOT COUNT!
BLAZAT!
THOOOM!

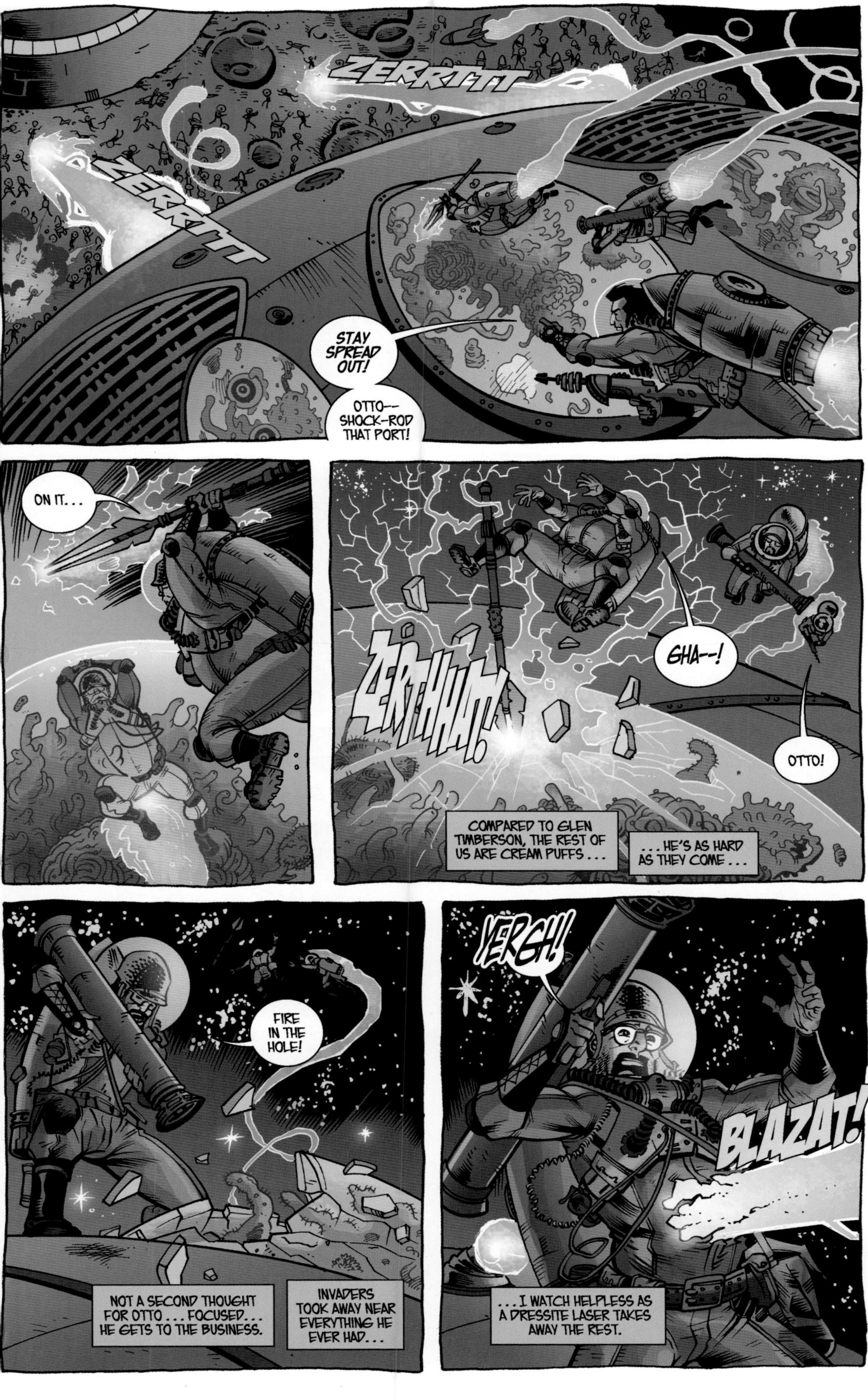
ZERRTTT
ZERRTTT
STAY SPREAD OUT!
OTTO-- SHOCK-ROD THAT PORT!
ON IT...
ZERTHHAT!
GHA--!
OTTO!
COMPARED TO GLEN TIMBERSON, THE REST OF US ARE CREAM PUFFS...
...HE'S AS HARD AS THEY COME...
FIRE IN THE HOLE!
NOT A SECOND THOUGHT FOR OTTO... FOCUSED... HE GETS TO THE BUSINESS.
INVADERS TOOK AWAY NEAR EVERYTHING HE EVER HAD...
YERGH!
BLAZAT!
...I WATCH HELPLESS AS A DRESSITE LASER TAKES AWAY THE REST.

≥COUGH≥
GET ON OUTTA
HERE . . .
≥COUGH≥

STUBBORN RAGE
KEEPS HIM ALIVE . . .

. . . LONGER THAN HE
HAS ANY NATURAL RIGHT . . .

GLEN!!

I KNOW AS
IT HAPPENS . . .

. . . IF I LIVE TA SEE
ANOTHER DAY . . .

. . . I'LL NEVER
RECOVER FROM
SEEING THIS . . .

. . . MY FRIEND GLEN
TIMBERSON WITH A GIANT
HOLE THROUGH HIS GUT . . .

I LOVE YOU,
LARRAINE . . .

TEK

. . . HIS FINAL
MOMENTS OF LIFE
SPENT IN UNIMAGINABLE
AGONY . . .

GLEN!!

GLI-THOOM!

. . . AS HE SAVES EVERY
GODDAMNED ONE OF US . . .

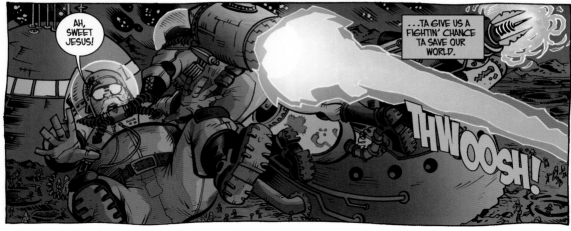

AH,
SWEET
JESUS!

. . . TA GIVE US A
FIGHTIN' CHANCE
TA SAVE OUR
WORLD.

THWOOSH!

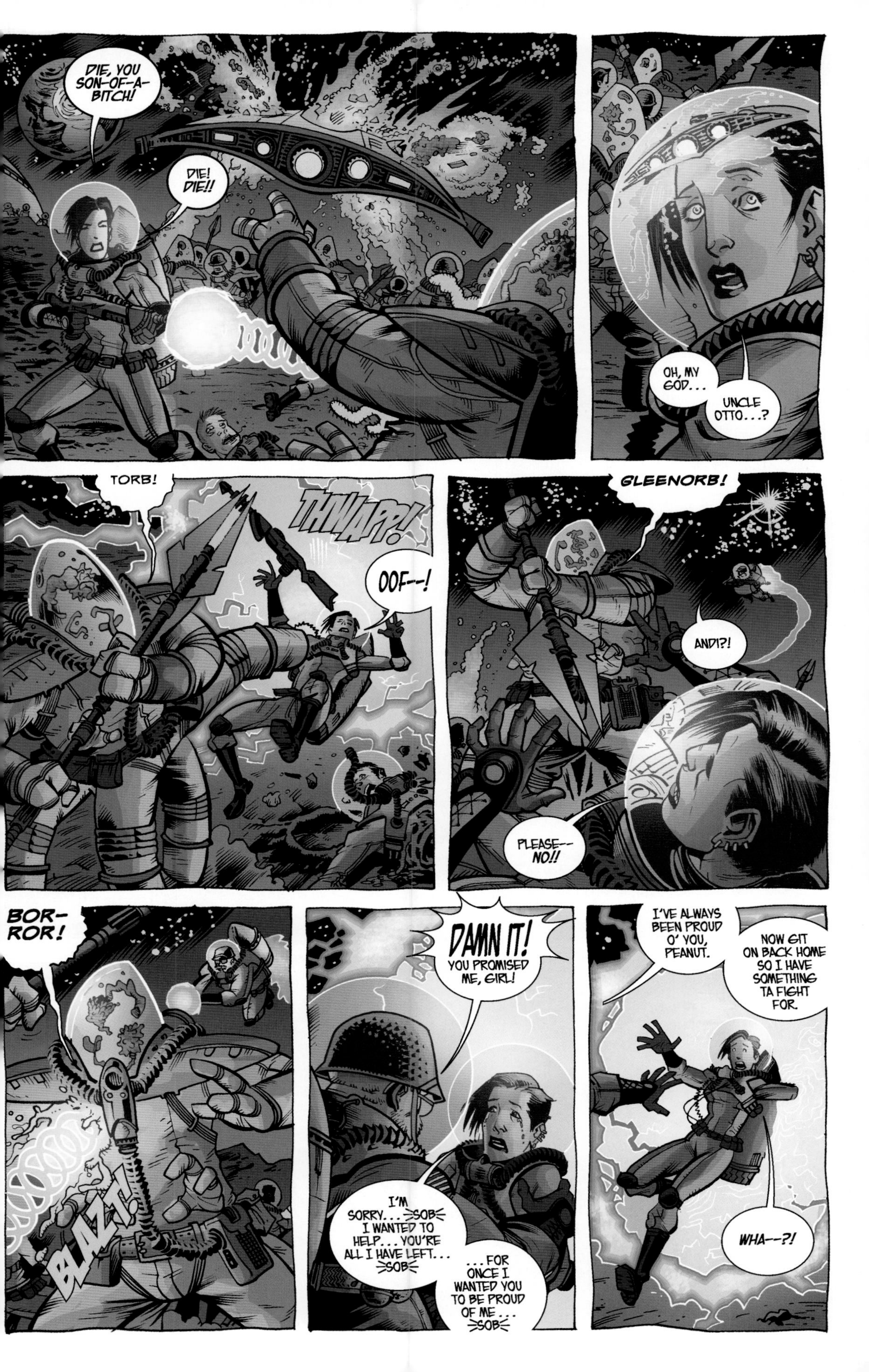
DIE, YOU SON-OF-A-BITCH!
DIE! DIE!!
OH, MY GOD...
UNCLE OTTO...?
TORB!
THWAPP!
OOF--!
GLEENORB!
ANDI?!
PLEASE-- NO!!
BOR-ROR!
BLAZT!
DAMN IT! YOU PROMISED ME, GIRL!
I'M SORRY... ≥SOB≤ I WANTED TO HELP... YOU'RE ALL I HAVE LEFT... ≥SOB≤
...FOR ONCE I WANTED YOU TO BE PROUD OF ME... ≥SOB≤
I'VE ALWAYS BEEN PROUD O' YOU, PEANUT.
NOW GIT ON BACK HOME SO I HAVE SOMETHING TA FIGHT FOR.
WHA--?!

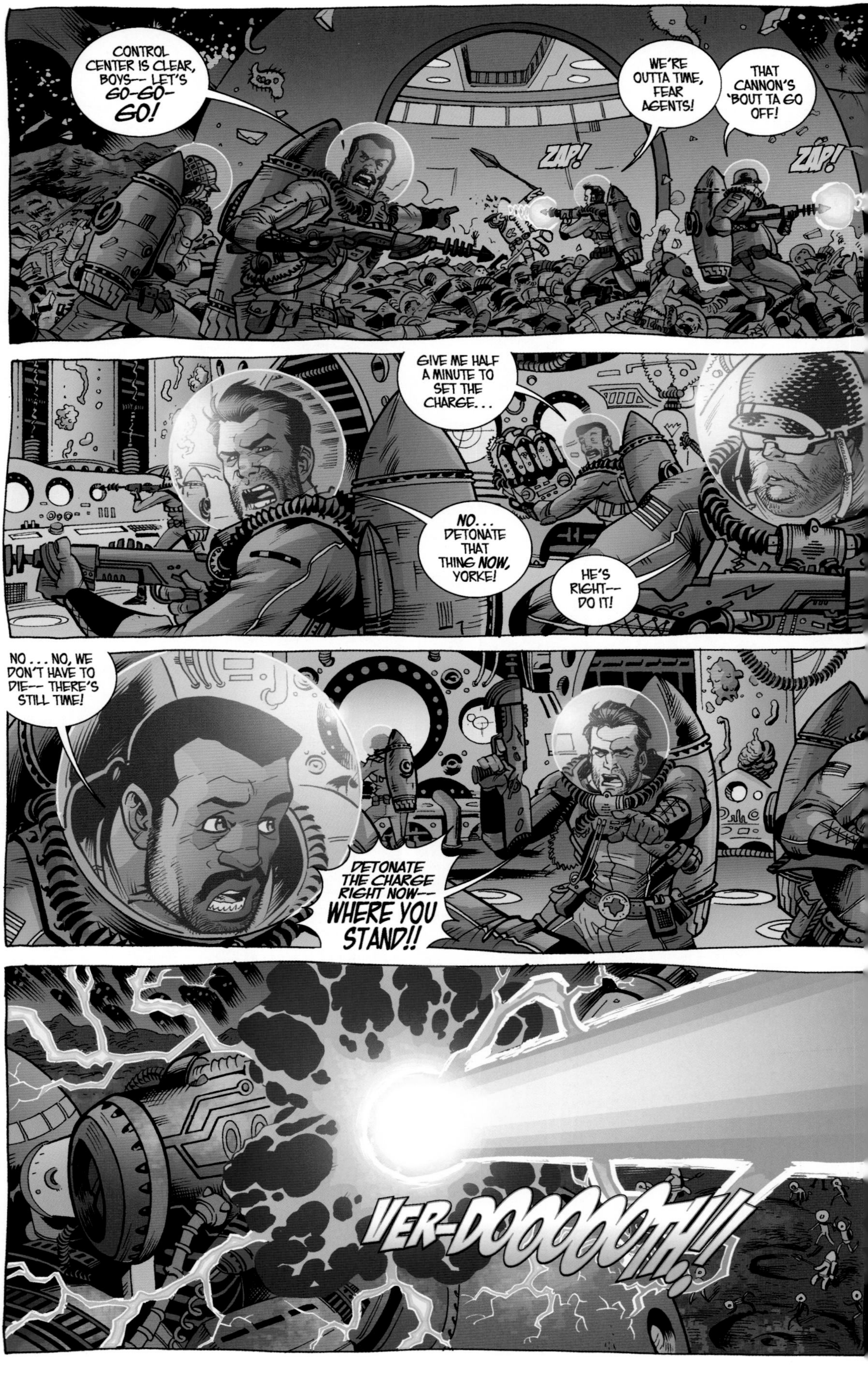
CONTROL CENTER IS CLEAR, BOYS-- LET'S GO-GO-GO!
WE'RE OUTTA TIME, FEAR AGENTS!
THAT CANNON'S 'BOUT TA GO OFF!
ZAP!
ZAP!
GIVE ME HALF A MINUTE TO SET THE CHARGE...
NO... DETONATE THAT THING NOW, YORKE!
HE'S RIGHT-- DO IT!
NO... NO, WE DON'T HAVE TO DIE-- THERE'S STILL TIME!
DETONATE THE CHARGE RIGHT NOW-- WHERE YOU STAND!!
VER-DOOOOOTH!!

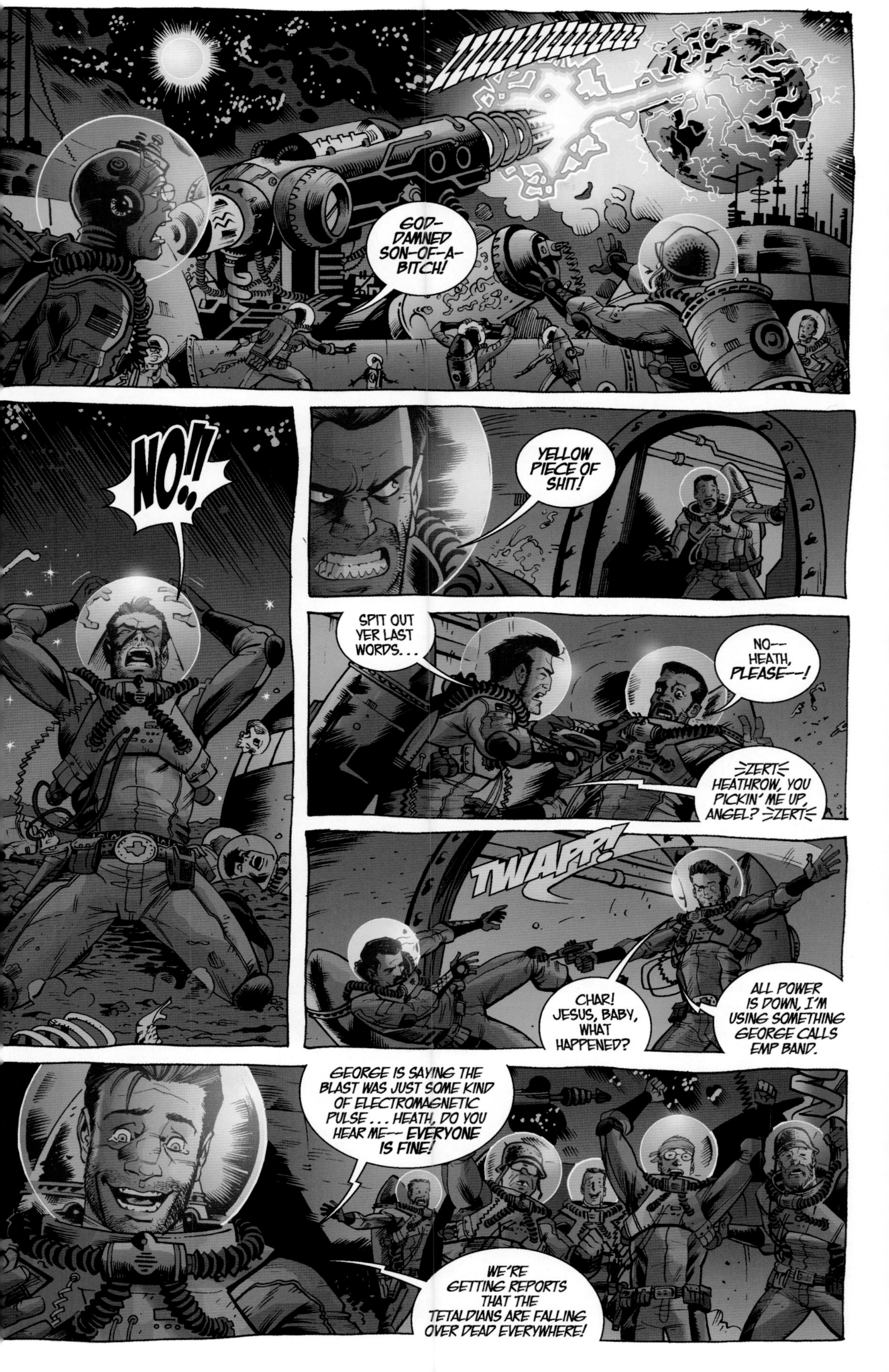
ZZZZZZZZZZZZZZZZ
GOD-DAMNED SON-OF-A-BITCH!
NO!!
YELLOW PIECE OF SHIT!
SPIT OUT YER LAST WORDS...
NO-- HEATH, PLEASE--!
ZERT HEATHROW, YOU PICKIN' ME UP, ANGEL? ZERT
TWAPP!
CHAR! JESUS, BABY, WHAT HAPPENED?
ALL POWER IS DOWN, I'M USING SOMETHING GEORGE CALLS EMP BAND.
GEORGE IS SAYING THE BLAST WAS JUST SOME KIND OF ELECTROMAGNETIC PULSE... HEATH, DO YOU HEAR ME-- EVERYONE IS FINE!
WE'RE GETTING REPORTS THAT THE TETALDIANS ARE FALLING OVER DEAD EVERYWHERE!

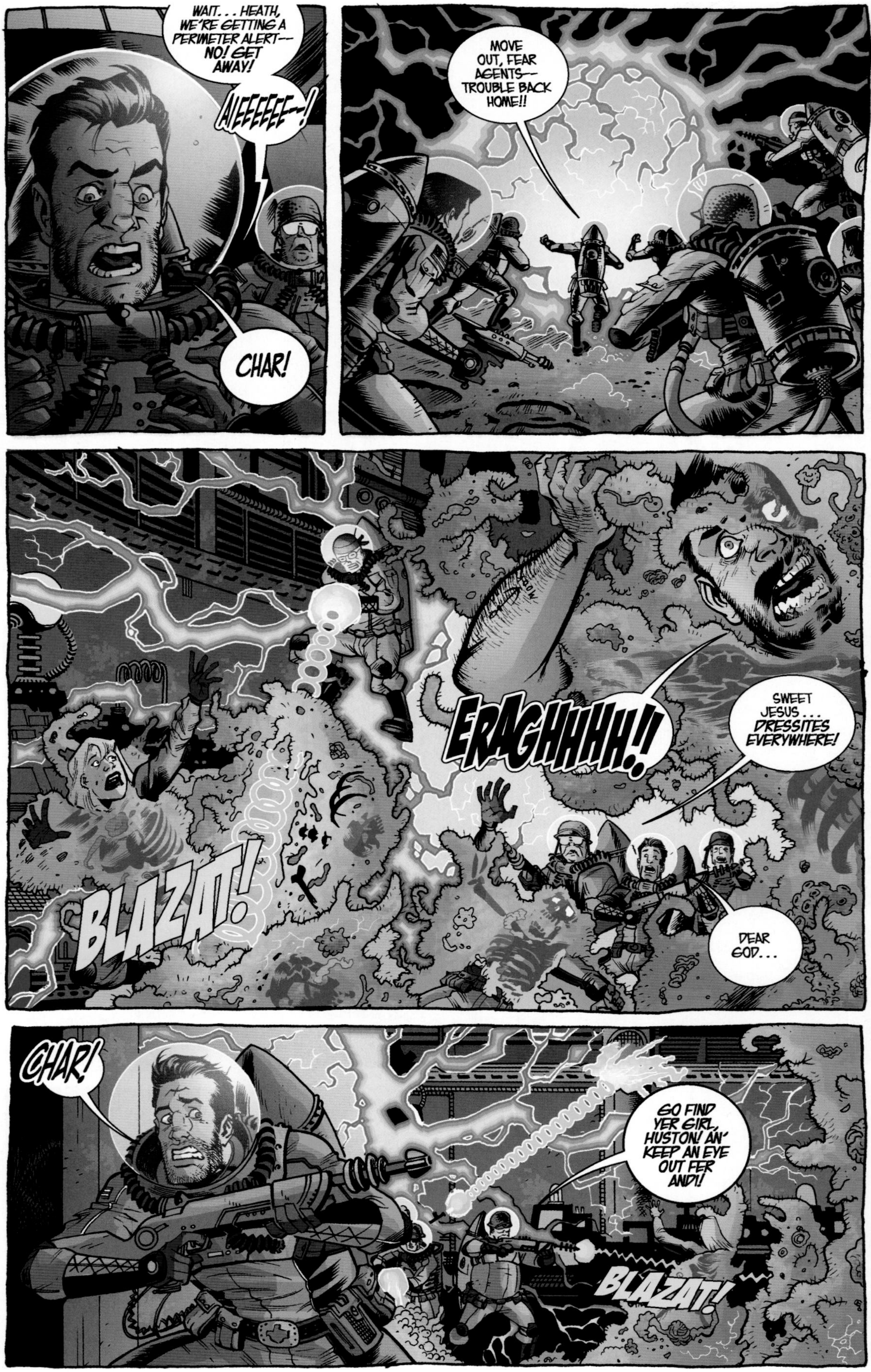
WAIT. . . HEATH, WE'RE GETTING A PERIMETER ALERT-- NO! GET AWAY!
AIEEEEEE--!
CHAR!
MOVE OUT, FEAR AGENTS-- TROUBLE BACK HOME!!
ERAGHHHH!!
SWEET JESUS . . . DRESSITES EVERYWHERE!
BLAZAT!
DEAR GOD. . .
CHAR!
GO FIND YER GIRL, HUSTON! AN' KEEP AN EYE OUT FER ANDI!
BLAZAT!

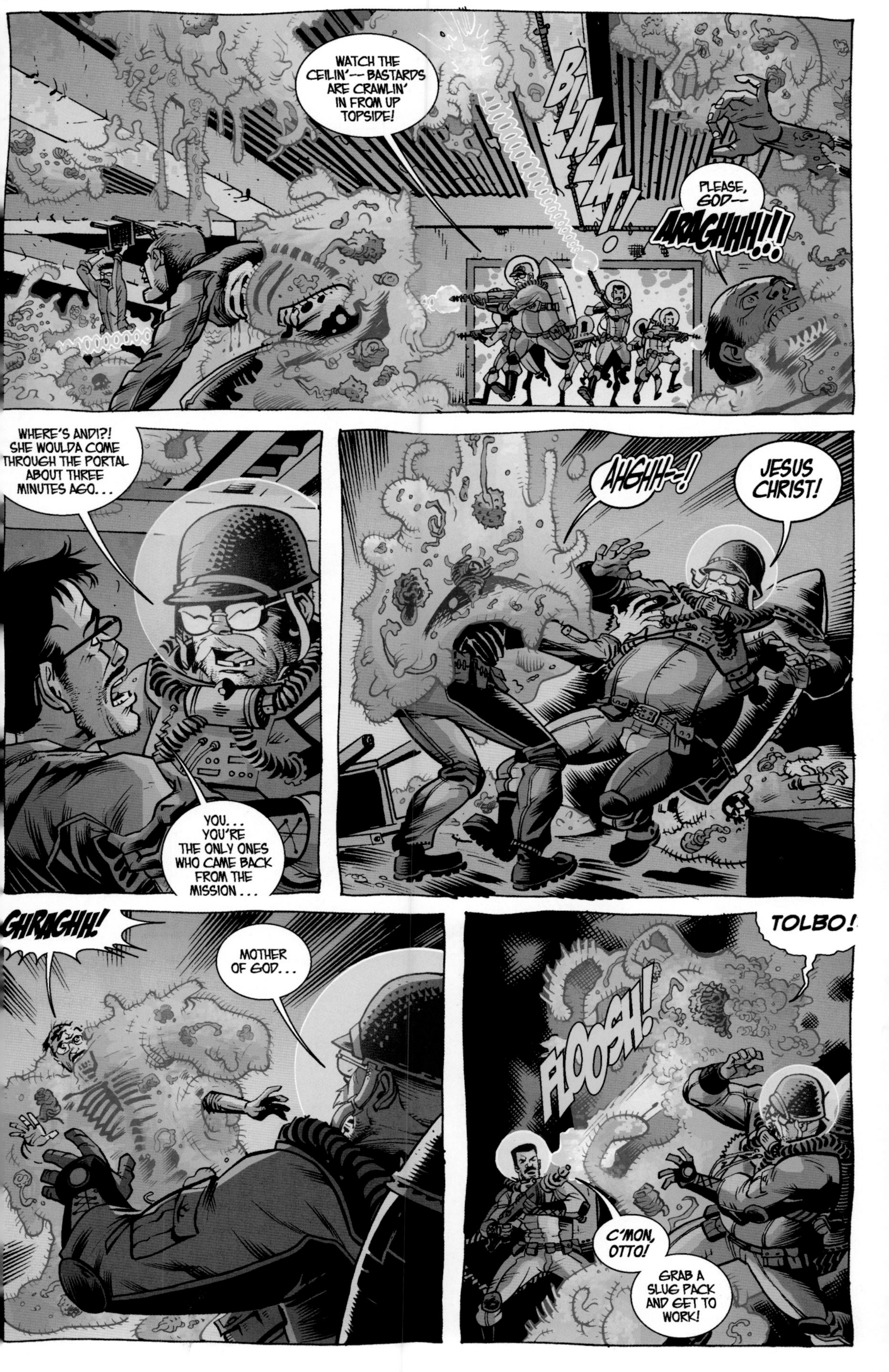
WATCH THE CEILIN'-- BASTARDS ARE CRAWLIN' IN FROM UP TOPSIDE!
BLAZAT!!
PLEASE, GOD--
ARAGHHH!!!
WHERE'S ANDI?! SHE WOULDA COME THROUGH THE PORTAL ABOUT THREE MINUTES AGO...
YOU... YOU'RE THE ONLY ONES WHO CAME BACK FROM THE MISSION...
AHGHH--!
JESUS CHRIST!
GHRAGHH!
MOTHER OF GOD...
TOLBO!
FLOOSH!
C'MON, OTTO!
GRAB A SLUG PACK AND GET TO WORK!

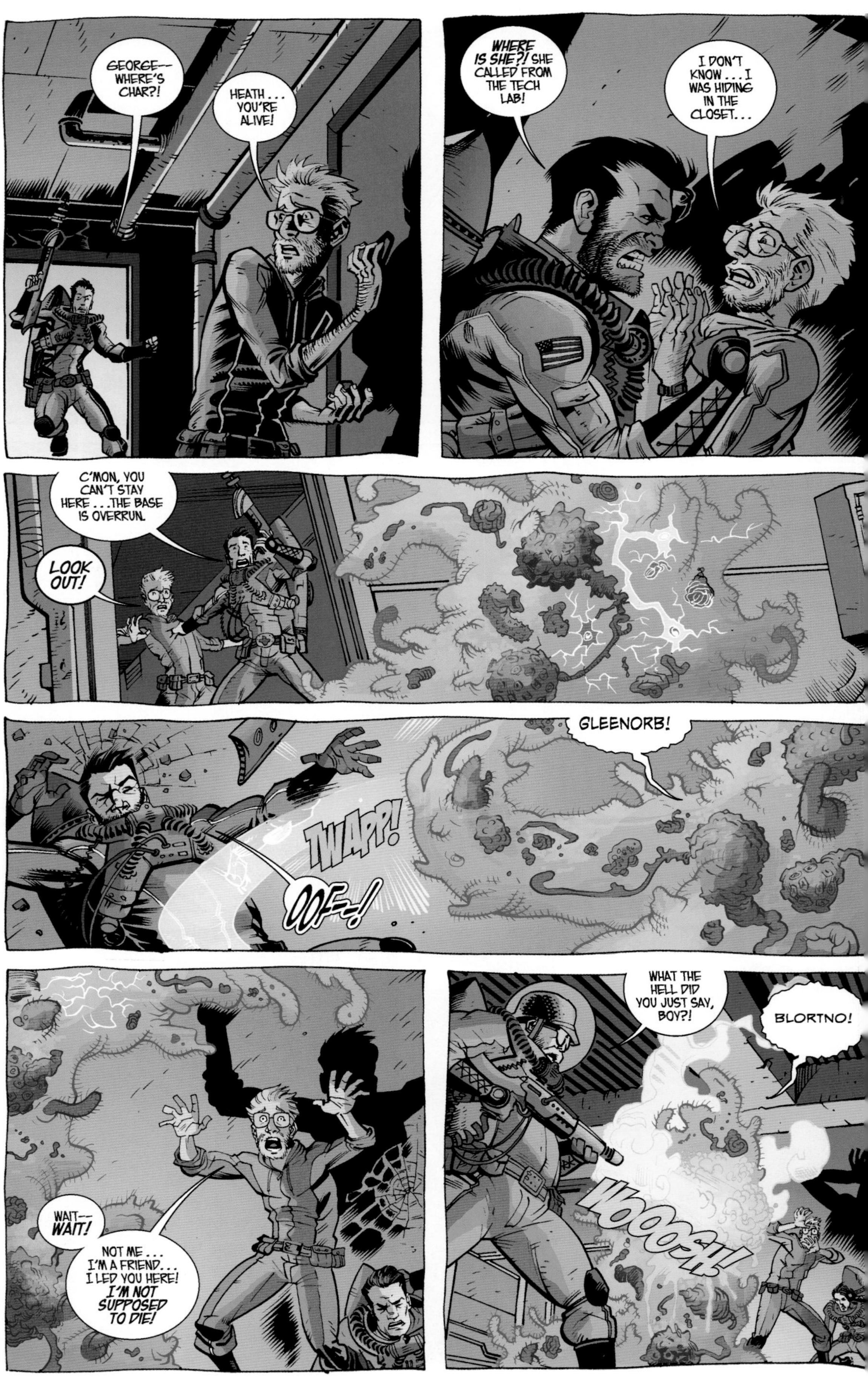
GEORGE--WHERE'S CHAR?!
HEATH . . . YOU'RE ALIVE!
WHERE IS SHE?! SHE CALLED FROM THE TECH LAB!
I DON'T KNOW . . . I WAS HIDING IN THE CLOSET. . .
C'MON, YOU CAN'T STAY HERE . . . THE BASE IS OVERRUN.
LOOK OUT!
GLEENORB!
TWAPP!
OOF--!
WAIT--WAIT!
NOT ME . . . I'M A FRIEND. . . I LED YOU HERE! I'M NOT SUPPOSED TO DIE!
WHAT THE HELL DID YOU JUST SAY, BOY?!
BLORTNO!
WOOOOSH!

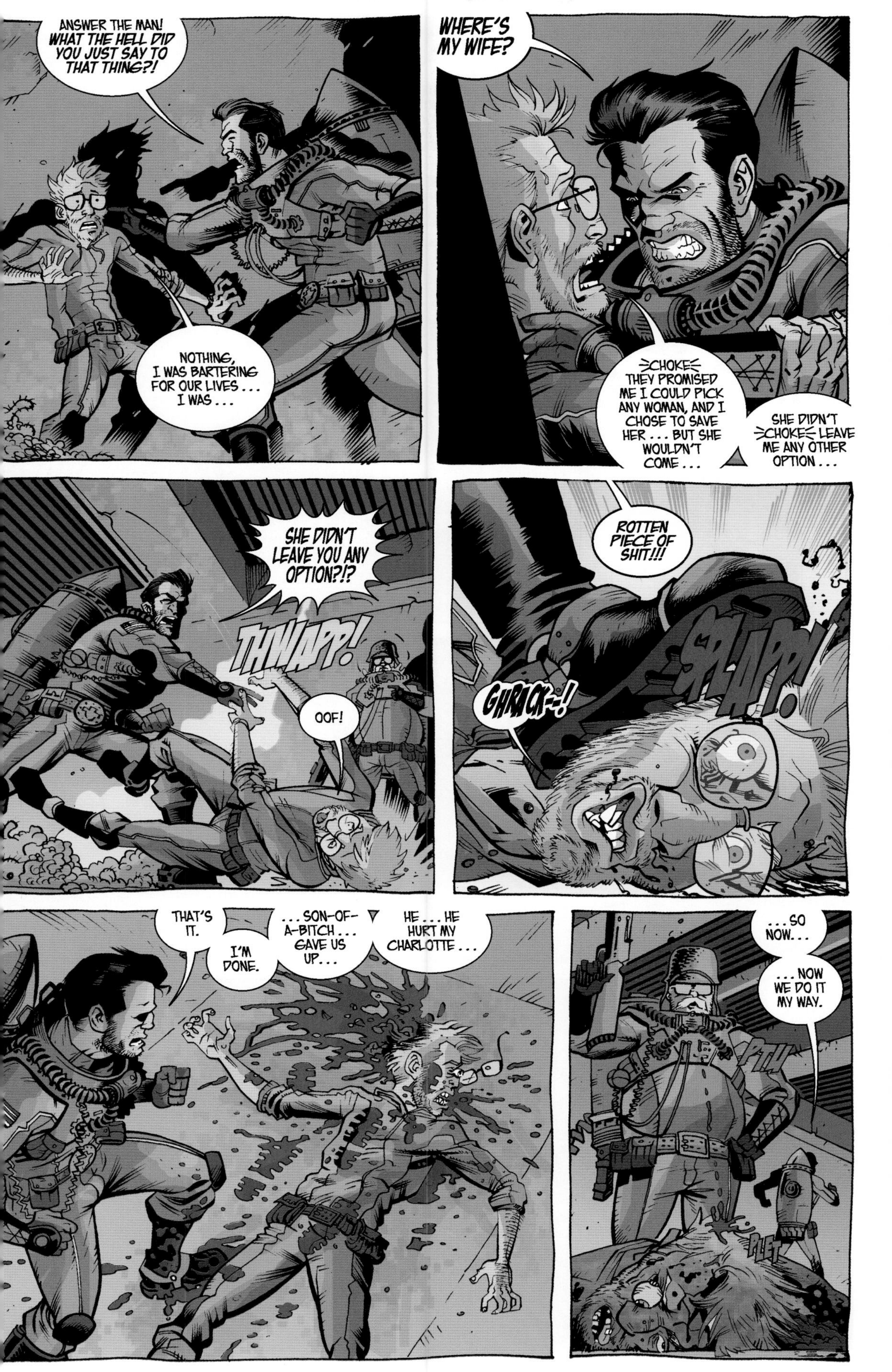
ANSWER THE MAN! WHAT THE HELL DID YOU JUST SAY TO THAT THING?!
NOTHING, I WAS BARTERING FOR OUR LIVES . . . I WAS . . .
WHERE'S MY WIFE?
CHOKE THEY PROMISED ME I COULD PICK ANY WOMAN, AND I CHOSE TO SAVE HER . . . BUT SHE WOULDN'T COME . . .
SHE DIDN'T CHOKE LEAVE ME ANY OTHER OPTION . . .
SHE DIDN'T LEAVE YOU ANY OPTION?!?
THWAPP!
OOF!
ROTTEN PIECE OF SHIT!!!
SPLAPP!
GHRACK--!
THAT'S IT.
I'M DONE.
. . . SON-OF-A-BITCH . . . GAVE US UP . . .
HE . . . HE HURT MY CHARLOTTE . . .
. . . SO NOW . . .
. . . NOW WE DO IT MY WAY.
PTU
PLET

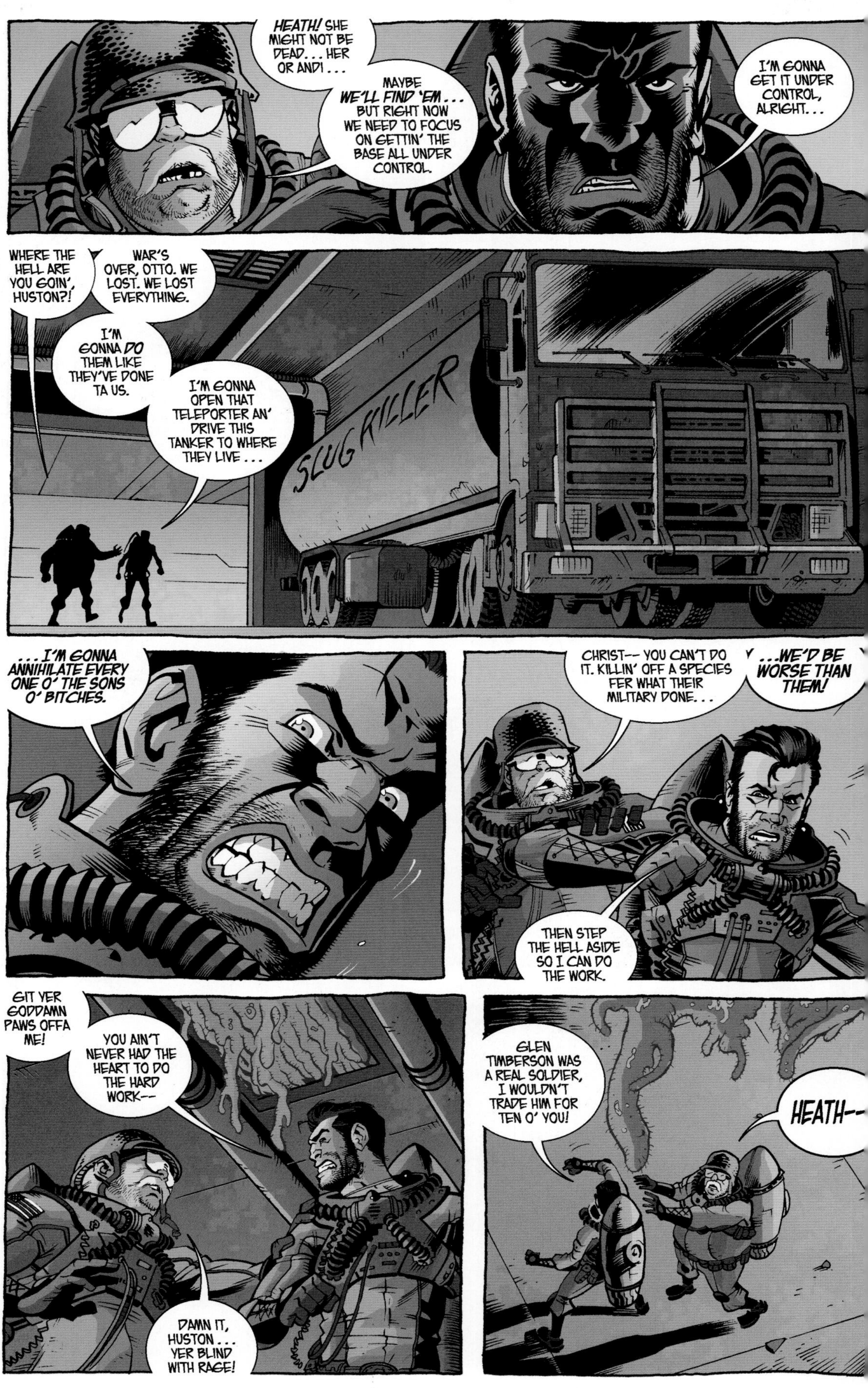
HEATH! SHE MIGHT NOT BE DEAD... HER OR ANDI...
MAYBE WE'LL FIND 'EM... BUT RIGHT NOW WE NEED TO FOCUS ON GETTIN' THE BASE ALL UNDER CONTROL.
I'M GONNA GET IT UNDER CONTROL, ALRIGHT...
WHERE THE HELL ARE YOU GOIN', HUSTON?!
WAR'S OVER, OTTO. WE LOST. WE LOST EVERYTHING.
I'M GONNA DO THEM LIKE THEY'VE DONE TA US.
I'M GONNA OPEN THAT TELEPORTER AN' DRIVE THIS TANKER TO WHERE THEY LIVE...
SLUG KILLER
...I'M GONNA ANNIHILATE EVERY ONE O' THE SONS O' BITCHES.
CHRIST-- YOU CAN'T DO IT. KILLIN' OFF A SPECIES FER WHAT THEIR MILITARY DONE...
...WE'D BE WORSE THAN THEM!
THEN STEP THE HELL ASIDE SO I CAN DO THE WORK.
GIT YER GODDAMN PAWS OFFA ME!
YOU AIN'T NEVER HAD THE HEART TO DO THE HARD WORK--
DAMN IT, HUSTON... YER BLIND WITH RAGE!
GLEN TIMBERSON WAS A REAL SOLDIER, I WOULDN'T TRADE HIM FOR TEN O' YOU!
HEATH--

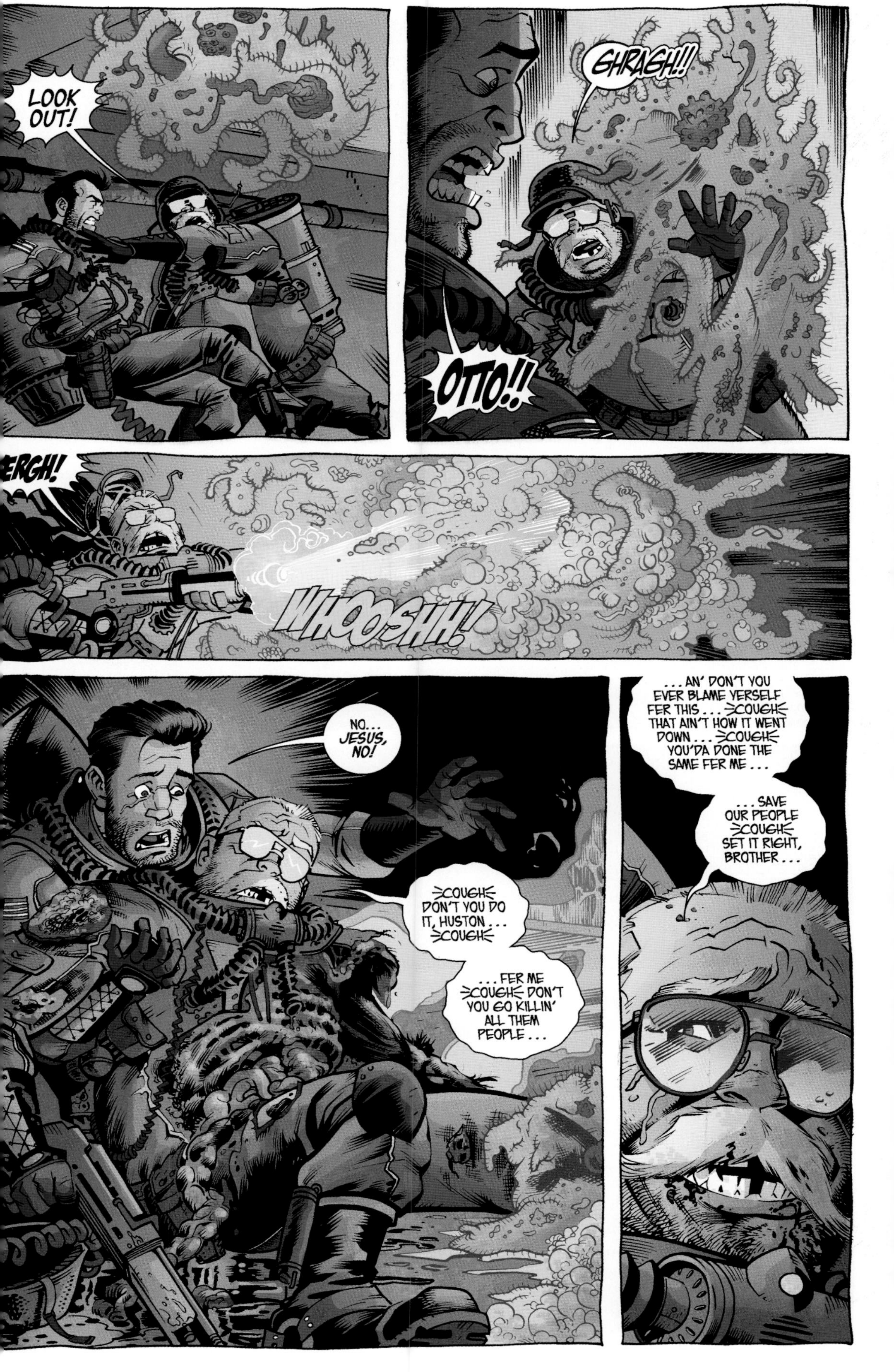
LOOK OUT!
GHRAGH!!
OTTO!!
ERGH!
WHOOSHH!
NO... JESUS, NO!
≶COUGH≷ DON'T YOU DO IT, HUSTON... ≶COUGH≷
...FER ME ≶COUGH≷ DON'T YOU GO KILLIN' ALL THEM PEOPLE...
...AN' DON'T YOU EVER BLAME YERSELF FER THIS... ≶COUGH≷ THAT AIN'T HOW IT WENT DOWN... ≶COUGH≷ YOU'DA DONE THE SAME FER ME...
...SAVE OUR PEOPLE ≶COUGH≷ SET IT RIGHT, BROTHER...

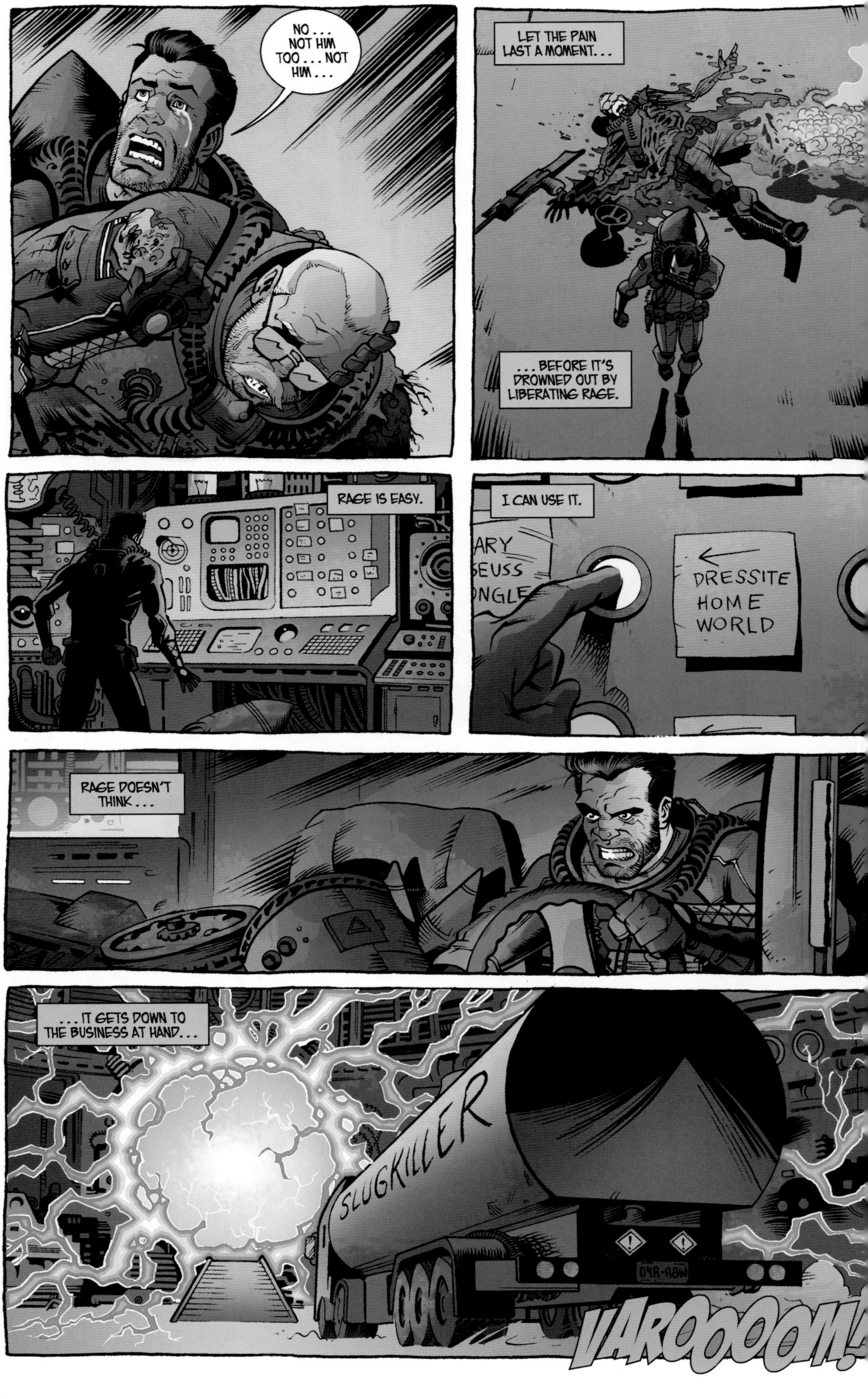
NO . . . NOT HIM TOO . . . NOT HIM . . .
LET THE PAIN LAST A MOMENT. . .
. . . BEFORE IT'S DROWNED OUT BY LIBERATING RAGE.
RAGE IS EASY.
I CAN USE IT.
DRESSITE HOME WORLD
RAGE DOESN'T THINK . . .
. . . IT GETS DOWN TO THE BUSINESS AT HAND. . .
SLUGKILLER
VAROOOOM!

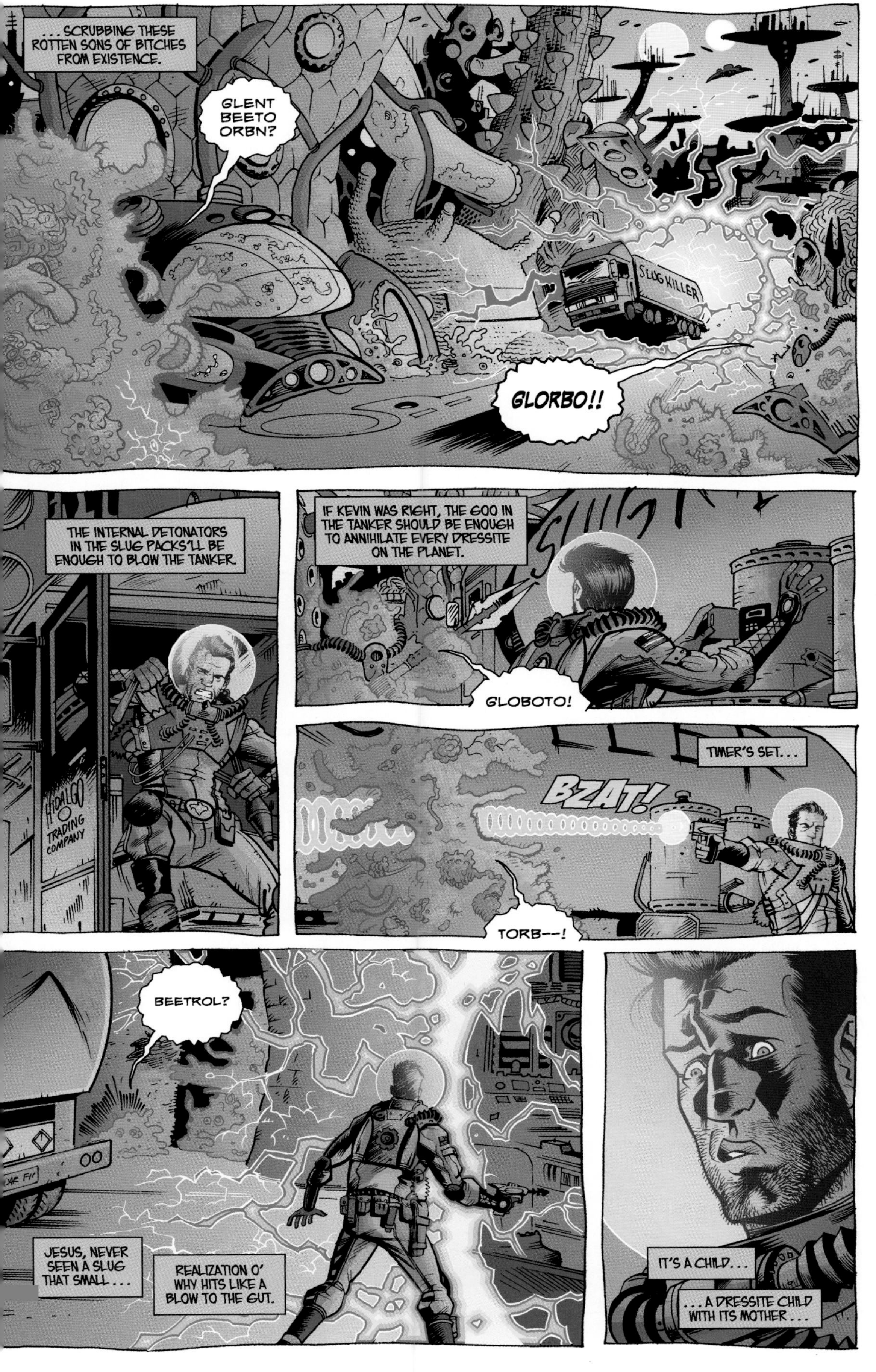
...SCRUBBING THESE ROTTEN SONS OF BITCHES FROM EXISTENCE.
GLENT BEETO ORBN?
SLUG KILLER
GLORBO!!
THE INTERNAL DETONATORS IN THE SLUG PACKS'LL BE ENOUGH TO BLOW THE TANKER.
HIDALGO TRADING COMPANY
IF KEVIN WAS RIGHT, THE GOO IN THE TANKER SHOULD BE ENOUGH TO ANNIHILATE EVERY DRESSITE ON THE PLANET.
GLOBOTO!
TIMER'S SET...
BZAT!
TORB--!
BEETROL?
JESUS, NEVER SEEN A SLUG THAT SMALL...
REALIZATION O' WHY HITS LIKE A BLOW TO THE GUT.
IT'S A CHILD...
...A DRESSITE CHILD WITH ITS MOTHER...

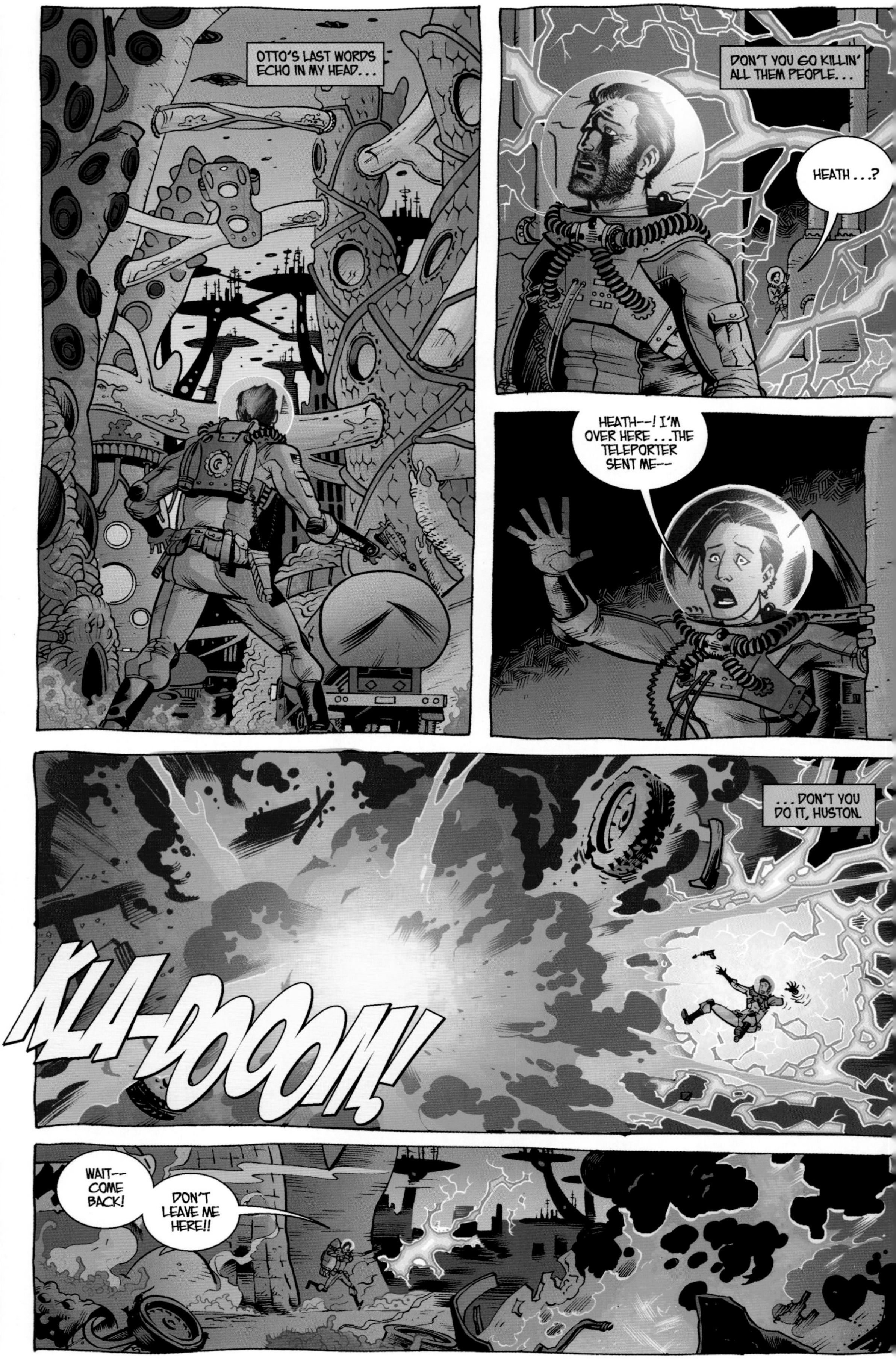

OTTO'S LAST WORDS ECHO IN MY HEAD . . .
DON'T YOU GO KILLIN' ALL THEM PEOPLE . . .
HEATH . . .?
HEATH--! I'M OVER HERE . . .THE TELEPORTER SENT ME--
. . . DON'T YOU DO IT, HUSTON.
KLA-DOOOM!
WAIT-- COME BACK!
DON'T LEAVE ME HERE!!

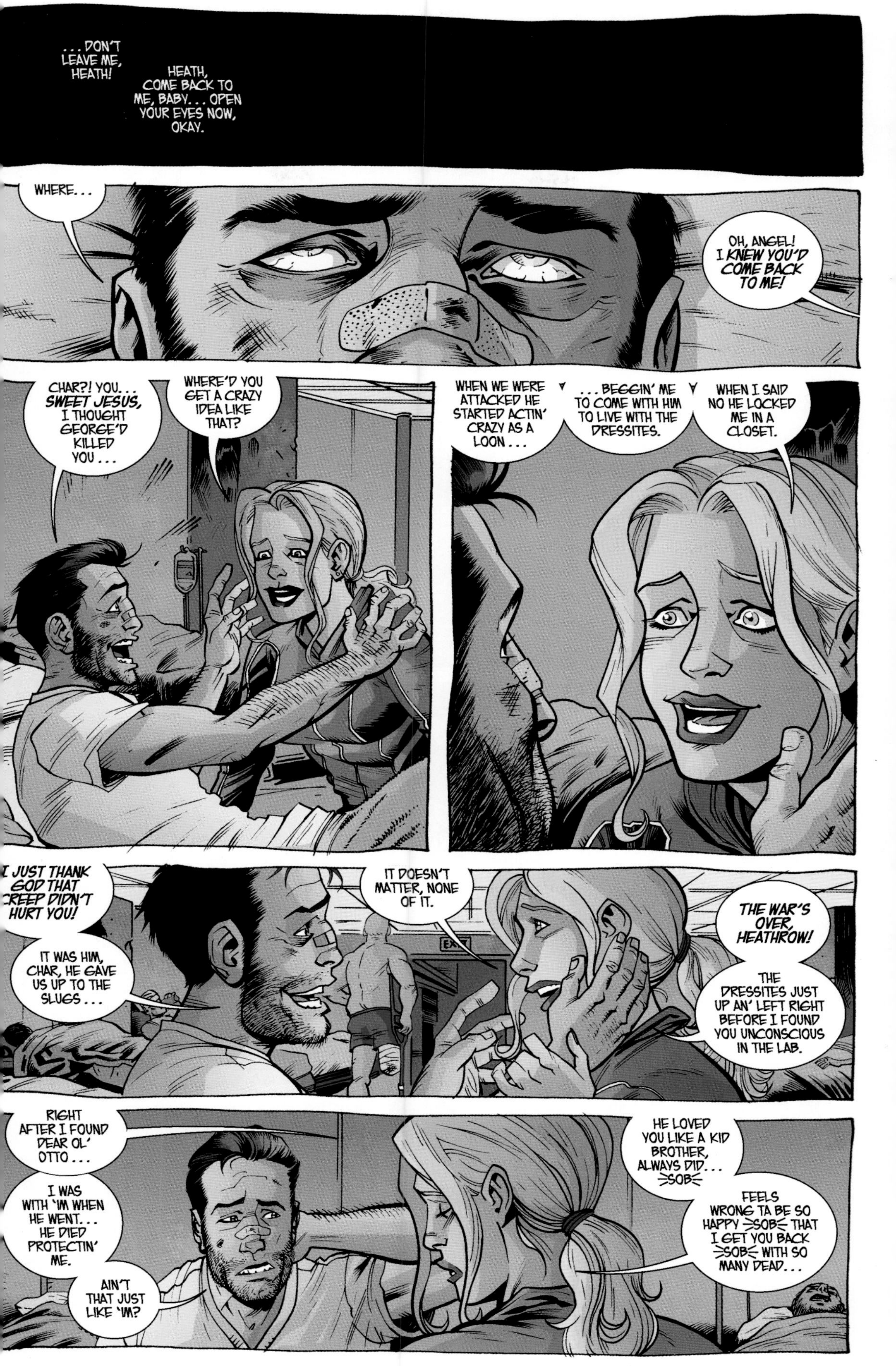
. . . DON'T LEAVE ME, HEATH!
HEATH, COME BACK TO ME, BABY. . . OPEN YOUR EYES NOW, OKAY.
WHERE. . .
OH, ANGEL! I *KNEW YOU'D COME BACK TO ME!*
CHAR?! YOU. . . *SWEET JESUS,* I THOUGHT GEORGE'D KILLED YOU . . .
WHERE'D YOU GET A CRAZY IDEA LIKE THAT?
WHEN WE WERE ATTACKED HE STARTED ACTIN' CRAZY AS A LOON . . .
. . . BEGGIN' ME TO COME WITH HIM TO LIVE WITH THE DRESSITES.
WHEN I SAID NO HE LOCKED ME IN A CLOSET.
I JUST THANK GOD THAT CREEP DIDN'T HURT YOU!
IT WAS HIM, CHAR, HE GAVE US UP TO THE SLUGS . . .
IT DOESN'T MATTER, NONE OF IT.
THE WAR'S OVER, HEATHROW!
THE DRESSITES JUST UP AN' LEFT RIGHT BEFORE I FOUND YOU UNCONSCIOUS IN THE LAB.
EXIT
RIGHT AFTER I FOUND DEAR OL' OTTO . . .
I WAS WITH 'IM WHEN HE WENT. . . HE DIED PROTECTIN' ME.
AIN'T THAT JUST LIKE 'IM?
HE LOVED YOU LIKE A KID BROTHER, ALWAYS DID. . . ≽SOB≼
FEELS WRONG TA BE SO HAPPY ≽SOB≼ THAT I GET YOU BACK ≽SOB≼ WITH SO MANY DEAD . . .

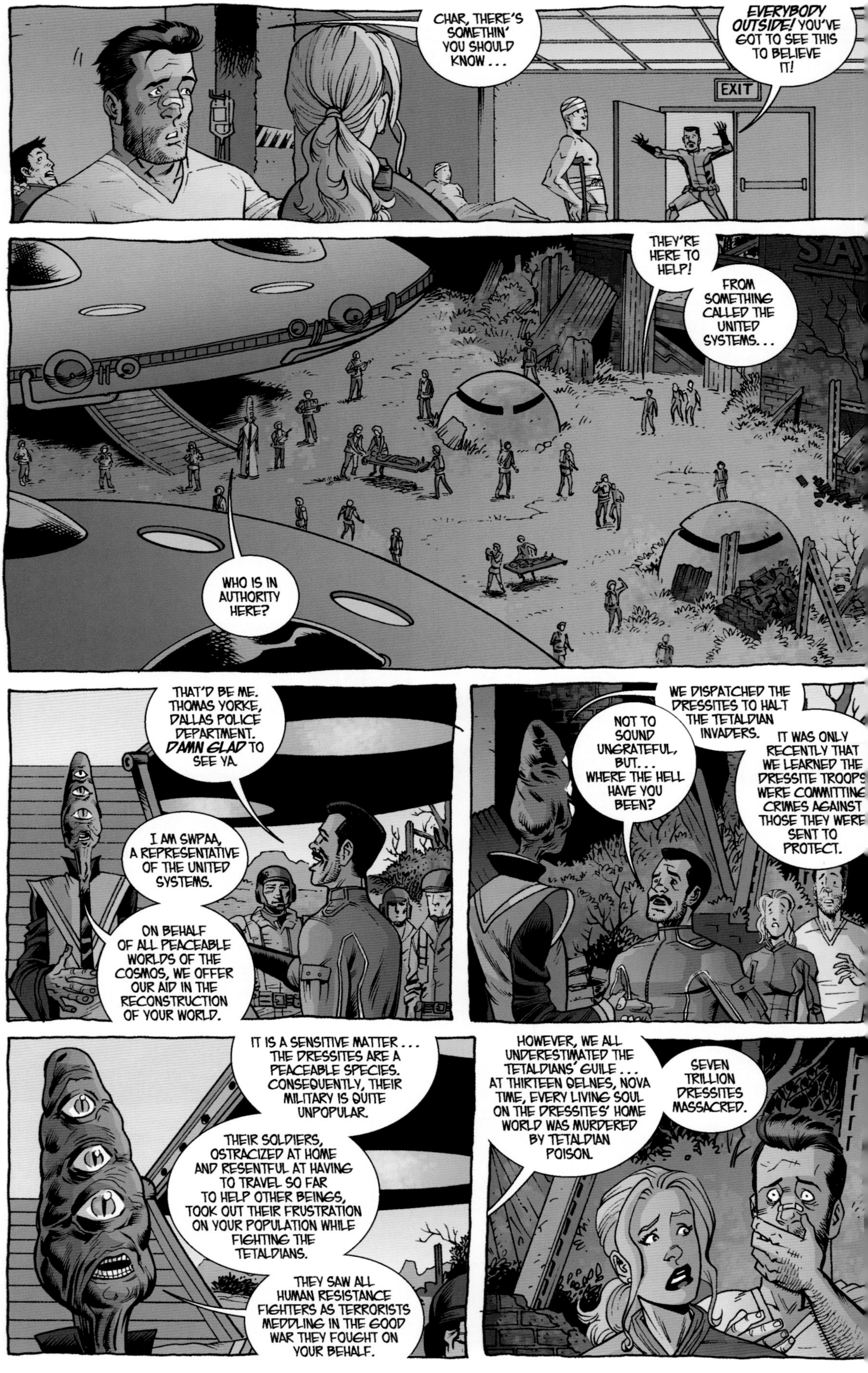
CHAR, THERE'S SOMETHIN' YOU SHOULD KNOW . . .
EVERYBODY OUTSIDE! YOU'VE GOT TO SEE THIS TO BELIEVE IT!
EXIT
THEY'RE HERE TO HELP!
FROM SOMETHING CALLED THE UNITED SYSTEMS. . .
WHO IS IN AUTHORITY HERE?
THAT'D BE ME. THOMAS YORKE, DALLAS POLICE DEPARTMENT. DAMN GLAD TO SEE YA.
I AM SWPAA, A REPRESENTATIVE OF THE UNITED SYSTEMS.
ON BEHALF OF ALL PEACEABLE WORLDS OF THE COSMOS, WE OFFER OUR AID IN THE RECONSTRUCTION OF YOUR WORLD.
NOT TO SOUND UNGRATEFUL, BUT. . . WHERE THE HELL HAVE YOU BEEN?
WE DISPATCHED THE DRESSITES TO HALT THE TETALDIAN INVADERS.
IT WAS ONLY RECENTLY THAT WE LEARNED THE DRESSITE TROOPS WERE COMMITTING CRIMES AGAINST THOSE THEY WERE SENT TO PROTECT.
IT IS A SENSITIVE MATTER . . . THE DRESSITES ARE A PEACEABLE SPECIES. CONSEQUENTLY, THEIR MILITARY IS QUITE UNPOPULAR.
THEIR SOLDIERS, OSTRACIZED AT HOME AND RESENTFUL AT HAVING TO TRAVEL SO FAR TO HELP OTHER BEINGS, TOOK OUT THEIR FRUSTRATION ON YOUR POPULATION WHILE FIGHTING THE TETALDIANS.
THEY SAW ALL HUMAN RESISTANCE FIGHTERS AS TERRORISTS MEDDLING IN THE GOOD WAR THEY FOUGHT ON YOUR BEHALF.
HOWEVER, WE ALL UNDERESTIMATED THE TETALDIANS' GUILE . . . AT THIRTEEN OELNES, NOVA TIME, EVERY LIVING SOUL ON THE DRESSITES' HOME WORLD WAS MURDERED BY TETALDIAN POISON.
SEVEN TRILLION DRESSITES MASSACRED.

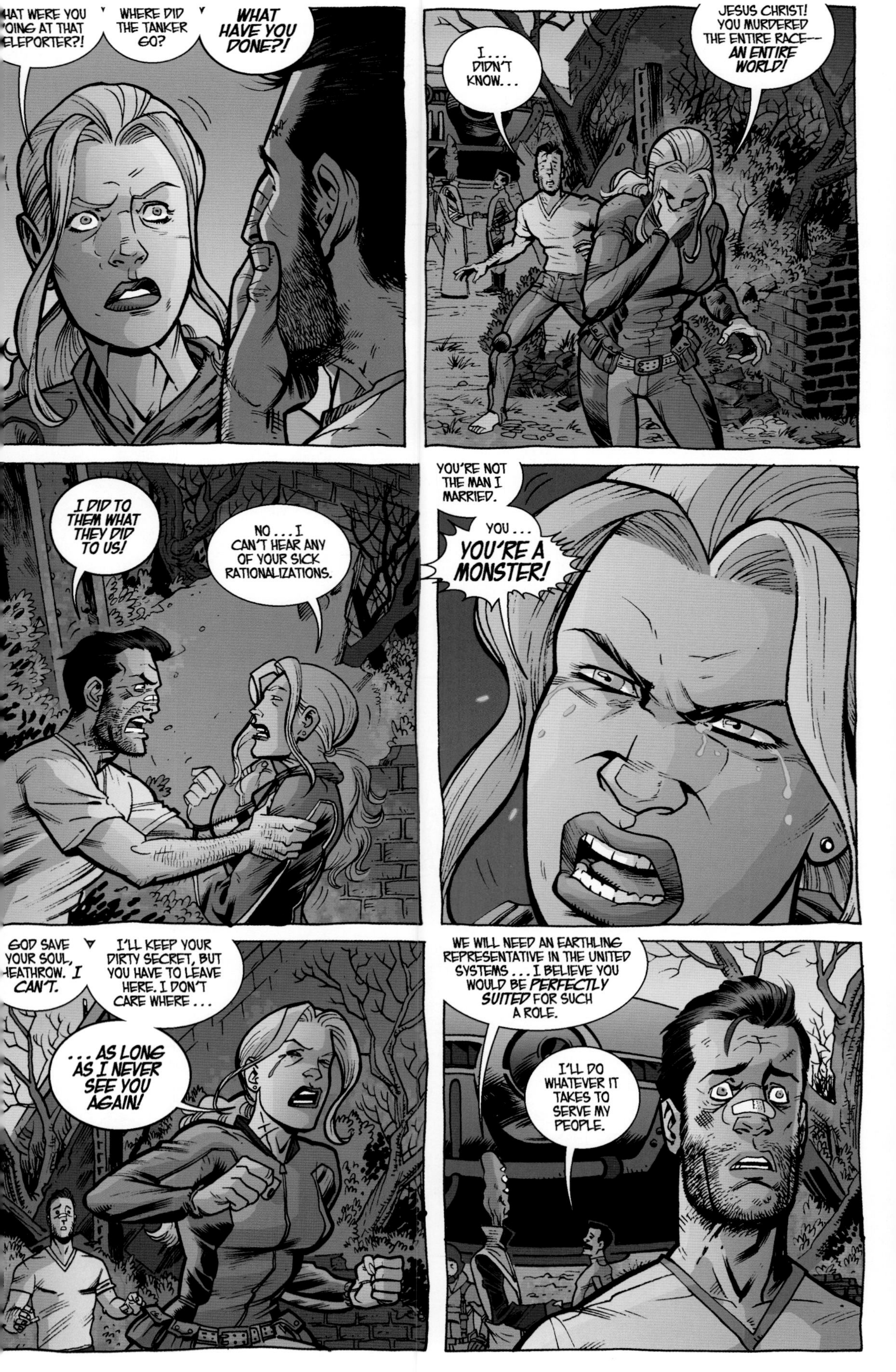
HAT WERE YOU OING AT THAT ELEPORTER?!
WHERE DID THE TANKER GO?
WHAT HAVE YOU DONE?!
I... DIDN'T KNOW...
JESUS CHRIST! YOU MURDERED THE ENTIRE RACE-- AN ENTIRE WORLD!
I DID TO THEM WHAT THEY DID TO US!
NO... I CAN'T HEAR ANY OF YOUR SICK RATIONALIZATIONS.
YOU'RE NOT THE MAN I MARRIED.
YOU... YOU'RE A MONSTER!
GOD SAVE YOUR SOUL, HEATHROW. I CAN'T.
I'LL KEEP YOUR DIRTY SECRET, BUT YOU HAVE TO LEAVE HERE. I DON'T CARE WHERE...
...AS LONG AS I NEVER SEE YOU AGAIN!
WE WILL NEED AN EARTHLING REPRESENTATIVE IN THE UNITED SYSTEMS... I BELIEVE YOU WOULD BE PERFECTLY SUITED FOR SUCH A ROLE.
I'LL DO WHATEVER IT TAKES TO SERVE MY PEOPLE.

MONTHS LATER...

HEY.

I'D HOPED YOU WERE GONE.

I'VE BEEN ON THE MOON DOING SOME HEAVY THINKING... DRINKING, WHATEVER.

BURIED ALL THE DEAD -- IT NEEDED TO BE DONE SO I DID IT.

BUT THE GHOSTS... THEY STAY WITH ME UP THERE... SO I THINK I'M GONNA GET THE HELL OUT OF HERE, FOR GOOD.

I WENT BACK TO THE OL' HOUSE TA SAY GOODBYE.

DIGGIN' AROUND IN THE RUBBLE I FOUND MY MAMA'S LOCKET.

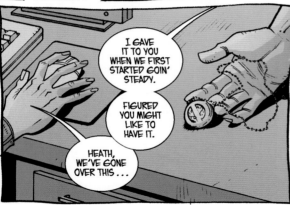

I GAVE IT TO YOU WHEN WE FIRST STARTED GOIN' STEADY.

FIGURED YOU MIGHT LIKE TO HAVE IT.

HEATH, WE'VE GONE OVER THIS...

I KNOW, CHAR. I AIN'T HERE TA BEG, JUST TA SAY GOODBYE.

GOOD LUCK GETTING THE HUMANITY SHOW BACK UP AND RUNNIN'.

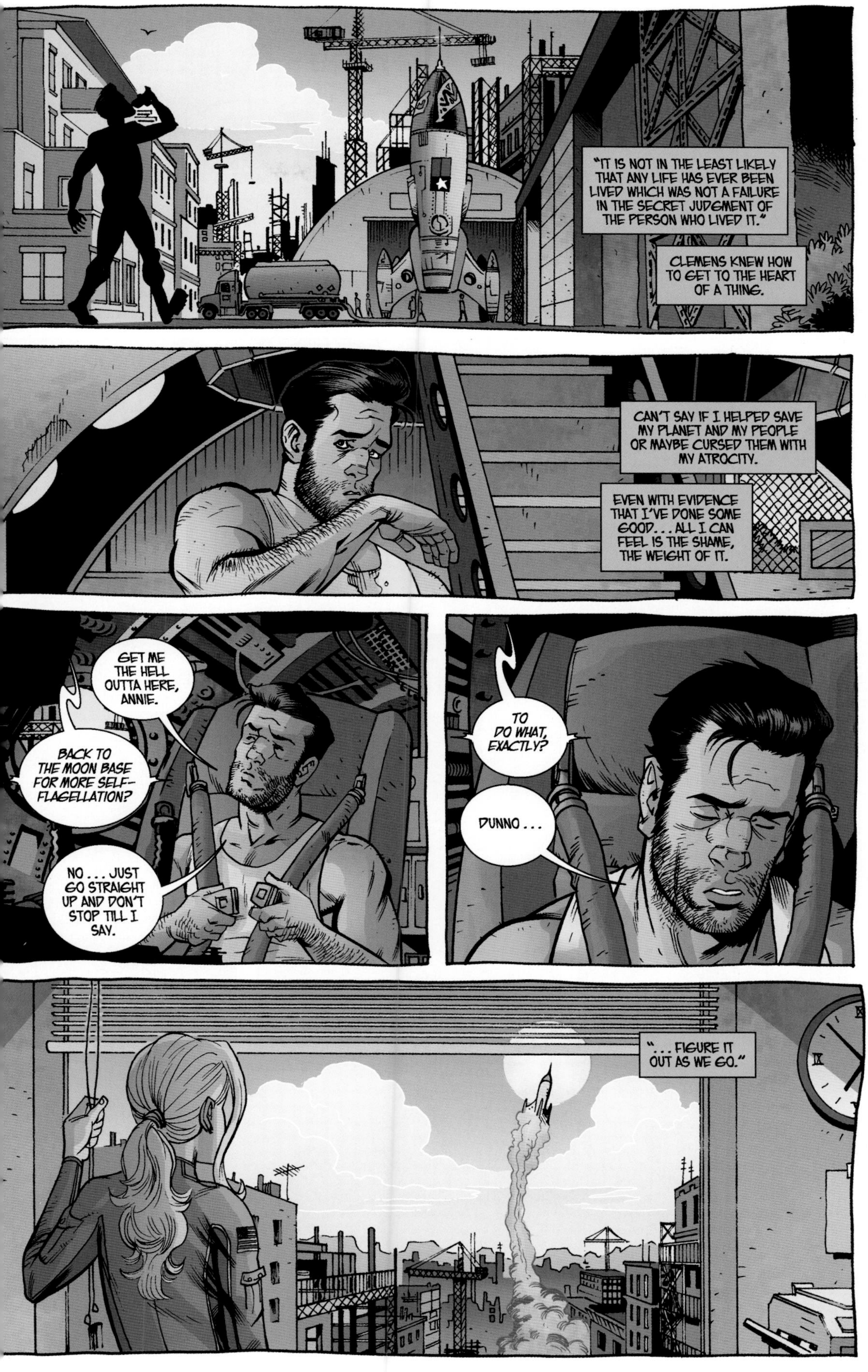
"IT IS NOT IN THE LEAST LIKELY THAT ANY LIFE HAS EVER BEEN LIVED WHICH WAS NOT A FAILURE IN THE SECRET JUDGMENT OF THE PERSON WHO LIVED IT."
CLEMENS KNEW HOW TO GET TO THE HEART OF A THING.
CAN'T SAY IF I HELPED SAVE MY PLANET AND MY PEOPLE OR MAYBE CURSED THEM WITH MY ATROCITY.
EVEN WITH EVIDENCE THAT I'VE DONE SOME GOOD... ALL I CAN FEEL IS THE SHAME, THE WEIGHT OF IT.
GET ME THE HELL OUTTA HERE, ANNIE.
BACK TO THE MOON BASE FOR MORE SELF-FLAGELLATION?
NO... JUST GO STRAIGHT UP AND DON'T STOP TILL I SAY.
TO DO WHAT, EXACTLY?
DUNNO...
"...FIGURE IT OUT AS WE GO."

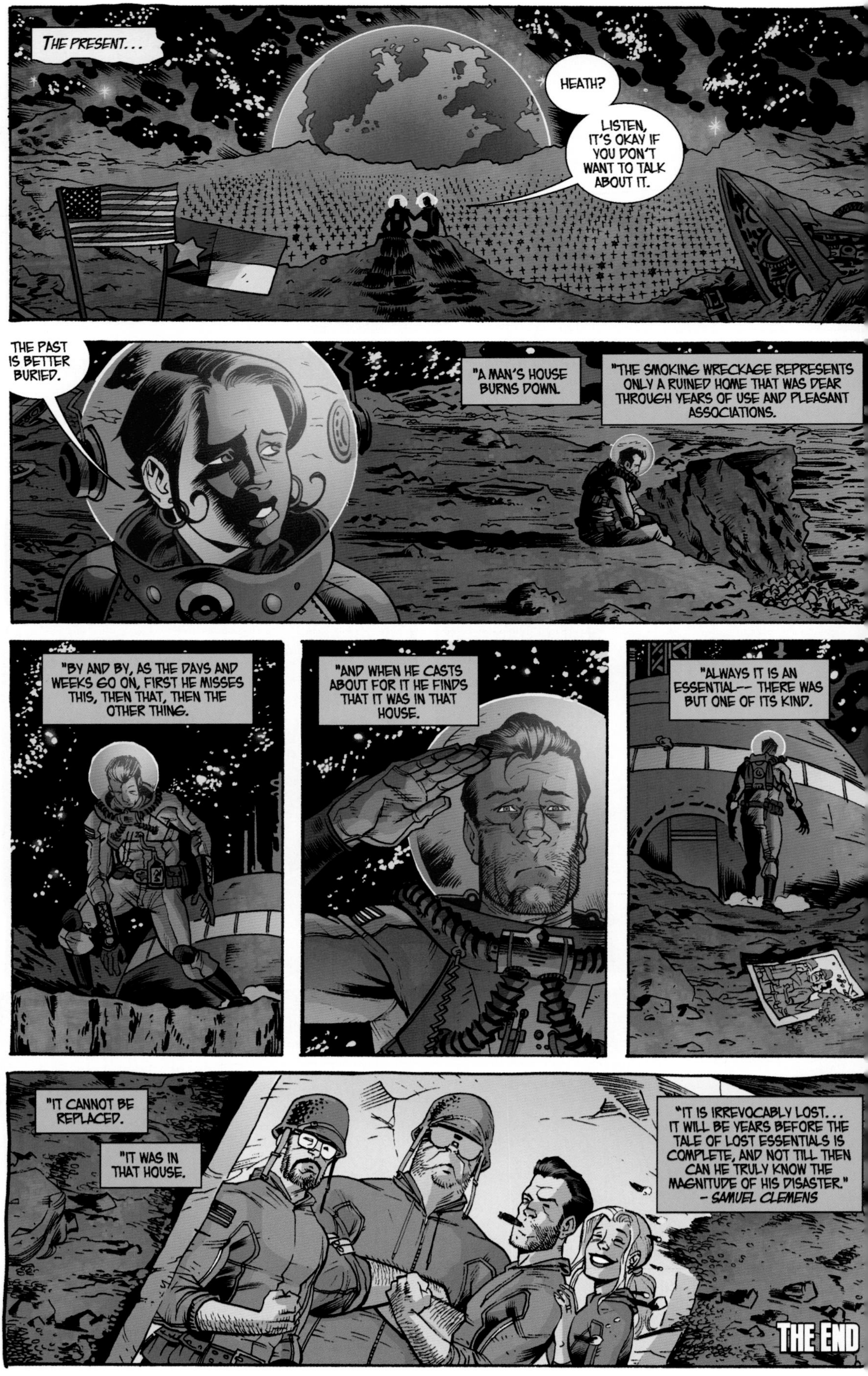
THE PRESENT...
HEATH?
LISTEN, IT'S OKAY IF YOU DON'T WANT TO TALK ABOUT IT.
THE PAST IS BETTER BURIED.
"A MAN'S HOUSE BURNS DOWN.
"THE SMOKING WRECKAGE REPRESENTS ONLY A RUINED HOME THAT WAS DEAR THROUGH YEARS OF USE AND PLEASANT ASSOCIATIONS.
"BY AND BY, AS THE DAYS AND WEEKS GO ON, FIRST HE MISSES THIS, THEN THAT, THEN THE OTHER THING.
"AND WHEN HE CASTS ABOUT FOR IT HE FINDS THAT IT WAS IN THAT HOUSE.
"ALWAYS IT IS AN ESSENTIAL-- THERE WAS BUT ONE OF ITS KIND.
"IT CANNOT BE REPLACED.
"IT WAS IN THAT HOUSE.
"IT IS IRREVOCABLY LOST... IT WILL BE YEARS BEFORE THE TALE OF LOST ESSENTIALS IS COMPLETE, AND NOT TILL THEN CAN HE TRULY KNOW THE MAGNITUDE OF HIS DISASTER."
- SAMUEL CLEMENS
THE END

PINUP GALLERY

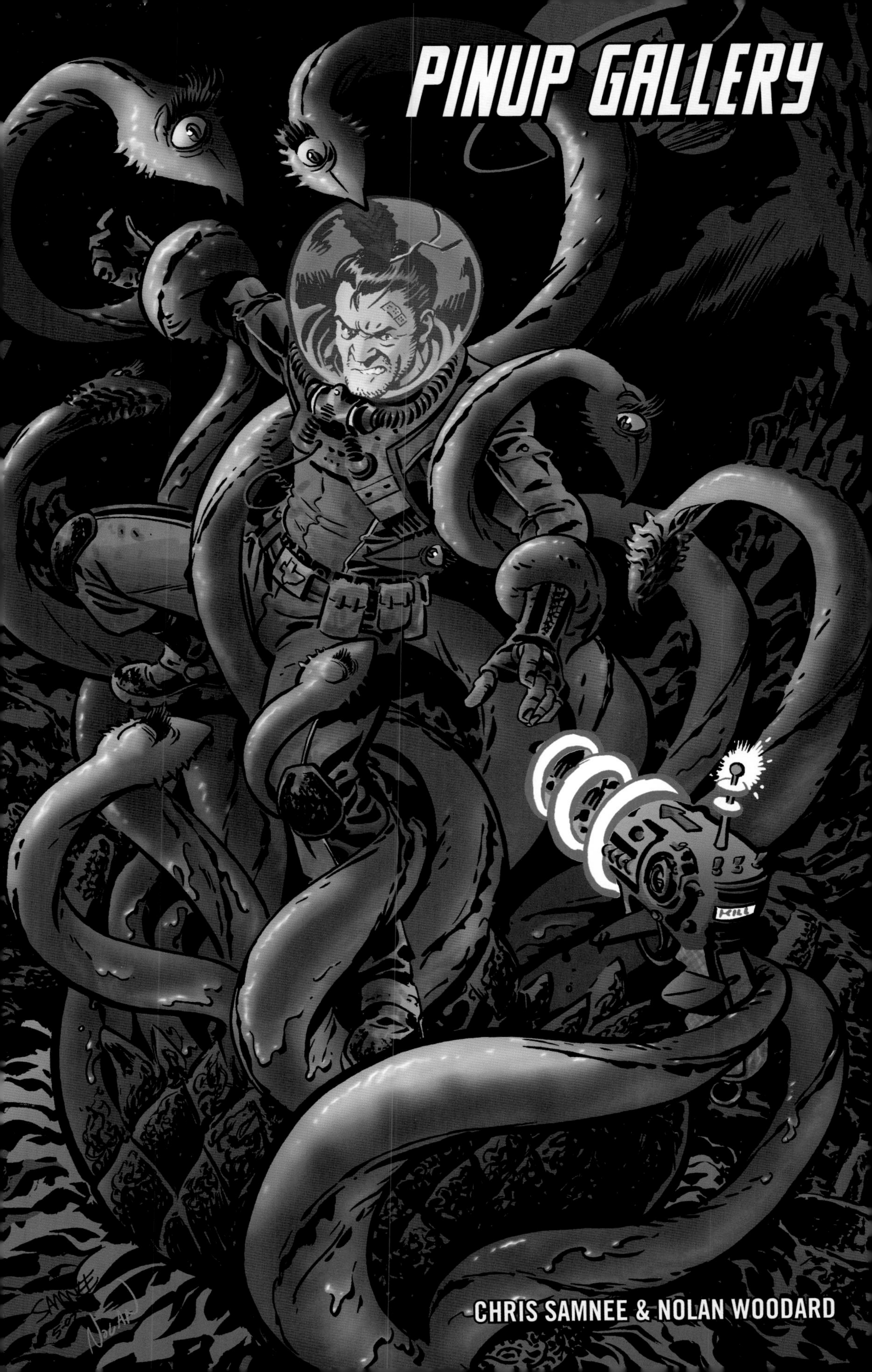
KILL

CHRIS SAMNEE & NOLAN WOODARD

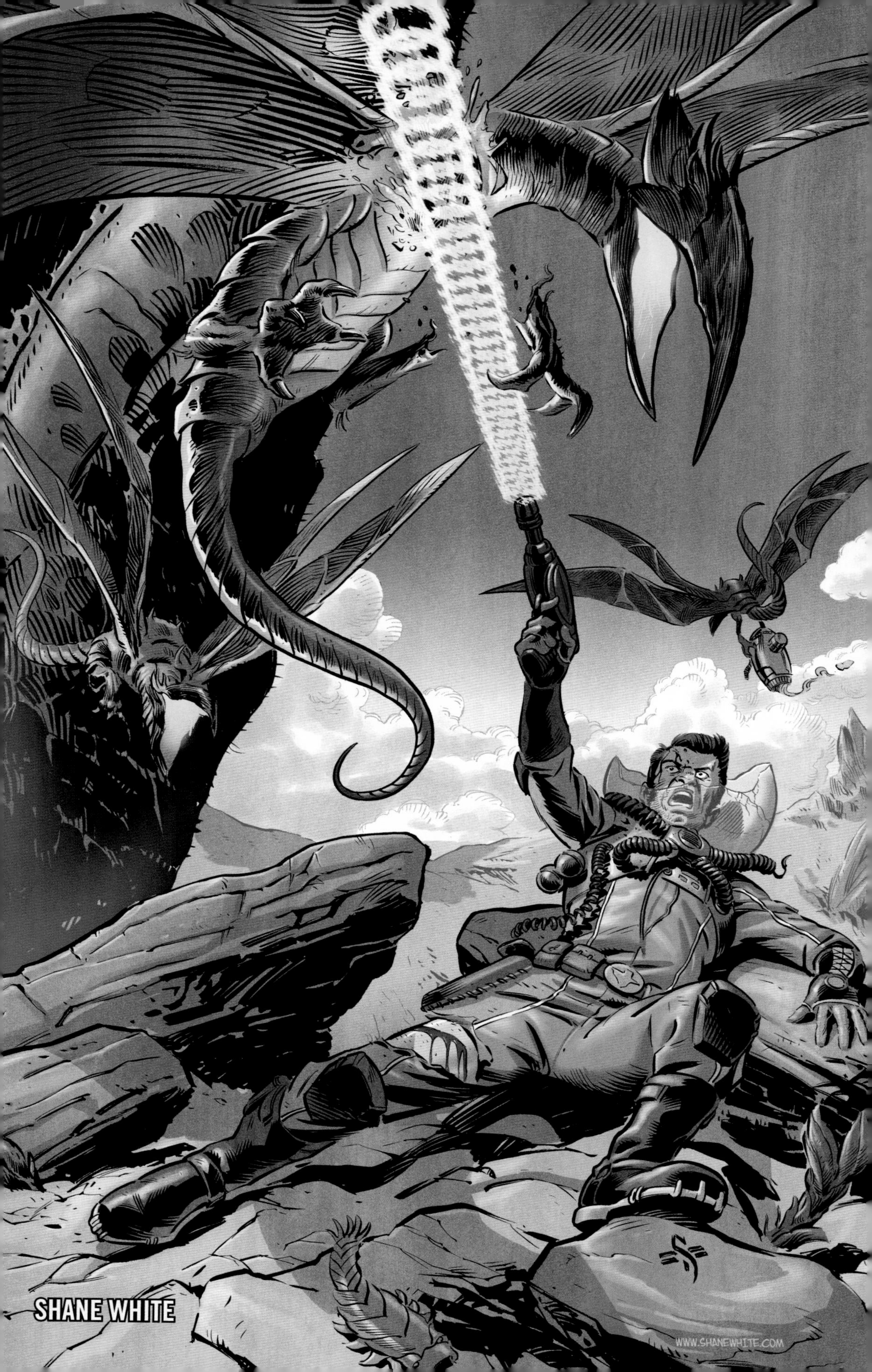
SHANE WHITE
WWW.SHANEWHITE.COM

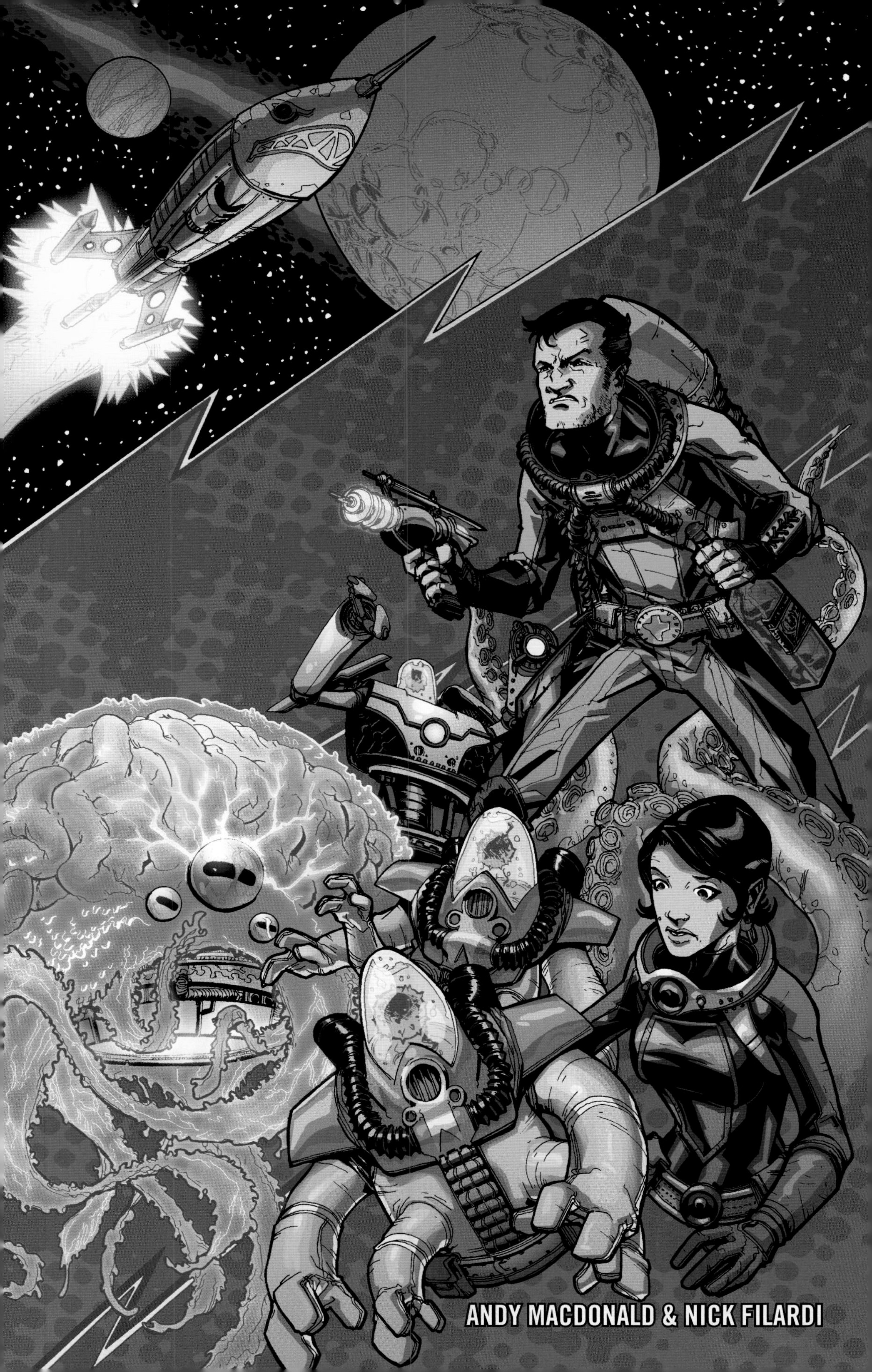
ANDY MACDONALD & NICK FILARDI

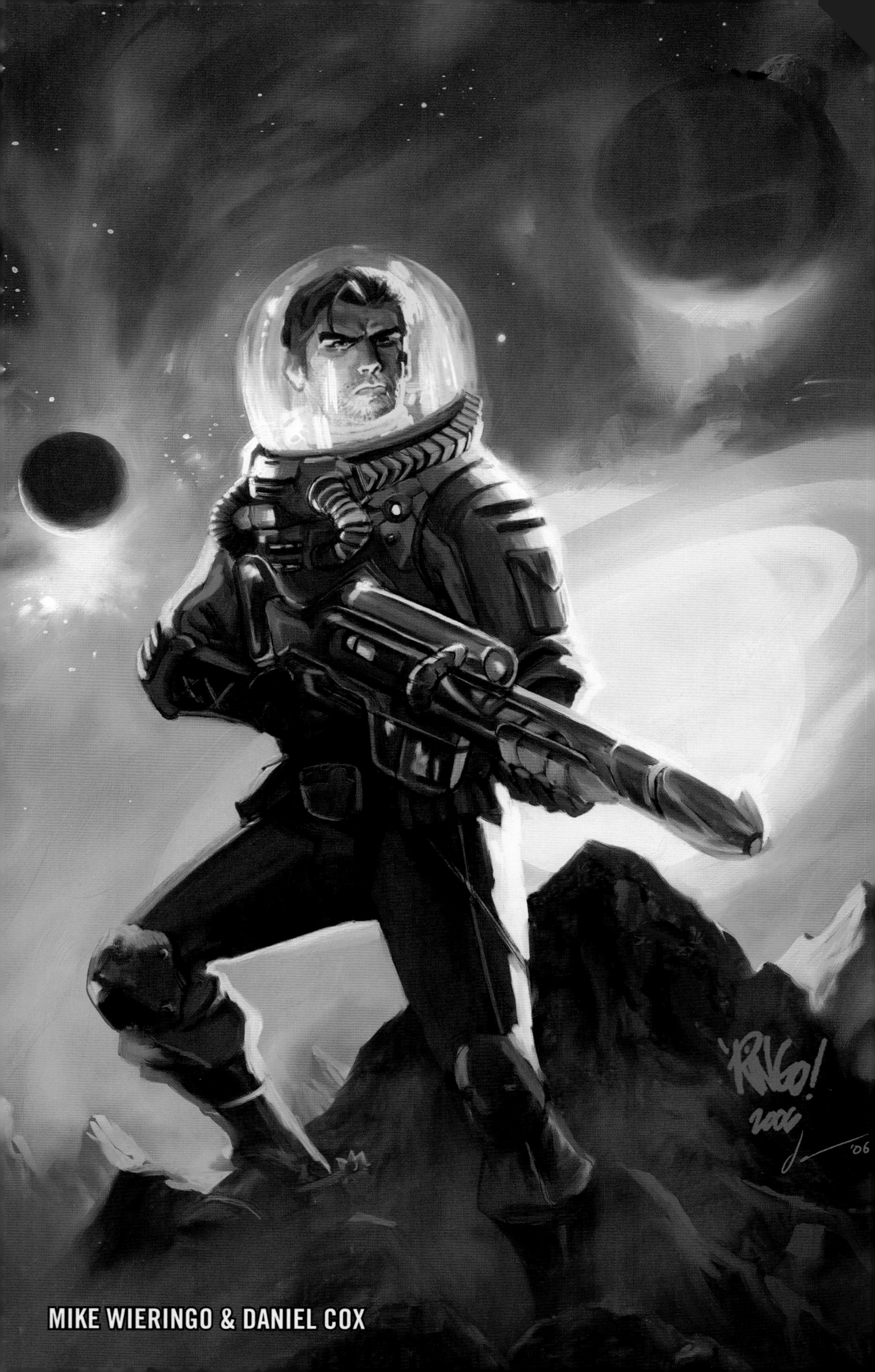

MIKE WIERINGO & DANIEL COX